ELEANOR BALDWIN AND THE WOMAN'S POINT OF VIEW

Eleanor Baldwin and the Woman's Point of View

NEW THOUGHT RADICALISM
IN PORTLAND'S PROGRESSIVE ERA

Lawrence M. Lipin

Oregon State University Press   Corvallis

Library of Congress Cataloging-in-Publication Data

Names: Lipin, Lawrence M., 1956– author.
Title: Eleanor Baldwin and the Woman's point of view : new thought radicalism in
    Portland's Progressive Era / Lawrence M. Lipin.
Description: Corvallis : Oregon State University Press, 2017. | Includes bibliographical
    references and index.
Identifiers: LCCN 2017017671 | ISBN 9780870719103 (original trade pbk. : alk. paper)
Subjects: LCSH: Baldwin, Eleanor Florence, 1854–1928. | Women journalists—Oregon—
    Portland—Biography. | Portland (Or.)—Intellectual life—20th century. | Portland
    (Or.)—Social conditions—20th century. | Journalists—Oregon—Portland—Biography.
    | Feminists—Oregon—Portland—Biography. | Progressivism (United States politics)—
    History—20th century. | Portland (Or.)—Biography.
Classification: LCC F884.P853 B355 2017 | DDC 305.42092 [B] —dc23
LC record available at https://lccn.loc.gov/2017017671

♾ This paper meets the requirements of ANSI/NISO Z39.48-1992
(Permanence of Paper).

Oregon State University Press
121 The Valley Library
Corvallis OR 97331-4501
541-737-3166 • fax 541-737-3170
www.osupress.oregonstate.edu

Contents

Preface

While in the throes of doing research for a previous book on the Oregon trade-union movement's changing relationship with nature, I spent what seemed like an eternity scrolling through microfilm in a small, windowless room at the Oregon Historical Society Library. The tedium was broken one afternoon when a younger patron noticed that we were both reading issues of the *Oregon Labor Press* from the Progressive Era. While talking about our reasons for interest in the source, I learned that she was seeking to establish the anti-Prohibition credentials of the Oregon labor movement. It did not take long before she found what she was looking for: an editorial supporting the decision of a state convention of the Oregon State Federation of Labor (OSFL) to oppose Prohibition, which affirmed her belief that the unions were and always had been a progressive force on this and probably other issues. Her motive for research was not clear to me, but the context suggested answers. Oregon had for more than a decade undergone a series of right-wing-sponsored ballot measures that had aimed to limit the rights of gays and lesbians, and it is likely that she associated religiously based efforts to control individual behavior with intolerance and rightwing politics more generally. It was not long after this encounter that I came across an account of a subsequent convention of the OSFL, one that had adopted a pro-Prohibition resolution offered by the mostly female United Garment Workers' Union. I thought about the young woman, who was probably happy to find that her attenuated research into the past had revealed a simpler narrative that validated her perspective.

This book has its origin in that moment, both temporally in that it was when I first came across the writings of the subject of this study, but also in the sense that my subject proved to be a complicated woman who defied any simple desire to find a usable and heroic past, though in most ways—not all—she is appealing to the modern progressive mind. A then-aging female journalist, Eleanor Baldwin first came to my attention when I found her defense of the Bolsheviks in a 1921 issue of the *Oregon Labor Press*. It was not that she expressed hope that a new regime of justice and economic democracy would result first in Russia and then later across the industrial world, as so many other leftists would, that caught my attention. It was how she did it. Her aim was to defend the Bolsheviks from the charge that they were against religion, a matter that was somewhat dear to her heart since so much of her moral compass, I would subsequently learn, was grounded in a peculiar version of the New England reform tradition. Critics, she wrote, had mistaken their antipathy for what she termed "the Church" for a soulless atheism. Here, the Bolsheviks represented progress not only in the realm of economic relations, but also in attacking the institutional power of patriarchal religious authority (and by extension to the Papacy). At the same time, Baldwin supported efforts to keep Catholic clergy and members of the monastic orders from teaching in the public schools. This was part of a broader effort by the Ku Klux Klan in the early 1920s to limit Catholic cultural influence, which included an attempt to close religious schools and force all children into the public ones, where they would assuredly be Americanized, safe from the influence of priests and nuns. Baldwin wrote about the "Corfu Incident" in the KKK's *Western American*, a condemnation of the Vatican's alleged role in consorting with Mussolini to arrange for the murder of Italian diplomats in Greek territory to justify the absorption of parts of Greece into the Kingdom of Italy and the Greek Orthodox Church by the Papacy. Baldwin's dalliance with the Klan offers a window into the puzzling mind of the Progressive Era radical who seems in our eyes to have been leaning in two mutually exclusive directions.[1]

I have often wondered what that young researcher in the Oregon Historical Society Library would make of Baldwin. She was an adamant supporter of labor rights, an unwavering opponent of finance capital and inequality, and an advocate of women's rights and independence. Moreover, she was uninterested in Prohibition and could express sympathy for the workingman who sought solace from alienation and misery in a dram of whiskey or a pint of beer. I suspect that the young woman in the library would find much that was admirable in Baldwin's thinking and would find her support for the Klan to be an unappealing coda to a much more progressive, even radical, life. In the aftermath of World War I, Baldwin looks less like a role model, for it is unlikely that any "progressive" today would identify with all of her positions. But this is the stuff of history, as the apparent anomaly reminds us how much cultural context shapes the actions of the individual human being.

This blending of what we might today consider progressive and conservative tendencies within the confines of populist movements is not new. Decades ago, Lawrence Levine chronicled the career of three-time Democratic presidential candidate William Jennings Bryan, inquiring how the champion of working people and small farmers against the corporate and banking elite could end his days defending an antievolution law in the Scopes trial. In that inquiry, Levine concluded that Bryan had changed less than the cultural landscape around him had, and that in the postwar era he retained his distrust for corporate authority. Before that, Southern historian C. Vann Woodward had explored the contradictory impulses that ran through the efforts of Georgia populist Tom Watson, who would spend the latter days of his career defending the Klan. That American populism itself has both left- and rightwing variants, meaning that these individuals were hardly unique, has been explored thoroughly by Michael Kazin. Moreover, in the locality of Portland, socialist Tom Burns has perplexed historians who have found his interest and support for the Klan inexplicable. Even William S. U'Ren, the so-called father of direct democracy in Oregon, who often railed against the forces of an unrestrained capitalism and who defended dissidents from an overly zealous justice department during World War I, became associated, if briefly, with anti-Catholic politics and the KKK. If Eleanor Baldwin did not travel a well-worn path, neither did she go it alone.[2]

Newspapers are filled with eccentric individuals who write letters to the editor; they are rarely worth extended study. But as I found Baldwin's name more and more in the pages of the *Labor Press* at the head of columns or at the end of letters to the editor, I found her increasingly compelling. Though she addressed many subjects, including restrictions on commercial fishing that were central to my earlier research project, it became evident that her main concern was to impress upon workers that the source of their poverty was what she considered the unnatural and aristocratic power that bankers held over them through the manipulation of money. Baldwin became something more than a commentator on current events, revealing intellectual links with the nineteenth-century greenback movement, which would have great influence on both the labor movement and the more farmer-based populist movement. I would soon find that she had published a tract on money and banking, which had become her life's work.

My curiosity piqued, I looked through the obituaries that announced her death in 1928.[3] Baldwin was remembered chiefly as an avid supporter of labor and as the writer of a daily woman's column for the Portland *Evening Telegram*. At that point, she seemed worthy enough of study that another self-imposed vigil of darkness and solitude in that windowless room of the Oregon Historical Society soon commenced. The engagement with her columns introduced me to a thoughtful woman who refused to conceptualize the women's column in the same way her employers probably had: as a mere instrument of commerce, an inducement for women to read advertisements and engage in sentimentality while disseminating household advice. Baldwin happily addressed women who broke the conventions of society, who chose occupations that were deemed male, and who engaged in spiritual and religious leadership. Most adamantly, however, she insisted that her readers think about society and government: she confronted them with the inequities of industrial society and urged women to study political economy. Beyond the column inches that she wrote for the *Telegram*, Baldwin engaged these themes with the Woman's Press Club, of which she was an active member, and her efforts to form a Woman's Political Study Group, which helped her put together her only published treatise, a monetary tract titled *Money Talks*. In an era in which women were struggling to gain the vote, Baldwin constantly addressed the relationship between individuals, the economy, and the state by providing her mostly female readers with a vision of full citizenship.

The obituaries also put me on the trail to her childhood and young adulthood, spent in New England. Information about her family lay waiting to be uncovered in local governmental offices and libraries in Waterbury and Naugatuck, Connecticut, but a deeper level of information came from her loquacious brother Henry, who was politically active in the Gilded Age as a perpetual candidate and speaker for Greenback-Labor, Union Labor, and Populist Parties, and who as a radical editor penned a long set of reminiscences of the Naugatuck of his and Eleanor's childhood. The two siblings made much of the abolitionist posture of the family, particularly that of their father, Lucius Baldwin, and for both the narrative of abolitionist triumph provided the optimism that the misery imposed by industrial capitalism too could be overturned.

But Baldwin had other and ultimately more important sources of optimism. The obituaries noted the importance of minister Henry Victor Morgan to her spiritual life. Baldwin attended his spiritual meetings when he lived in Portland for a few years in the first decade of the century, and he conducted the funeral services that were held at her home. Like Baldwin, Morgan left the Methodist Church and adopted a New Thought spirituality that combined mind cure as a salve for the individual with an assuredness that the collective mind could cure what ailed society. And though some New Thought ministers were male, like Morgan, many of the most prominent New Thought leaders were female. Baldwin lived briefly with Morgan and with fellow female journalist Clara Colby, who also was active in New Thought circles, and it was not long before Portland had a significant group of New Thought writers, many of the most important of them women. The more I learned about this community and American metaphysical religion, the more it became clear that Baldwin's sociology reflected a kind of New Thought socialism. At the same time, Baldwin's own writings reflected a tension within the New Thought tradition, one that she sought to guide in a radical direction.

What did not become clear was the nature of Baldwin's personal life. She never married. Today, we are much more cognizant of the ways in which communities of women could provide quiet space for deep, spiritual, and passionate relationships between women, sometimes in clandestine relationships, sometimes in more observable "Boston marriages." The absence of personal material on Baldwin leaves us with many questions that I am unable to answer. She left behind little to inform us about her personal life, but she was prolific in documenting her beliefs. And that is what this book attempts to provide. Baldwin, as a public writer, links significant communities in Portland, some that have received a good deal of recent attention, like the labor and women's movements, and others, like the New Thought community, that still await careful and systematic study. Attention to Baldwin's intellectual production allows us to see Progressive Era Portland in greater complexity while providing us with a broader vision of an active participant in the local women's rights community and of the political potential of a female reading community.

And as much as she has left behind with regard to her thoughts about economic inequality or about the criminal justice system, she has left little that would help explain her latter-day affinity for the Klan. What was it that made the Catholic Church at that moment seem to be the institution that threatened to stop the spread of liberty and equality in its tracks, when she had long lamented the power of bankers? Careful attention to her previous writings may not prepare the reader adequately to understand this intolerant turn in her thinking, and yet in that silence it may also help us understand how the KKK divided the Oregon labor movement. Though Baldwin may suggest some of the reasons why reasonable people on the left momentarily found it viable to work with the Klan, the resulting contradictions will still leave us puzzled.

One develops many debts when engaging in a project like this, for sometimes the research process can resemble looking for a needle in a haystack. I have become over the years indebted to many of the staff at the Oregon Historical Society, most notably Scott Daniels, who helped me reason through the existence of materials that might shed light on Baldwin's connections in Portland. In Connecticut, I benefited from the helpfulness of Renata Vickery, the archivist at Central Connecticut State College, and of Bridget Mariano at the Naugatuck Historical Society, who had found Henry Baldwin's reminiscences and generously made them available for me on my arrival. I have also profited from the generosity of other scholars. While I was unable to benefit from Kristin Mapel Bloomberg's forthcoming biography of Clara Colby, she generously shared a number of items regarding Baldwin that she came across during her own research. More regularly, Kimberly Jensen took time from her own marvelous work on women during the World War I era to listen to me talk about this project, to provide encouragement, and to send me copies of articles written by Baldwin that had escaped my notice. Thanks are also due to Eliza Canty-Jones for helping me conjure a local bibliography.

The project also benefited from the labor of two smart Pacific University students who were paid by the College of Arts and Sciences but in whose debt I remain. When I could no longer take the time to take notes from microfilm, I began to photocopy Baldwin's columns, and then Catherine Prechtal transcribed them into searchable documents from which I would write. For a time, Catie knew Baldwin's mind better than I did, and her enthusiasm for many of the columns further convinced me that this project was worth pursuing. When it became clear that Baldwin had contributed much more to the Portland *Labor Press* than I had originally thought, Arianna Blunt went through numerous reels of microfilm searching for the many columns that she wrote for that weekly newspaper during the second and third decades of the twentieth century. The efforts of these two intelligent young women ensured that I would be ready to write this book when I became eligible for sabbatical.

There are other Pacific people to thank. Social Science Administrative Assistant Pam Kofstad helped facilitate the student work for this project, finding means to make sure that students were properly compensated and that the originals from which Catie worked were carefully stored. For these and so many other helpful turns that Pam has provided me over the years, I am grateful. I also owe thanks to the members of the Faculty Development Committee of the Pacific University Arts and Sciences College, who awarded me a sabbatical as well as a faculty development grant, which allowed me to travel to Connecticut and Massachusetts to research Baldwin's family. In addition, I owe thanks to Director of the School of Social Sciences Sarah Phillips, who saw clear paths where I saw only bureaucratic roadblocks. Chapter 1 could not have been written without that institutional support, and without that this book would not have been viable.

As lonely as the research and writing process can be, it is ultimately sustained by the friends and colleagues that we are fortunate enough to gain over the years. Many of them have probably long forgotten that they listened to me babble about Baldwin and encouraged me to take on this study. William Robbins was among the first, and his questions over the years about the project helped motivate me to finish it. Mark Eifler has probably forgotten that he expressed interest in this book at its earliest stages, but he always has provided good cheer and friendship; he has also bought me no small number of pints of locally crafted beer. Moreover, he was the first person I knew who took Donald Trump's candidacy seriously (Mark was right and I was wrong). At my own institution, I have been kept on my feet and engaged by the intellectual community and friendship of a group of wonderful scholars and teachers, colleagues including Richard Jobs, Martha Rampton, Cheleen

Mahar, Jeff Seward, Jules Boykoff, and Aaron Greer, all of whom, each in his or her own way, have made my years at Pacific a great pleasure. Eva Guggemos gave chapter 1 a helpful reading, while my daughter Ella did the same for chapter 4; in both cases, the verdict was that I needed to be much clearer. I hope that what has made it into print shows that I have taken their criticisms to heart. In addition, Robert Johnston and an anonymous reader for the press gave the entire manuscript reads that were at once generous and helpful. Thanks are due to Pacific University physicist Stephen Hall for explaining developments in turn-of-the-century physics that my subject misunderstood, but to no greater extent than I have. And I owe a deeper thanks to Chris Wilkes, Pacific's former vice provost for research, whose good cheer and encouragement were always the proper remedy for those moments when I asked myself, "what is the point of this study?" The project has also benefited from the support of many good folks at the Oregon State University Press. Mary Braun encouraged this project when it was at its incipient stages, and copy editor Ashleigh McKown helped fix my gravest violations of the rules of grammar and syntax.

Last and not least, I owe so much to my partner and wife, Sylvie Horne. This is the third book that I have written, and in both previous instances I thanked her, but it seems senseless to thank someone who has shared your life for over thirty-five years. Together we have raised two bright and lively daughters, sharing our concerns and our joys, and over the years there have been plenty of both. I still smile stupidly when I see her at the end of a long day of teaching or writing. At a certain point the difference between us is hard to judge; I am no longer certain for what she is responsible and what I am. Thanking her is like thanking myself; it feels redundant. I just have the good sense to thank my lucky stars that she walked into my life and has never left.

ELEANOR BALDWIN AND THE WOMAN'S POINT OF VIEW

Introduction

Eleanor Florence Baldwin was a writer, though nothing she wrote has stood the test of time. Nor did any of her writings bring her much fame in her own day. Yet, however obscure she remains historically, she was not ignored. She wrote constantly, and most of her writings were published and read by others. Baldwin was a journalist, one of the few but growing number of women who gained employment writing newspaper copy during the Progressive Era, and who for three years wrote a daily women's column for the editorial page of a Republican Party newspaper in Portland, Oregon. In those columns, Baldwin condemned capitalists for selfishness and greed and for bringing misery to others. She called on them to exercise self-control over their acquisitiveness, but she otherwise argued against restraint. For instance, she rejected strict discipline of children, imposed particularly on boys by Victorian parents and teachers, and in the same vein she condemned harsh punishment of criminals, placing the blame for their crimes on society rather than on the failing of the individual. Equally important, she rejected the need to impose restraints on women, calling for the establishment of institutions that would not only enable women to enter occupations that had formerly been reserved for men, but also allow such women to live comfortably on their own, outside of the family unit. For Baldwin, there was little need for the kind of Victorian restraint that had cloistered so many women within the home; she provided her readers with a clear sense that knowledge and thought were the only things necessary for evils to be stripped away and for a better society to emerge. In some ways, she was the quintessential radical progressive, confident the social order was corrupt and unnatural, perverted by the powerful, and yet optimistic that social evils could be overcome. Similarly, she reflected the emphasis on literacy, study, and the production of knowledge that grew out of both the expanding realm of social science and the women's club movement, the latter of which furnished support for both woman's suffrage and for a broader list of social reforms. While male editors of turn-of-the-century newspapers hoped that a woman's page or column would bring female eyes upon the ads for the dazzling array of goods being offered by department stores, increasingly the papers' largest advertisers, many of the newspaper women they hired to write them had their own agenda. Eleanor Baldwin was one of them.[1]

In the years after she lost her column in 1909, Baldwin continued to write to influence public opinion while she sought to support herself. She found employment for a short while editing a magazine, *New West*; wrote for a rival daily newspaper in Portland; worked in stints as a stenographer; and produced a series of columns for the *Oregon Labor Press*, the organ of the Oregon State Federation of Labor and the Portland Central Labor Council. In these years, she turned her intellectual attention to the writing of a monetary tract that located the source of poverty and unemployment in the machinations of bankers who used paper money and credit to extort value from working people. These years also saw her oppose World War I. Prior to US entry into the conflict, she wrote a short story that posed the problem of war as a matter of propaganda that dulled the natural moral senses of the men fighting it, which could be sharpened by the appearance and thoughts of antiwar advocates. After the carnage had ended, she would blame the war on bankers and arms producers, and she would defend the Bolshevik experiment in Russia. Writing for a labor newspaper, her condemnation of the wealthy intensified, building on the general understanding that had already been present in the woman's column a decade before.

If Baldwin has been forgotten until now, historical invisibility was an occupational hazard. Only recently have historians like Alice Fahs and Elizabeth Faue put the light of scholarship on the women who entered newspaper work at the turn of the twentieth century. Hundreds of female journalists entered the newspaper industry during this time, yet few gained much in the way of renown in their own day. Newspaper writing was like that in general, but women writers suffered other obstacles. Female journalists were usually relegated to either sensationalistic reporting or to the "woman's page," which historian Fahs suggests embarrassed these educated and capable women because of its "seemingly endless features about society women or its silly decorating projects that involved making furniture out of boxes." Fahs reminds us that the woman's page was hardly the creation of women; it was the male editors interested in "an expanded female readership" who called it into being.[2] But Baldwin was not relegated to such work; instead, she produced about three hundred columns a year, the vast majority of them appearing prominently on the editorial page of the Portland *Evening Telegram*. While many newspaper women used their access to print to go beyond the fluff of the woman's page, Baldwin had a daily venue in which to help create a progressive female reading public. The columns rarely focused on household advice. Instead, they addressed a wide variety of socially relevant subjects, and as such they provide a rich documentary record for understanding the political potential of a kind of female readership, while offering insight into the kinds of discursive communities to which female journalists could contribute if they were given the opportunity.

Through her column and her participation in a network of organizations, Baldwin was deeply immersed in multiple communities in Portland. Her support for woman's suffrage and gender equality was evident in her actions, her writings, and her associations. Baldwin delivered a pro-suffrage speech at a downtown auditorium during the successful campaign of 1912 that ridiculed a female opponent, Miss I. T. Martin of New York, for asserting that women could not understand economic matters like currency and the tariff. In that speech, Baldwin chided men for making issues overly intricate, a means by which men and institutions drew cover for corruption, and she pointed out that both men and women needed to be responsible for governance if they were to construct a "humane world."[3] During the campaign, Baldwin addressed smaller groups of suffrage supporters at "parlor meetings" of the Political Equality League.[4] After the success of the 1912 campaign, Baldwin would make a point of being among the first women to register for the vote in early 1913.[5]

But as was the case for many other active women, suffrage was only one of many public issues with which she was concerned. Five years earlier, she joined the Portland Woman's Club, and from time to time notice was given in the press that she was to give a talk on literary or political themes at meetings of the organization, the leadership of which was increasingly oriented toward social reform and public health issues during the Progressive Era.[6] As late as 1920, she was elected corresponding secretary of the Woman's Press Club and was long an active participant in the intellectual life of that organization.[7] When she gave a talk in 1915 titled "The Dead Level" before the Woman's Press Club, the report in the *Oregonian* declared that she "maintained her usual standard of excellence."[8] She gave talks to an early local version of a parent-teacher association, known as the Home Training Association, on several occasions.[9] And she was known to lecture, as she did in November 1918 on "Modern Novels and Periodicals," to the Women's Christian Temperance Union.[10] In a twenty-year period, Eleanor Baldwin's activities within the sphere of women's organizations ranged from the literary to the political, from the assertive demand for women's rights to the need for parents to be concerned about the welfare of their children, from the rights of prisoners to the rights of workers. She covered a lot of intellectual ground.

While Oregon women's historians have long been fascinated with the efforts of pioneer Abigail Scott Duniway's multidecade fight for suffrage, recent scholars have examined activist women like Esther Pohl Lovejoy, Marie Equi, Caroline Gleason, and Beatrice Morrow Cannady, all of whom sought to transform or ameliorate the harsher and more inequitable elements of urban society.[11] The relationship between inequalities rooted in race, class, and gender has been well established in the historical literature, and it was evident among women of varying political stripes, ranging from social workers to members of women's clubs, many of them concerned that poverty enforced brutal conditions on urban children. As Maureen Flanagan has written of the women who comprised this progressive force in Chicago, they "turned their attention from the private world of the home to the public world of the state" in an effort "to create a city that worked for all its residents."[12] The politicizing effect of such organizational work led women to become the movers and shakers of social justice progressivism.[13] Portland women, like their compatriots in Chicago, addressed problems that afflicted the growing city, ranging from law enforcement to public health, from labor conflict to housing and recreation.

Baldwin's columns, titled "The Woman's Point of View," reflected this broader level of female activism. For instance, she highlighted the efforts of social worker Valentine Prichard, who ran the People's Institute settlement house, which in self-conscious imitation of Chicago's Hull House offered an array of services to poor children and medical care to children and adults.[14] Others like Millie Trumbull, a suffrage activist and a prominent opponent of racial violence directed at Portland's small black population, worked under the auspices of the Oregon State Congress of Mothers to fight child labor, lobbying both the legislature and working-class parents to keep children out of the factories. This too received publicity through Baldwin's typewriter, and her commitment extended further than the frequent column about such organizational efforts; she was the auditor for the organization.[15]

In attempts to understand the breadth of women's activism in the Progressive Era, historians have made distinctions between social feminists or "maternalists" who sought to protect women and children and equal rights feminists who sought to remove all barriers to female opportunity. While the latter would come together to establish the National Woman's Party, which made the Equal Rights Amendment the basis for their politics, social feminists tended to support laws, like Oregon's ten-hour-day law, which limited the exploitation of women at work. Portland women were divided about these matters like women everywhere; for instance, Clara Bewick Colby, the editor of the *Woman's Tribune*, denounced the Oregon law, claiming, "The state has no right to lay any disability upon woman as an individual."[16] Historians have also made distinctions between sentimental maternalists who organized the Congress of Mothers and progressive maternalists like Jane Addams and Florence Kelley who sought to reform economic conditions by ameliorating the lives of working families in settlement houses and by passing laws limiting economic exploitation of working people. And yet the community of women's activism was more fluid than these distinctions might suggest. Molly Ladd-Taylor, speaking of progressive and sentimental maternalists, warns her readers that "the distinction between them must not be drawn too sharply." Likewise, Seth Koven and Sonya Michel point out that maternalists were not concerned solely "with the welfare and rights of women and children but also generated searching critiques of state and society." Despite their differences in emphasis, women in Portland and across the country engaged in institution building that would become the basis for a social welfare state that would more thoroughly arise later in the twentieth century. Many Progressive Era institutions that provided welfare and aid to dependent populations were rooted in female activism.[17]

Baldwin's interests were at least as broad as the realm of female reform, and the columns that she wrote were ecumenical, revealing the political potential of female readership. What is most interesting about

Baldwin's journalism, however, is that it sought to expand the interests of the female reform community toward radical political economy, developing a searching radical "critique of state and society." Her suffrage speech defending the ability of women to comprehend the intricacies of currency and tariffs reflected this broader interest. Her pamphlet *Money Talks* was said to have been formulated in sessions of a woman's political economy group that she was instrumental in establishing with the purpose of, as she put it, "getting at the bottom of the money question."[18] When Baldwin lost her column with the *Evening Telegram*, she began a long-term relationship with the *Oregon Labor Press*, which connected her to a distinct source of local radicalism, but at the same time she continued to lecture for Women's Club meetings and to serve as an officer of the Oregon Woman's Press Club.

Historian Robert Johnston has uncovered the petit bourgeois and working-class coalition that engaged in a long-term effort to limit the power of corporations and the wealthy in Portland. Such opposition to the dictates of capital had been rooted in similar cross-class alliances throughout much of the country in the late nineteenth century, threatening the profits of businessmen, and it was only at the turn of the century that the modern corporation spread throughout much of the economy and capitalists grew more dominant in their efforts to restructure the channels of economic power.[19] Johnston's Portland was a hotbed of radical petit bourgeois progressivism in the early era of corporate domination, and Baldwin's own politics and perspective provide a broadened sense of what middle-class radicalism might have meant.[20] This tradition coalesced in Portland around the reformism of Mayor Harry Lane and around the electoral efforts of William U'Ren, who sought to revolutionize landholding patterns in the state through the passage of radical political economist Henry George's "single tax."[21] This leftwing populism was closely associated with Oregon's early establishment of the tools of direct electoral democracy: the referendum and initiative.

These movement communities, one characterized by female activism and the other by a mostly male-dominated labor movement, tend to be treated separately by historians. Baldwin provides a voice that shows how these movements may have built upon each other. It has long been recognized that populist, socialist, and women's rights activists could sympathize with each other's reforms. Many prominent socialists and radical democrats showed up at suffrage conventions to demonstrate support for women's rights. U'Ren caused a stir at the 1905 meeting of the National American Woman Suffrage Association, held in Portland to coincide with the Lewis and Clark Exposition, when he outlined the potential of the recently adopted democratic tools of the initiative and referendum for gaining the vote for women, and socialist Tom Burns informed the same gathering that the socialists were the only party that had a plank in its platform calling for woman suffrage, asserting, "Men have made a failure of government . . . now let the women try it."[22] Seven years later, the Oregon State Equal Suffrage Association would run a successful suffrage campaign, enjoying the support of U'Ren allies like Will Daly, the president of the Oregon State Federation of Labor, and Alfred Cridge, a longtime Populist Party member and advocate of the single tax. Conversely, physicians Marie Equi and Esther Pohl Lovejoy, both of whom rose to professional status from working-class origins, blended their advocacy for woman suffrage with a larger social justice progressivism that allowed the latter to be appointed city health officer by reform Mayor Harry Lane, and which would lead the former to become a casualty of the Red Scare. Equi found herself under surveillance of the Federal Bureau of Investigation because of her unabashed support for radical labor and her opposition to US entry into the war.

Woman's suffrage was just one part of a larger progressive project to establish a more equitable society. Rebecca Mead has argued that in part it was the ability of suffrage advocates in the American West to mine these kinds of relationships that distinguishes them from the more conservative leadership of national leaders like Carrie Chapman Catt, who feared that such links with radicalism would tar the movement as unrespectable.[23] Strategy may have followed the norms of community politics in the radical progressive city. Some of that progressivism grew out of populist electoral communities that had supported the establishment of direct democracy. As Charles Postel makes clear in his recent interpretation of the populist movement, more women joined the Farmers' Alliance than the Women's Christian Temperance Union, the largest of the nation's women's organizations, and the populist movement provided a forum for discussions of female political equality and economic independence.[24]

The kind of middle-class politics that Johnston uncovers in Portland was strongly opposed by the Portland establishment, especially the *Oregonian*, the leading local Republican newspaper, and the *Telegram* was perhaps an unlikely venue for a radical political discourse. Under the same ownership as the *Oregonian*, the *Telegram* was shaped to appeal to those who might have been interested in a more reform-oriented politics, in part out of a desire to limit the readership for an afternoon Democratic Party newspaper, which would come with the establishment of the Oregon *Journal* in 1902. The moralistic reformism of the newspaper—expressed in support for vice commissions and Prohibition—probably reached its acme under the editorship of John F. Carroll, whom historian George Turnbull describes as a "crusading type of editor" who "had a high sense of public responsibility and a keen desire to make their newspaper serve the public to the limits of its powers." It was Carroll who hired Baldwin.[25]

Baldwin's prominence on the editorial page of a newspaper dedicated to moral reform provided her access to readers who took seriously matters of female morality. While that might seem like a cultural straightjacket, it proved to be an opportunity for Baldwin, who never succumbed to the acceptance of limits on female political and economic power. And that is not as contradictory as it might seem, as many Victorian women, some of them better educated than she, embraced the social purity of Victorianism while supporting female suffrage and challenging the powerful in an effort to support the interests of the poor. Women like Florence Kelley and Jane Addams, who used the settlement at Hull House in Chicago as a female family that could support their efforts to ameliorate the conditions of the poor, embraced Victorian codes of sexuality and restraint; for many women, morality opened the door to female influence. Much as in other places, women's expanding influence was felt in the local corridors of power; the success of the suffrage campaign in 1912 reflected this influence.[26] Baldwin wrote for a community of women that was increasingly comfortable with female exertions of influence. And she made overt the class connotations of many female benevolent reforms.

Radicalism as a Family Inheritance

Radicalism was a familial cultural posture for Baldwin, who grew up in New England fully immersed in some of the significant reform movements of the nineteenth century. That Yankee upbringing would inform her writing and her political activity. Her father was an abolitionist who had left the Methodist Church, for which he had been an itinerant minister, because of his antislavery principles. Both Eleanor and her older brother Henry remembered the centrality of abolition within their households, and both saw the end of slavery as a sign of subsequent liberations to come. Both worked with the labor movement. Henry served as a high-ranking official within the Greenback-Labor Party, was elected to office on the Union Labor Party ticket, and was a chief official for the developing People's Party of the 1890s. While Eleanor was forced to operate outside of electoral politics, she embraced similar philosophies. She understood that allegedly free human beings were held in metaphorical shackles, some of which were imposed by oppressive institutions that sought to perpetuate and expand their own power at the expense of common people. For Eleanor and at least three of her siblings, the sources of such oppression were bankers and their ability to manipulate money and credit to transfer the value of labor created by working people to their own vaults.[27] And the destruction of slavery gave Eleanor and Henry reason to hope that these sources of injustice would also be overturned.

This was by no means the common intellectual route. Only a few of the more prominent abolitionists—Wendell Phillips was such an exception—understood the logic of abolition as applicable to the inequalities generated by wage labor and industrial capitalism. For many who engaged in the abolitionist crusade, slavery was a singular evil because it prevented the individual from making the moral choices that confronted all potential believers: whether to choose good or evil, salvation or damnation. Whereas the slave had little control over his or her own moral purity, as overbearing masters could determine such matters, abolitionists pointed out that wage laborers had no compulsions forced upon them by an employer, and they often pointed to the failure to engage in moral purity and temperance as the source of working-class poverty. The Baldwins were hardly alone in rejecting this free-labor analysis; Alfred Cridge, a mainstay of the Portland single-tax movement that held intellectual sway over the Oregon State Federation of Labor, had a similar familial inheritance and personal trajectory that was rooted in abolition.[28] Such latter-day abolitionists understood that there were logical connections between the two movements.

And that logic seems to have informed Eleanor Baldwin's opposition to corporate capitalism and her support for the Bolshevik Revolution in the aftermath of World War I. Yet her latter-day anti-Catholic radicalism would be expressed in the context of the rise of the second Ku Klux Klan, and it was articulated within the same radical idioms that she had developed previously about reform. Her growing articulation of an anti-Catholic political position was expressed without any acknowledgment on her part that it was incompatible with her earlier abolitionism or her simultaneous defense of the Bolsheviks.

New Thought and the Metaphysics of Anticapitalism

If the daughter of an abolitionist understood that wage labor and banking placed restraints on freedom, she also believed that human beings were held in bondage by fetters imposed by the mind, or a mind that remained unenlightened and unaware of its connection to higher forms of truth and divinity. While Baldwin wrote about political economy and spoke of social progress, her method was much more idealist than materialist, for she believed that the new social order would come as a result of an orientation of the collective mind toward progress and equality. Much of her social vision was ingrained in her religious practices. She departed from her father's Wesleyan Methodism and made her way toward the metaphysics of the New Thought movement, sometimes called "the Boston Craze" by contemporaries, which helped shape her thinking about capitalism, gender, and social progress. Her affiliation with the New Thought community intensified over the years through her close connection to "Divine Science" minister Henry Victor Morgan, a former itinerant with a strong socialist inclination who temporarily resided in Portland, only to take up a permanent position with a congregation in Tacoma in 1912. New Thought was integral to her social vision and her public writings, requiring some understanding of this tradition.

New Thought grew out of the mind-cure philosophy of Phineas T. Quimby, whose teachings would influence the rise of not only New Thought but also Christian Science. The emphasis was on the ability of individuals, guided by a clairvoyant, to tap into spiritual power to overcome disease and debility. New Thought teachings would stress the importance of thought as a material force, as thought particles generated by individuals who were all connected to the divine would attract each other and eventually overcome negative thoughts that kept individuals impoverished and disease ridden. As William James, who understood the emerging tradition as optimistic and efficacious, put it:

Most mind-curers here bring in a doctrine that thoughts
are "forces," and that, by virtue of a law that like attracts
like, one man's thoughts draw to themselves as allies all
the thoughts of the same character that exist the world
over. Thus one gets, by one's thinking, reinforcements from
elsewhere for the realization of one's desires; and the great
point in the conduct of life is to get the heavenly forces on
one's side by opening one's own mind to their influx.[29]

A good deal of historical attention has evaluated the degree to
which New Thought was consistent with the logic of consumerism,
thereby furthering the development of a mass consumer culture. Many
historians have stressed that there was sufficient evidence of this, arguing that New Thought offered a thoroughly American embrace of prosperity and success, encouraging the acquisition of consumer goods and
reinforcing the values of consumer capitalism.[30] There is probably no
better example of what they meant than the midcentury work of Norman Vincent Peale, whose *Power of Positive Thinking*, first published
in 1952 and consistently reissued since then, blended the teachings
of the New Thought tradition with applied psychology to assert the
power of mind in connection with God's higher energy to improve one's
life. As scholar Catharine Albanese argues, metaphysical practitioners,
including New Thought adherents, "have used 'mind'—their own and
others', including God's—as instruments that walk a fine line between
spiritual expansion and this-worldly comfort and success."[31] There are
reasons why New Thought books frequently get shelved in the self-
improvement rather than the religion section of bookstores.

Other historians have produced a more nuanced understanding of
the origins of the movement, one recognizing that New Thought immediately got woven into discussions of gender and civilization, developing within its rather unwieldy tent both those who sought to limit
desire according to the dictates of an older Victorian women's culture
and those who sought to liberate women from such constraints and allow them to seek the satisfaction of desire. It is the latter position that is
usually associated with consumer society. Female New Thought leaders,
like Ellen Hopkins and Elizabeth Towne, took opposite positions on this
subject, and most scholars agree that the long-term tendency within
New Thought was toward the latter's position, which when considering

Mary Baker Eddy's insistence on the evil influences of the body was a sign of a growing chasm between the two movements.[32]

Yet we should recognize that this more "modern" approach to desire and the self did not in itself mean that consumerist indulgence had immediately replaced Victorian restraint. Many of the leading New Thought writers, like Ralph Waldo Trine, embraced a fuller sense of self-expression while supporting reforms that would severely limit the behavior of capitalists. Historian Richard Weiss captures these contradictory elements, noting that the "New Thoughters rebelled at the separation of individualism from the egalitarian ideal. Their argument with social Darwinists was not that the latter denied individualism, but simply that they restricted it to the 'fittest.'"[33] The "survival of the fittest" had created a harsh and unequal environment, which many New Thoughters perceived to be the result of industrial change and corporate consolidation; they blamed industrialists for fomenting the increasing class conflict that they witnessed in turn-of-the-century America. Many of their forays into socioeconomic criticism reveal an affinity with Edward Bellamy's 1888 book *Looking Backward*, which provided a utopian tract in the guise of a novel in which natural evolution led to a peaceful replacement of capitalist society by a Christian socialist one, without the confrontational politics of labor radicals and socialists on the one hand, and private industrial militias and the army on the other. For instance, one writer declared that the new industrialists "have been the unconscious agents of the Supreme in the necessary work of systematizing and organizing productive industry; and in the end their work will contribute immensely toward increased life for all. Their day is nearly over; they have organized production, and *will soon be succeeded by the agents of the multitude, who will organize the machinery of distribution.*"[34] New Thought provided one source of a new liberal synthesis with its acceptance of state regulation, which was different from its nineteenth-century laissez-faire version. In many regards, New Thought sociology reflected the most optimistic qualities of turn-of-the-century social justice progressivism.

Though a self-identified New Thoughter, Baldwin was ecumenical in her treatment of metaphysical regimes, writing affirmatively about spiritualism and theosophy as well as New Thought, and she particularly emphasized the efforts of female spiritual leaders working within these traditions, ranging from Christian Science to theosophy.

In Baldwin's columns, these developments provided evidence that the world was moving in a more divinely inspired direction and that women were playing an important and necessary role in that transformation. Baldwin understood, as did many others in this emerging tradition, that individual health was inextricably interwoven with social improvement.

Nor was she the only New Thought–influenced writer or activist of note in Portland, which had a substantial metaphysical contingent in the early twentieth century, though that community still awaits thorough historical treatment. In 1910, the census reveals that Baldwin lived with two New Thoughters: socialist minister Henry Victor Morgan, who would gain a considerable following in Tacoma, where he took up permanent ministerial duties in 1912, and feminist newspaper editor Clara Bewick Colby. But the New Thought circle spread well beyond Baldwin's own personal acquaintances. Suffrage activist Abigail Duniway Scott was active in spiritualist circles, and the same can be said of single-taxer William U'Ren.[35] Of the Portland New Thought writers, perhaps the best known was Elizabeth Towne, who relocated around the turn of the century from Portland to Holyoke, Massachusetts, when she married a New Englander. There, she wrote and published a magazine, *The Nautilus*, for years, and she would publish at least two of Baldwin's writings. Towne was also active in national meetings of the New Thought Alliance. Also prominent in Portland New Thought circles was Lucy A. Rose Mallory, who for decades beginning in the 1880s produced the *World's-Advance Thought*, dedicated to New Thought and other metaphysical traditions, including spiritualism. In her woman's column, Baldwin frequently mentioned both women, reprinting excerpts from their writings and recommending their publications to her readers. Mallory, in turn, often republished columns that Baldwin had previously written for the *Telegram*. Mallory also published news of others like her, who understood that disease and poor health were spiritual rather than physical problems.

With grounding in the rejection of the regular medical community, New Thought held an ambiguous relationship with science, one that reminds us how the world of wonder and enchantment had not been left entirely behind by advancements in scientific knowledge.[36] Both Baldwin and Mallory were animal rights activists, and both denounced medical researchers who relied on animal experimentation. Yet Baldwin argued that some recent scientific discoveries were consistent with religious understandings that stressed the interconnectedness of body and spirit, of the ever-present existence of divinity within human beings. This had long been the case in the metaphysical community. Spiritualists of the mid-nineteenth century had made an analogy between the "rappings" that first caught public attention in the 1840s and the telegraph, then a new phenomenon, because both provided two-way communication between parties who could neither see or hear each other.[37] Scientific research in particle physics would continue to stimulate thinking, if loosely understood, about how thoughts could migrate in the "ether" and effect change in "matter." And this tendency would influence Baldwin's own contribution to thinking about currency, as she would argue that the actual function of money was equivalent to the flows of electricity through the ether. Without the perverting influence of bankers and banker-inspired law, money was a result of the productive energies of human beings; it was a mere reflection of human creativity, imagination, and labor. It was as if bankers had built dams on previously free-flowing rivers to create bottlenecks in the productive economy. Her currency tract, *Money Talks*, infused the Greenback-Labor tradition with New Thought spirituality, and, accordingly, Elizabeth Towne published it.

Baldwin's embrace of New Thought religiosity intensified her belief that a more just future was inevitable, and it transformed her own journalism into a practice that would help to bring it about. A turn toward the spirit that connected all being, as New Thought leaders perceived, would remove humanity from the baser material motives that led to so much greed and inequity. When Baldwin condemned the capitalist for exploitation, she seemed to take a different approach than when she took on religious and spiritual themes, but her New Thought assumptions about spirit and matter informed her larger view of society, giving her confidence that social progress would mean a more just and nonexploitative world. She believed that as people came to think correctly, tapping into the universal spirit, materialism and greed would be overcome without class conflict and struggle. Baldwin's metaphysical bent intensified the optimism that so many middle-class progressives brought to their reform efforts. And her efforts to get readers to take political economy seriously reflected the means by which a better society would replace the current one.

Progress and the Progressive Era

We know little about women like Eleanor F. Baldwin. Though she was articulate and left a series of developed writings, to gain any sense of her personal life, the historian must sew together a bare narrative from the few biographical scraps that her nonprofessional existence has left behind. A single woman, she had no children to collect and donate her correspondence. Whatever personal papers that remain were donated by the Portland labor movement when it vacated its Labor Temple to either the Oregon Historical Society (OHS) or to the University of Oregon. Rather than personal relationships, these mostly reflect her long-standing interest in currency reform. While her achievements outside of her prolific writing may have been unexceptional, the evidentiary record and the clues provided in her columns suggest that her life was characterized by the struggle to maintain an independent economic existence, and it was reflected in her column's material about women. Her writings provide important insight into the female communities that sustained progressive reform in places like Portland, allowing us to appreciate the optimism and potential complexities of progressive reform. And her ability to support both the Klan and the Bolsheviks in the aftermath of World War I demonstrates just how complex the progressive reaction to unprecedented bloodshed could be.

Despite these complications, the Progressive Era speaks to modern liberals or progressives in dialects that are mostly understandable to contemporary ears; it is perhaps a reflection of the conservative turn of national politics at the turn of the twenty-first century that it once again does so in louder tones. There was a period when historians, particularly those on the left, were often dismissive of progressive reformism. When a liberal consensus about the uses of the state had a hold on national politics in the 1950s and 1960s, progressive and New Left historians grew critical of the corporatism that seemed to go along with it; they objected to the growing bureaucratization of political and economic life, and in many cases to the conformity of culture that they associated with it. These historians worked to overcome what they considered overly simple populist narratives that described progressivism as a democratic uprising of the people against a previously unrestrained set of "robber barons" in an effort to establish a more just and egalitarian society. Many of them found a much more complicated set of motivations for the expansion of government at the beginning of the twentieth century, and some of them, like James Weinstein and Gabriel Kolko, emphasized the support of some of the most important corporations in the land for legislative innovations like the Federal Trade Commission Act and the Meat Inspection Act, arguing that it was in the corporate interest to develop a more stable and regulated environment. As late as the 1970s, it was from the left that some of the most critical historical portraits of progressive reform emanated.[38]

But in recent decades the postwar political consensus about the virtues of the liberal state has broken down, and with the subsequent weakening and even withering of that state, inequality has rapidly increased, approaching levels that have not been witnessed since the Gilded Age, when there was little in the way of a formalized role for the state or federal government in social welfare, and when whatever social safety net that existed was from the combined efforts of small, private groups, local charities, and municipal governments. Amid contemporary assaults upon the liberal state, historians have rediscovered an appreciation for its democratic sources. In returning to histories of sustained political democratic activism, historians like Alan Dawley have reminded readers of the roles played by social justice progressives, even if they recognize that they did not control the agenda as much as earlier generations may have believed.[39] These reform communities energized individuals who felt confident that the world was inexorably on its way toward a more enlightened social order, and who believed that industrial evils would be abolished in the way that chattel slavery had been by an earlier generation.[40] Many of these fighters for social justice took on child labor and the unprecedented levels of inequality that industrialization and the Gilded Age had bequeathed the United States. If these are matters that remain relevant to us today, then Baldwin's approach to inequality and injustice should ring in familiar tones.

As Americans today find themselves in a new Gilded Age, characterized by growing social and economic inequality, neo-progressives have organized protests against the so-called one percent, who have, according to French economist Thomas Piketty, seized a share of national income that is reminiscent of the class structure of the late nineteenth century and, perhaps worse, reflective of the gross inequalities of the old regime of aristocratic Europe, dominated as it was by a class of unproductive "rentiers."[41] The haunting parallels with regard to disparities of wealth and power raise questions about how previous generations understood the forces arrayed against them. Again, the Progressive Era waxes in importance, and it is not merely the left that looks back to that time. The right too has increasingly focused on the Progressive Era, and Woodrow Wilson in particular, as the source of all that it believes is a perversion of the American republic and its nonstatist origins.[42]

This book turns to that era by examining the writings of a female journalist who undoubtedly would have sympathized with the protesters who gathered in Zuccotti Park to protest the financiers who, they asserted, rigged the economy to benefit themselves at the expense of what they termed the ninety-nine percent. While it may surprise some readers that Baldwin articulated much of her criticism in a daily woman's column, it serves as a reminder of the possibilities that women's culture held for resistance to finance capitalism. Historically obscure, Eleanor F. Baldwin used her position as a newspaper writer to articulate some of the sources of radical reform.

But Baldwin interests us not only for the way that she put the woman's column to use. Attention to her spasmodic journalistic production over a longer period also provides us with insight into sources and complexities of reform communities, which helps us to think about the unfolding nature of American reform from the Civil War to the modern world of corporate capitalism. She understood her own political commitments to have been rooted in the abolitionist reform climate of Civil War Massachusetts, which had culminated in the destruction of the slave regime and in the creation of a broader basis for freedom. Paying attention to her writings provides an intriguing exploration into the way that an abolitionist minister's daughter might move from abolition to labor and currency reform. Baldwin is interesting to us in part because she offers what some might see as a consistent approach to human freedom and inequality, as each of these movements sought to remove barriers to human fulfillment and social equality, but others might see as intolerance in her characterization of the Catholic Church as such an impediment.

Baldwin's writings provide a window into the relationship of that radicalism to postwar reaction. As they played out in Portland, the categories of labor radicalism and Klan reaction were not exclusively alternative paths. Oregon labor was divided by the rise of the Klan, as was much of the state.[43] That Baldwin's own sense of self continued well into middle age to be rooted in the abolitionism of her father and her native New England makes her seemingly contradictory writing in the Oregon Klan–affiliated *Western American* all the more intriguing, though it may not explain precisely why she took up the mantle of anti-Catholic crusader late in life.

Yet prior to the war, Baldwin's optimism reflected that of many other progressives, which helps distinguish the turn of the twentieth century from our own time. Progressives believed not only in greater state action but also, in ways that might seem contradictory, that natural law and science were leading the world inexorably toward progress. In many instances, state action was required to put society back on the natural law path from which it had deviated, but once that was done theirs was a teleological view of the future. Progressives did not all agree about how a better world would emerge, but a good many of them shared a belief that their efforts would enable natural forces to reclaim their determining impact on human societies in a way that was clearly progressive. The word "progress" reflects a broader cultural set of assumptions that is harder to hold on to in the wake of the carnage of two world wars and the growing awareness of the environmental consequences of industrialization: that the Western world, or at least the United States, was ever evolving toward greater things and a better life for its citizens.

And that is the value of a book about a woman writer like Eleanor Baldwin. This book focuses on her ideas and her mode of expressing them, which led her to address different radical communities active in Portland and in other places, communities that sought, sometimes successfully, to democratize American society. The reader will not find in these pages much about the development of progressive institution building, whether it was done by female reformers and rights activists or by a mostly male trade-unionist leadership. But that same reader will find a deeply articulated sense of what was wrong in capitalist America, and the optimism that anything that had been derailed could be put back on the right track. Whether or not we agree with Baldwin's assessment of the things that needed to be overcome—and I doubt any reader will sympathize with her on all accounts—the confidence with which she refashioned older ideas to meet new contingencies commands our attention.

1
The Spreading of Abolitionist Roots
THE BALDWIN FAMILY'S MORAL ECONOMY

On a Saturday in early February 1907, the old and venerable play *Uncle Tom's Cabin* was twice performed at the Helig Theater in downtown Portland before crowded houses, once in the afternoon and then again in the evening. The leading Republican Party daily newspaper, the *Oregonian*, treated the performance as a trifle, albeit a popular one, noting the demand for tickets suggested that "All the children (including many old ones) in the city are going to see Uncle Tom and Little Eva." Even a parade was associated with the production. Its popularity notwithstanding, the play had become hackneyed and clichéd; Alfred Kazin described the dramatic renderings as "garish dramatizations" that "emphasized the most melodramatic, seemingly improbable incidents in the novel."[1] By the early twentieth century, the story no longer resounded with the moral fervor that had led to both its writing and its reading in the mid-nineteenth century. And coverage of it in the strongly Republican newspaper suggests just how much the cultural context in which the play was received had changed since then.

The Republican Party had formed in the 1850s out of the wreckage of the second party system, the health of which depended on the ability of politicians to avoid sustained agitation over the issue of slavery. Both Democrats and Whigs found it necessary to stifle slavery talk to maintain the ability of their parties to compete nationally for votes, but Stowe's novel was just one of a series of political and cultural provocations that made that strategy no longer feasible. Increasingly, Southerners perceived a North dedicated to eradicating slavery, and more and more Northerners perceived a Southern plot to make slavery national, and the conflicts over slavery's extension into new territories like Kansas made both scenarios seem increasingly credible. The new party drew former Whigs like Abraham Lincoln and former Democrats like Lyman

Trumbull together for the explicit purpose of preventing the spread of slavery into western territories. As the war broke out and extended longer than anyone had expected, Republicans fulfilled the worst fears of Southern whites by aiming at the source of rebellion—abolishing slavery and replacing it with free labor—and in the immediate years after the war, it would be congressional Republicans who staked their own and their party's future on a defense of the civil rights of the freed men and women who lived in the former states of the Confederacy.[2]

Yet since then the Republican Party had lost its fervor for civil rights. The causes were complicated and interwoven. The immigration of millions of immigrants from southern and eastern Europe and their settlement in northern and midwestern industrial cities awakened nativist fears that had earlier been raised during the era of mass Irish immigration. Many nativists understood this population as the source of industrial conflict, though few unions were controlled or constituted mainly of these populations until the twentieth century. In the wake of the massive nationwide railroad strikes that broke out in the summer of 1877 in response to the last of a series of wage cuts, bringing confrontations between army units recently removed from the South and local populations of workers, E. L. Godkin demonstrated just how quickly Republican minds could be changed. Godkin was the founding editor of *The Nation*, a journal established in commemoration of the Union victory over the Confederacy. A supporter of Republican civil rights measures in the 1860s, Godkin lost faith in the American democratic experiment, and his calls for harsh repressive measures in the industrial cities demonstrated early on where many Republicans would end up:

> Some of the talk of the laborer and his rights that we have
> listened to on the platform and in literature during the last
> fifteen years, and of the capacity even of the most grossly
> ignorant, such as the South Carolina field-hand to reason
> upon and even manage the interest of a great community,
> has been enough, considering the sort of ears on which it
> now falls, to reduce our great manufacturing districts to the
> condition of the Pennsylvania mining regions, and put our
> very civilization in peril. Our superiority to the Ashantees or
> the Kurds is not due to right thinking or right feeling only,
> but to the determined fight with the more enlightened part

of the community has waged from generation to generation against the ignorance and brutality, now of one class and now of another.[3]

The forces of segregation and disfranchisement that we associate with Jim Crow would consolidate as white Southerners realized that Northern Republicans were increasingly less likely to take political risks that might destabilize economic growth. More and more racial theory in the Northern academies seemed to support white supremacy in the South. When the Supreme Court handed down its landmark ruling in *Plessy v. Ferguson*, the bench was occupied by almost exclusively Northern Republican appointees, and the most important dissent was registered by Kentuckian John Marshall Harlan.

For these reasons, it is not surprising that the Republican editors of the *Oregonian* treated the performance as an opportunity to engage in racial mockery, printing a mostly incoherent review in full dialect as if it were lifted from the script of a minstrel show. The reviewer, said to be "Jimmy, the Office boy," was impressed that "dere were real colored mens and ladies on de stoig." The review wandered from subject to subject, at one point turning to song and dance:

> De coon songs an' dancing was prutty good, but Dollar Bill
> Smith hez frein's dat can skin dem anny day. Uncle Billy
> Reese, even if he ha a flat wheel, can beat dem fellers doin' de
> cake walk, just you ask William Reese, an' he aint no brother
> of Uncle Billy's neither. . . . De bes' part of de show wus
> when one of the fellers what takes de part of de liar Marks an'
> doubled an' sold songs and threw in a picture of Little Eva all
> fer ten cents.[4]

For many white Americans, a performance of *Uncle Tom's Cabin* in the early twentieth century was, at best, an insignificant cultural event.

Yet in some minds it retained great importance. For journalist Eleanor Baldwin, who wrote her daily column in a rival Republican daily, the *Evening Telegram,* the theatrical event was worthy of extensive comment, and she used it to articulate a narrative of sustained progress in which moral improvement was teleologically associated with historical development. She asked her readers to ponder how important it was that "well-dressed, comfortable looking colored people" were able to purchase their seats "just as white people did," reminding them that fifty years before this would have been unthinkable. Social progress, if one was willing to pay attention, was on display in Portland on that evening, if not in general, in the form of an integrated audience.

For Baldwin, the play and the novel retained their original cultural and political salience. She seized the opportunity of the performance to remind the mostly female readership of her daily column, "The Woman's Point of View," how dedicated and morally inspired women could make a difference. The author of the novel, Harriet Beecher Stowe, had wielded the gender conventions of midcentury Victorian culture to construct a world in which slavery unleashed male passions for lucre and sex. In that novel, innocent female slaves were at the mercy of greedy and immoral white men who had forsaken the moral guidance of their mothers. No clearer example could there be than the wicked Simon Legree, who provided the epitome of slaveholder immorality by brutally exploiting his slaves both sexually and economically. Legree was haunted by the memory of his dying mother, whom as a younger man he had callously disregarded. Stowe used female domestic influence as a pure stream from which flowed moral conscience, and she also portrayed male logic and reason as the means by which the flow of conscience could be dammed up, and a great moral wrong could be made to seem like the right and necessary thing. In the final pages, Stowe spoke to her mostly female readers, urging them to ignore the rational pleadings of male politicians and ministers and to listen to their own maternal understandings, to their feelings, to "see to it that they *feel right*," that slavery was wrong and to plead the case of the slaves.[5]

These gendered constructions of morality still held deep reservoirs of meaning for the Progressive Era columnist. Baldwin reminded her readers how Stowe had utilized the tools of Victorian domesticity toward revolutionary ends, pointing out that the novelist "did not have a mathematical mind," a failing that did not inhibit her ability to effect change, for "there was no need of long division in the writing of a book that spoke to the heart." Instead, Stowe had marshaled the emotional qualities of the moral mother. Her preparation for this great task was "taking care of her children, doing her own housework, and attending to the duties of the parish that belonged to a minister's wife." Baldwin characterized Stowe, author of the best-selling novel of the nineteenth century and daughter of a prominent Calvinist minister, as a "poor, obscure, minister's wife," who labored in the "backwoods of the Middle West." Unexceptional, Harriet Beecher Stowe stood for the kind of female influence that any right-thinking woman might wield.

When Baldwin pointed out that Stowe had stood up against "a besotted and infidel clergy" and the bearers of "financial and political power" to challenge the status quo in the cause of moral regeneration, she was not merely discussing the mid-nineteenth century. This was no simple reminiscence of the great moral crusade to end slavery. For Baldwin, Stowe's novel held allegorical meanings for the efforts to reform the present. Assessing the novelist's impact, Baldwin asserted, "This woman gave black slavery in the United States its death blow," following that with the rhetorical query, "Black slavery, did I say?" as if she had slipped unconsciously, but it was the answer—"Yes, *only* black slavery"[6]—that was her main point, that wage labor under the industrial regime amounted to another form of slavery; it too was a social evil that needed to be overcome. She made other distinctions that held potential meanings for the present, as when she distinguished between the "surging tide of impetuous young patriotism" exhibited by Union soldiers and the "black and deadly undertow of mercenary motive" or those "men who saw ways to make money out of a war." In fact, she claimed that these war-borne fortunes were the evolutionary seeds out of which the trusts and corporations—the source of economic power in industrial society—had formed, "against which the whole nation is now preparing to defend itself." The column concluded with the hope that another murderous conflagration could be avoided, suggesting the specter of class conflict, in the hopes that self-sacrificing patriotism would be sufficient to oppose "the hyena-like greed that stops at no misery or suffering that can be turned into material wealth for itself."[7]

In deploying the nineteenth century's best-selling and arguably most important American novel as a source of hope and inspiration for a new crusade against what many in the nineteenth century had called "wage slavery," Baldwin was doing something more than filling necessary space in a newspaper column that she wrote six days a week for over three years. In fact, it was a reflection of her own family history, something that she from time to time remarked upon. Eleanor Baldwin hailed from New England, born to a Connecticut minister's family in Naugatuck, one of the river-valley towns that lacked a plenitude of

fertile, arable soil but possessed in some abundance water-power potential along streams and rivers that led men away from the unyielding
land and toward the manufacturing activities that we associate with
the Industrial Revolution. Her father, Lucius Baldwin, did not benefit
from such economic opportunities; instead, he was a struggling farmer
and former itinerant preacher who maintained close relations with the
local Methodist meeting. Her older brother, Henry Chalmers Baldwin,
would grow up in that household during the height of sectional conflict,
would volunteer and fight in the Connecticut Fifteenth Regiment of the
Union Army, and would in later days make the same allegorical use
of the moral crusade against slavery in a period of growing economic
inequality. For Eleanor and Henry Baldwin, abolition would stand for
more than the end of slavery: it became a historical precedent in which
human beings put aside self-interest and acted out of moral conscience;
it was a precedent for fighting the powerful who disregard the needs
of their fellow human beings. And it was rooted in the memory of
the small town in which they were raised. To understand the terms
by which Eleanor would address the contemporary world of the early
twentieth century, we need to travel across the continent, back to the
nineteenth century, to find that Eleanor walked a similar path that other
family members had often followed.

The New England Preacher's Family

Originally from nearby Meriden, Connecticut, Lucius Charles Sylvanus
Baldwin married Maria Willard, the daughter of a Methodist preacher
from Winchester, New Hampshire, in 1829. It is likely that Baldwin
met his future wife during his days as an itinerant Methodist preacher.
Once settled in Naugatuck, the couple would have fourteen children:
Henry was born ninth in 1842, and Eleanor, born in 1854, was the
last.[8] In those years as a young husband and father, Lucius bought land
in Naugatuck and established himself as a farmer, though as his son
Henry remembered, it was a struggle to make ends meet. The land, he
recalled, was poor and "sterile," and its trees produced only knotty,
wormy apples," that others sometimes refused in trade. Henry's "Aunt
Molly" rejected a half-bushel of the apples, telling his father, "You may
take them back, Mr. Baldwin, they are miserable things."[9] To support
so many mouths, Lucius had his children work outside the home at a
fairly young age. Henry was eleven when he was first hired out to work

and board with neighbor John Hopkins, who paid him four dollars a month for farm labor, and when that contract came to an end with the harvest in October, Henry was then shipped off to do chores, mostly woodcutting, for "Aunty Ruthy" Spencer, though not for wages but rather for his board. Other Baldwin children engaged in productive labor to supplement the family's income or to relieve the family of the cost of their subsistence. Older brother Hervey Watson, eight years Henry's senior, left farm labor behind with an apprenticeship with Captain David Smith in his joinery shop, and he would parlay those skills into a career as a builder in the postwar era.[10] Lucius and Maria's daughters also toiled for wages in the developing workshops of antebellum Naugatuck; the eldest, Jerusha, worked in a button shop large enough to employ what the young Henry, probably in error, recalled was about a hundred young women and girls.[11] That the census taker would find the then-sixteen-year-old Eleanor living as a domestic servant in the household of her married older sister, Esther, in Lynn, Massachusetts, in 1870 may have resulted from Maria's death in 1868 and that of Lucius two years later. But working, and even residency, outside of the family home had been the norm for the Baldwin children since before she was born.[12]

This pattern of mixing farm and workshop was a common one in the community. Others found that wages could augment the meager subsistence that could be coaxed from the ground. Henry recalled that another resident of Pond Hill, William Taylor, supplemented what he could raise in the field by working in one of the early rubber-producing shops in town, because, as he recalled, "It was beyond the range of human possibilities that any man could raise enough on these barren and rugged lots to support a family."[13] Agriculture and manufacturing blended throughout the community, as many master craftsmen relied on boys, like the young Henry, to take care of their fields while they worked in their shops. As historian Constance McLaughlin Green puts it, "Farms were something to fall back on; the men of the [Naugatuck River] valley were by natural inclination and gifts more mechanics than farmers, the shops almost always reopened and men joyfully accepting the challenge of the workbench."[14]

Henry and Eleanor grew up during an era in which Naugatuck experienced significant socioeconomic change. Though Green portrays the small town as retaining more of the harmonious elements of the small village than other places undergoing industrialization in the late nineteenth century, attributing this characteristic to the persistence of local ownership over industrial plants, she allows that the transformations were significant. Assessing the period during which Henry lived almost his entire life, she concludes:

> The village of about 300 families in 1844, virtually all Yankee, all Protestant, almost all in reasonably comfortable circumstances, with a common, simple standard of living, had become by 1893 a town of about 1,100 families, nearly half of them foreign-born and Roman Catholic in religion. Most striking difference of all was the disparity of wealth.[15]

Though their reactions to these social and economic changes were in many ways distinguished and determined by gender, Henry playing the much more public role as a third-party politician and occasional newspaper editor, the two Baldwin siblings responded to the new industrial order by trying to revivify the remembered cultural values of the old, something that Eleanor would continue to do in her early twentieth-century women's column.

Those values were a family inheritance. While his father's feeble efforts to scrape by on unforgiving land loomed large in Henry's memory, that is not how Lucius Baldwin made his greatest mark on Naugatuck society. That was accomplished through his service as the first circuit preacher assigned by the Methodist Episcopal Conference to the immediate vicinity. By the early 1830s, the elder Baldwin relocated to the small village of Salem Bridge, as Naugatuck was then known as an outlying district of the town of Waterbury. For years the local "class" met in the Pond Hill School before local Methodists were able to raise the money for a church building.

Their father's Methodism bequeathed Henry and Eleanor the experience of being outsiders and disturbers of social order. Congregationalists had settled Connecticut in the seventeenth century, bringing from England their Calvinist theology and penchant for social cohesion, an educated ministry, and acceptance of one's spot within the social hierarchy. With their Arminian theology, which stressed the ability of individuals to determine their eternal destinies and an itinerant and often uneducated ministry, Methodists appeared to threaten the sources of social stability in late eighteenth- and early nineteenth-century New England, and these central aspects of the early faith had a profoundly leveling effect on Methodist communities.[16] In the 1830s, the Methodist class at Pond Hill drew the ire of local pastor of the Congregational Church, Amos Pettingill, who denounced it as an anarchic, egalitarian, and heretical threat to society. Local Methodists remembered Lucius for ably defending them from the Congregationalist assault. Baited by a local follower of Pettingill, who challenged him to preach on the spot from the same text that the Congregationalist pastor had used to denounce the Methodists, Baldwin demonstrated that though he might not have been college educated, he was well versed in the text and well endowed with the spirit, responding, "without a scrap of manuscript . . . smash[ing] the logic and successfully combatted the arguments of his predecessor so well that the wonderful sermon of Pettingill was never heard of thereafter."[17]

The Methodist penchant for stressing voluntary individual conscience over the bonds of tradition and hereditary church affiliation was capable of further upsetting the equivalence of parish and town that had been breaking down in Puritan New England since the upheavals associated with the Great Awakening of the eighteenth century. Yet fears that Methodist activity would lead to moral decline were probably misplaced, as Methodists sought to encourage the individual believer to overcome the temptations of sin. Lucius Baldwin illustrated this emphasis on personal rectitude. In his public writings about his father, Henry offers little warmth, noting that the elder Baldwin held to a strict moral compass, one that correlated worldliness with sinfulness. Lucius had warned the adolescent Henry that the center of town—despite Henry's recollections and the later historical portrait drawn by Green of Naugatuck as a harmonious, industrious village—was a "'sink of iniquity' where profanity and New England rum fairly tainted the atmosphere."[18] Henry recalled that strong paternal strictures against violation of the Sabbath, against drinking, and against profanity were forcefully articulated, and righteousness by family and community members was expected. Thirty years after the fact, Henry recalled his father administering a "bloodcurdling" reproof to a couple of boys who had the audacity to spend a Sunday afternoon fishing and the misfortune to be caught at it. Henry thought there was something old fashioned about his father's moral stubbornness, and in his own writings he would associate much religious moralizing with hypocrisy, celebrating those who fearlessly embraced free thinking and practicality, as he did in his approval of his neighbor John Bird, who had been thrown out of an orthodox church for using common sense in the face of an impending rainstorm and "saving some hay from being spoiled on the Sabbath."[19]

The familial commitment to abolition was another thing altogether; it would be honored by the next generation. Eleanor would remember her father as a participant in the Underground Railroad, harboring runaway slaves, and Henry would recall Lucius's commitment to the Wesleyan Methodist Connection, an abolitionist group that departed from the Methodist Church over the issue of slavery in 1843 and soon thereafter endorsed the abolitionist candidate for president, David Birney of the Liberty Party in 1844.[20] That schism may have come at some cost for abolitionist Methodists like Baldwin, as principle led them to cut social ties that they had long worked to build. When Lucius cast his lot with the Wesleyans, he explained to the readers of *The True Wesleyan* that he had "hesitated too long" in leaving the Methodist Episcopal Church (it had been only a few months since the break), which he described as "an intolerant, slaveholding church," because "old attachments are hard to be broken off."[21] A longtime Methodist, Baldwin joined a relatively small Northern cadre of twenty thousand abolitionists who had left what had by then become the nation's largest Protestant denomination. Later, after reading Henry's recollections of his father, an elderly local, P. S. Stevens, wrote Henry that Lucius's speeches on slavery "left impressions which have never been forgotten; he was a man that did not spell negro with two g's."[22] There were good reasons why Henry and Eleanor would remember and hallow their father's antislavery commitments.

But the single most extended story that Henry told about the family's antislavery posture was a domestic one, one that anticipated the 1907 column his sister would write: the reading by his mother of *Uncle Tom's Cabin* when he was about ten years old. Here the patriarchal Lucius was replaced by the otherwise rarely mentioned mother, Maria, whose reading alternately made the children laugh and cry in turns; Henry remembered they would "cry when Uncle Tom's sufferings were recounted and laugh at the pranks of Topsy." The reading, and others like it, grew in importance over the years, and in the mid-1880s,

Henry declared that this most overtly political of the sentimental novels produced by women writers "was the cause of the war." He explained:

> The sentiment engendered by that book in the minds of
> the youth of the land from 1850 to 1860 made the devotion
> and sacrifice necessary for that four years of bloody strife
> possible, and without that sentiment the armies of the North
> would never have conquered. Harriet Beecher Stowe's pen
> was the most potent agency of all in the abolition of slavery,
> for without it there would not have been a moral sentiment
> in the North to back up the Lincoln proclamation. When that
> hour arrived there were a million men in the North to whom
> every slave holder became a "Legree."[23]

The memories of the battle against slavery bound brother and sister with the memory of their father and mother. It would continue to inspire both of them to work for reform in an increasingly corporate-dominated economy that had rid itself of chattel slavery but that had established new forms of oppression and inequality. Yet theirs was not the clearest of paths toward a progressive future.

Henry Chalmers Baldwin and the Fight against Industrial Inequality

The Civil War took Henry away from the local farms and workshops of Naugatuck. In the wake of Union General George McClellan's unsuccessful Peninsula Campaign of the spring of 1862, in which the Confederate Army turned back a Union threat against Richmond, Virginia, Henry and others in the Naugatuck Valley joined Company H of the Fifteenth Connecticut Regiment. Enlisting as a corporal, Henry saw considerable early action at the disastrous battle of Fredericksburg, in which well-entrenched Confederates commanded by Robert E. Lee cut down waves of advancing Union soldiers. Captured in the aftermath of battle near the end of the war, Baldwin spent the last two months of the conflict as a prisoner, and he would escape the battlefield with only minor wounds. Like it did for so many Gilded Age males, the war experience remained a part of Baldwin's identity, and in later years he would be repeatedly elected an officer at reunions of the Connecticut Fifteenth, serving as historian and then later as president. In 1893, he would pen his recollections of his army experience, in which he reflected upon laughable and colorful incidents as well as the "suffering and heroism worthy the sublimest period of civilization's growth."[24]

More revealing to his later commitments is the one surviving letter that he wrote to Naugatuck from his period of enlistment. In the wake of the battle at Fredericksburg and the Emancipation Proclamation, Baldwin supported the decision by union generals to follow up and deploy black soldiers on the field of battle. Speaking of General Benjamin Butler, he articulated a pragmatic, if callous, assessment, writing, "I dont care how many negroes he arms or how many get their heads broke if it will help end the war." What he did care about was that civilian merchants and peddlers were seeking profit at the expense of the soldiers. He wrote to Charles Lewis, "Our friends from the North show their love for the soldier in a curious manner by bringing down a cargo of articles as soon as are paid off & in nine cases out of ten seem hardly content 100 percent profit" on their goods, a demonstration of the self-interested manner in which he and the other soldiers in the regiment had been "forgotten by the Patriotic men of New England."[25] Twenty years later, he would publicly reflect on the same inequities, noting that men like fellow Naugatuck recruit Luzerne Woodin, who lost his life defending the "'sacredness' of that flag he loved so well," were paid in paper money, but that the "bond-holder and gambler" who extended credit to the government insisted on being paid in gold.[26] Thirty years later, the eldest of the Baldwin daughters, Celia, recalled Henry's doubts about the meaning of his service, quoting him, "Had I foreseen the use that would be made of our victory I would never have lifted a finger to win the war." Celia would add that the war had brought forth "the quick rise of American plutocracy, which without the war would have taken at least a century and might never had come."[27]

This disdain for human selfishness and greed was characteristic of the way that Baldwin (and at least some of his siblings) interpreted social change as he entered the world of politics as a dedicated Greenbacker and labor advocate during the Gilded Age. But he entered politics not as a frustrated mechanic encountering an increasingly banker- and corporate-dominated society, but rather as a highly successful attorney who was in the process of developing a regional reputation. When he first returned to Naugatuck after being mustered out of the army in 1865, he returned to work on the farm and dabbled in manufacturing.

As late as 1870, soon after his father's death, he was found to be living in his brother Monroe's household, working as a laborer.[28] In an expression of personal ambition, he gave that up and left home for not very distant New Haven, where he entered Yale University Law School. In the years after his 1872 graduation, Baldwin parlayed his legal education into an ever-growing law practice. When Baldwin was in his fifties, the writer of *The Citizen Souvenir*, a local piece of collective biography, described him as the "senior member of the bar in Naugatuck." In 1889, Baldwin opened an office in New York City, working there as many as three days a week, and in 1895 he opened one in Waterbury, all the while maintaining his practice in Naugatuck.[29] By the time of his death in 1897, he and his wife Millicent had a son and two daughters, the eldest nineteen years old.[30] In so many ways, Henry Baldwin seemed to embody the qualities of the Victorian bourgeois professional.

Local postmortem accounts reaffirm this image of conventionality, stressing his reputation for honesty, while at least one noted that he was widely renowned for possessing a prodigious memory and great oratorical powers. But they also stressed, while distancing themselves, his dedication to the labor movement and to currency radicalism. In this, the obituary writers captured Baldwin's long-term commitment to monetary reform and anti-banker politics, a posture first expressed when he was one of the leading organizers of the Connecticut Greenback Party during the late 1870s and mid-1880s. In both 1880 and 1884, Baldwin toured the Northeast in support of Benjamin Butler's presidential candidacy on the Greenback-Labor Party ticket, and he himself ran as that party's candidate for governor in 1880 and for congressional representative from Connecticut's second district in 1884.[31] These commitments would not die with that party; they would be revived in the 1890s when Baldwin became a leading advocate of the newly organized People's Party, founded in 1892, which would pursue many of the Greenback-Labor Party's positions, namely, the fight against banker domination of the economy and a defense of working people. He attended the founding Omaha Convention of that party, and as chairman of the Connecticut People's Party, in 1896 he endorsed fusion with the Democrats and the nomination of William Jennings Bryan.[32] For decades, Henry Baldwin fought political battles aiming to limit the influence of bankers.

Conflicts over money and banks had long roiled Americans and their politics, so long as the market economy had bound them ever more closely and connected them to the rest of the Atlantic world. Such conflicts began to have a formative political effect three decades prior to the Civil War, during the administration of Andrew Jackson, when "Old Hickory" vetoed a bill to re-charter the Bank of the United States (BUS) in 1832. The bank was a quasi-public institution whose power was increased by the placement of governmental treasury funds, collected chiefly from tariff payments and land sales, in its vaults. Those payments were made in what passed for money, the paper notes issued by hundreds of banks across the country that promised that the bearer would receive the face value of the note in gold should it be presented to the bank's cashier. Some of the banks passing paper money were sound, but many of them printed vastly more notes than they could reasonably redeem in hard currency or specie, leading many observers to note that the difference between a banker and a counterfeiter was not always clear. The immense size of the governmental treasury deposits permitted the BUS to increase its own note-issuing capacity while performing some of the regulatory functions of a central bank. Its administrators took notice of the bank notes that accumulated in its vaults, and when there seemed to be too many of them, they presented the notes to the issuing bank for redemption in specie. If the smaller bank could not fulfill its obligations, the bank thus had the power to put it out of business; it had been Congress's intention that the bank administrators fulfill this function when it chartered the bank soon after the War of 1812. Yet many bankers sought the freedom of economic life without the restraining influence of the Bank of the United States. One could be a banker and despise it.[33]

But when Jackson vetoed Henry Clay's bill to re-charter the bank, he did not emphasize the virtues of freeing up banking from the regulatory control of a central bank; instead, he attacked the bank as a "Monster," a source of aristocratic power that had no place in a democratizing America, and in doing so he politically energized the plebeian democrats who sought a more egalitarian economy, instantly invigorating the antimonopoly tradition. On the one hand, the veto and the subsequent battles over banks and treasury deposits led to the crystallization of party divisions, casting the Whigs as the defenders of the Bank and of an orderly economy and society with some direction from government and Protestant religious institutions, and the Democrats as the party of individual freedom, both economic and cultural. On the other hand, it crystallized a distrust of bankers generally among farmers and urban workers; many such people, Jackson among them, distrusted all bank notes, perceiving in them means by which manipulative and unproductive bankers stole the earnings of hard-working producers. An older language about the ways in which "parasitic" bankers and speculators robbed those who produced goods through their labor, which political economists like Adam Smith had agreed was the source of wealth and value, one that worker associations like unions had perpetuated, was revived and brought into the main body of political discourse by the bank veto.

The Civil War transformed the nature of the debate over currency. To fight the war, the Republican Party, which had united over a determination to keep slavery bottled up in the South while it adopted the nationalistic qualities of the Whig economic program, issued greenbacks to facilitate the Union war effort. In the aftermath of the war, the Republican-dominated government began to articulate a retrenchment policy that aimed to retire the greenbacks it had issued to help finance the Union effort and to put the nation's economy back on a specie standard, a policy that alarmed debtors because it promised to shrink the money supply and make it harder to pay off their loans. Radical monetarists put forth a series of recommendations that would become the basis for Greenback Laborism, Alexander Campbell's inconvertible bond proposal chief among them. The proposal was for the government to issue bonds that would pay 3 percent interest and would be "'interconvertible' with governmentally issued greenbacks." The scheme addressed the questions of banker power, as Campbell believed that exorbitant interest rates would be prevented because the rising demand for money would lead holders of the bonds to cash them in, thereby making additional money available for loans. The proposal grabbed ahold of the labor movement during the Civil War era. Andrew C. Cameron, editor of the Chicago-based *Workingman's Advocate*, became a convert to the inconvertible bond scheme in 1866, and two years later the leading trade unionist, iron molder William Sylvis, joined Cameron in arguing that the Campbell proposal was the solution to labor's woes. In the late 1860s and early 1870s, the National Labor Union, a confederation of trade unions and reform organizations, repeatedly endorsed the inconvertible bond scheme. The spread of the greenback doctrine through the labor movement, historian Irwin Unger explains, was due to the growing belief "that usury steadily concentrates the national wealth in the hands of money lenders" and that this "was the key to the great labor puzzle."[34] It was the commitment to a Jeffersonian notion of equal rights by working people and middle-class reformers alike that propelled Henry Baldwin, Eleanor's older brother, to become a prominent leader of the Greenback Labor forces in Gilded Age Connecticut.

Though this movement rejected the hard currency position of earlier reformers, the movement built on the old antiaristocratic discourse of the anti-bank forces of the Jacksonian era. Bankers seemed to monopolize economic power and thereby to violate the natural laws that granted common people the opportunity to improve their lives through labor. The Greenback-Labor movement revitalized the antimonopoly tradition in American politics by urging the replacement of bank notes by a government-issued supply of money. The movement generated economic analysis, for political success depended on understanding the inner workings of banking and finance. As political scientist Gretchen Ritter puts it, "For anti-monopolists money was social and political while for the financial conservatives, it was natural and objective."[35] As Henry wrote of gold in the 1880s:

> not because of any intrinsic quality inhering in the metal
> itself but because human legislation has temporarily endowed
> that particular metal with a power which it denied to all
> other substances, and that is the power to redeem the debtor
> from the tyranny of the creditor. It is legislation and not
> nature which makes gold preeminently valuable.

It would be Eleanor's most fervent political objective to lift the veil over bank-issued money and expose it as an unnatural means of transferring wealth from labor to capital. Sympathetic to other reforms that grabbed the interest of labor reformers, she and her brother Henry remained imbued with the absolute necessity of removing the shackles imposed by bankers on working people.

Debtors found it increasingly difficult in the wake of the monetary contraction policy of the federal government to pay their creditors, whom Henry Baldwin described as "men ready to speculate in the blood and tears of their fellows." The problem was that legislation had ensured that there was "a much larger inflation of credit (which is what the banker lives on) than money, and thus an enormous tax was laid on labor in the shape of shaves, discounts, bonuses and interest, all terms used to disguise the thief of usury and make him look respectable."[36] The problems afflicting producers, therefore, were grounded in legislative action, and they were likewise susceptible to political solutions, like those offered by the Greenback or Greenback-Labor Parties.

Baldwin described his loyalty to the Greenback-Labor movement in ways that reflected his commitment to justice for working people. In 1884, he explained to the New York labor newspaper editor John Swinton that his support for James Weaver, the nominee of the Greenbackers in 1880, and for Benjamin Butler, who would become the nominee in 1884, was grounded in their being "hated by the bankers and millionaires," and that they "both regard the industrial classes as worthy of as much attention at the hands of Congress as the note shavers and stock gamblers."[37] That the democratic republic had degenerated into a government for and by the rich was a constant theme in Baldwin's writings to the labor paper. He lamented during the fall of 1885, "We have permitted our Government to pass into the hands of the most barbarous, soulless set of bloodsuckers that ever cursed any people—viz., the usurers."[38] As Baldwin saw it, Americans had experienced a fall from a state of republican grace and were now suffering from a depraved government and society.

Despite his abolitionist and New England childhood, characteristics that usually led young male reformers to avoid the Southern-dominated Democratic Party, Baldwin's early political experience was characterized by at least some allegiance to the party of Jackson, and much of that seems grounded in his association of banking with illegitimate power. This was evident in a memorial he wrote after the death of former Greenback candidate Peter Cooper. Baldwin saw that Cooper had lived during tumultuous and formative periods in American history, noting that he was "in business when the old national bank was chartered in 1816 and lived through all that period when that robber institution robbed the people of this nation up to 1836."[39] Perhaps this attachment to the party of Jackson explains his willingness to embrace and push for populist fusion with the Democrats after the latter had nominated William Jennings Bryan, making a break with the conservative Cleveland administration that had further contracted the currency by ending the federal government's silver purchases in 1893 to bolster gold reserves. Whereas he had denounced both the Republican and Democratic Parties as "corrupt and unworthy of support" during the 1880s, Baldwin hailed the Democratic platform of 1896 by celebrating it as the first Democratic ticket in twenty years "that has smacked of Jeffersonian and Jackson Democracy," and he predicted that a Democratic victory would allow "the United States to win its independence from the international gold syndicate and assume control of its own money."[40] But Baldwin's efforts would be for naught, as William McKinley handily defeated Bryan in November.

Nowhere is this attachment to Jacksonian themes more complicated than in the defense he wrote of Andrew Johnson, the Tennessean who served as Lincoln's vice president during his second term and who thereby assumed the presidency after the assassination, for the New York labor organ *John Swinton's Paper* in the late fall of 1885. Calling Johnson the "truest friend the toiling masses ever had in the White House," Baldwin blamed his poor historical reputation on "the bond-holding, stock-gambling, money-trading pirates, who have for the past twenty years had the management of our national finance, been enabled to perpetuate the lies that have been told" about him. That Johnson in the White House had earned the enmity of Republicans for his efforts to quash the intent of Congress and to support Southern states' efforts to impose a form of second slavery on recently freed African Americans was completely absent in Baldwin's account; so was the racist invective that the then-president engaged in during the 1866 congressional campaign as he sought to rally voters in opposition to the growing propensity of Republicans to impose federal authority to protect the rights of former slaves, or "Freedmen." Despite the counterrevolutionary positions taken by Johnson, Baldwin blamed the deteriorating conditions for labor in Gilded Age America on the eclipsing of Johnson's strong influence by Republicans who first neutralized him in an impeachment trial and then replaced him in the White House with the politically feckless Ulysses S. Grant. Baldwin believed that Grant gained the presidency by promising "to assist in carrying out" the schemes of bankers. "Grant was their man," he asserted, and one of Johnson's virtues had been that he saw through this. Two years after the 1869 Credit Strengthening Act moved the treasury toward retirement of the war-issued greenbacks, signed into law by Grant, Johnson had written:

Slavery has disappeared South of Mason and Dixon's line only
to reappear North of the line in the shape of a funded debt
of two billions, the holders of which will hereafter prize the
whole producing class, North and South, just in proportion
to the docility they manifest under the crucial application of
the thumb-screws, to make them bleed *golden* drops of blood
from the finger ends of labor in the shape of interest.[41]

In quoting Johnson in this way and defending his historical reputation, Baldwin departed from the path that is often associated with
the New England tradition, portraying illegitimate power in Jacksonian
terms, associating it not only with a "Slave Power," as Republicans had
done, but with a "money power." As Eric Foner noted decades ago,
the Republican Party briefly unified Northern society to fight against
the Southern slave master, the agent who was perceived by many
Northerners to be corrupting the flow of liberty and opportunity for
free labor in the republic by attempting to spread slavery across the
continent.[42] Whether or not Baldwin ever supported the Republican
Party is unclear, and in the 1880s he expressed nothing but contempt
for the proslavery position taken by the Democrats in the 1850s. But
as he grew more active in the Gilded Age, he articulated the antiaristocratic themes previously associated with radical workingmen in the
antebellum Democratic Party, arguing that it was the unholy alliance
between government and the wielders of credit and bank notes that was
responsible for the perversion of democratic society.

It is unclear whether it was Henry's penchant for monetary radicalism and the language he used to denounce grasping capitalists that
led him to support the Gilded Age struggles of industrial workers, or
whether it was the opposite, but by the time John Swinton began printing his labor newspaper in the mid-1880s, Baldwin was an unabashed
supporter of the effort to improve wages and conditions for working
people. In mid-1884, amid labor troubles at the Baltic Mills in eastern
Connecticut, Baldwin wrote Swinton of his own tour of "that child-
killing institution" six years earlier. He wrote that he had come there to
"address workers on industrial reform," and found enthusiasm among
local working people, who encouraged him to tour the factory the next
day. What he found was a Dickensian scene of "scores of little pale-
faced girls, of from eight to twelve years of age, almost all barefoot, and

apparently with nothing on but a calico gown" on a "frosty" morning. Wages were abysmally low, the men earning but eighty-seven cents a day, while the girls were paid between ten and fifteen cents for twelve hours of labor. Baldwin recalled that his "eyes became too misty to see plainly" as he witnessed the misery and deprivation around him. His account was filtered through his Democratic and Greenback political lens, as he concluded after looking "in the faces of the slaves in that mill" that Republican Party promises that a protective tariff would improve the condition of American labor had amounted to nothing, asking "could 'free trade' render their condition worse?"[43]

A year later, Baldwin recounted for the readers of the New York–based labor paper the results of a strike in Naugatuck's "Big Shoe Shop," a rubber factory capable of putting out "ten thousand shoes per day." Though the account was lacking in specifics about the cause of the conflict and the eventual settlement, Baldwin praised the Knights of Labor for its resolution, and he characterized the "several hundred men and women" who had joined the two Knights assemblies that had been organized for their "intelligence and prudence." In ways that support Green's historical account of Naugatuck as a harmonious industrial village, Baldwin portrayed the Naugatuck factory owners as reasonable men who, "on closer acquaintance with the K. of L., say they wish all their help belonged to it." Baldwin saw the instance as broadly instructive, lecturing: "Intelligent, *organized* labor will always command respect, while disorganized and ignorant labor can and will be kicked and cuffed by greedy capitalists, *ad libitum*." Growing unity "of the toilers of the land" under the banner of the Knights of Labor, Baldwin asserted, would put the private armies of Pinkerton detectives and agent provocateurs, "like Othello, out of a job, and subjects for a charity hospital or the penitentiary."[44]

As the Knights of Labor nationally experienced meteoric growth in the wake of their successful strike in 1885 against the Gould Railroad system in the Southwest, Baldwin increasingly tied his own radical ambitions to that organization. In the late winter of 1886, Baldwin spoke in front of a crowd of one thousand in Bridgeport, Connecticut, and praised the effect that the Knights of Labor had on the context in which labor organized, terming it a "wonderful change." Baldwin claimed, "Working people are no longer denounced for attending to their own affairs, even if on Sunday they preach the brotherhood of man." He took the occasion to call for structural change that would replace capitalism with "universal co-operation," and in the meantime he laid out a reformist program that included fewer hours of labor, a graduated income tax, and governmental ownership "of the three agencies of industry, money, the telegraph and the railroads."[45]

The public reputation of the Knights, and of the labor movement in general, was shaken by the events that occurred during the eight-day agitation in Chicago in early May of that year. A bomb exploding in Haymarket Square at a protest meeting against the use of city police to protect the McCormick Company and its use of strikebreakers killed a policeman, and the state of Illinois arrested and convicted a group of anarchists associated with the organization developing the meeting. Their trial was replete with judicial prejudice against the defendants, and they were sentenced to death. For the labor movement, the events at Haymarket Square became divisive. Some distanced themselves from the anarchists; one of those who did was the head of the Knights of Labor, Terence Powderly, who sought to protect his organization from any sign that it had been complicit in the violence. That would not be the case for Baldwin, who was then the editor of the radical Naugatuck *Agitator*, and who spoke of "capital's foul conspiracy" to have the Chicago anarchists forever silenced, reminding his local readers that the abolitionist John Brown, executed by the state of Virginia prior to the Civil War, had been remembered as "a fearless defender of human rights," while those who did the bidding of "the respectable worshipers of property" in executing August Spies and Albert Parsons, whom he termed "pioneers of progress," would be "consigned to ignomy."[46]

As class tensions increased nationally in the wake of Haymarket, labor tickets put up by the Knights of Labor competed for office across the country, in small towns as well as in the metropolis. Perhaps the best known of these was the running of radical political economist Henry George for the mayor's office in New York City by that city's Central Labor Council. In his 1877 treatise *Progress and Poverty*, George had blamed private land ownership for stifling the natural workings of the marketplace and causing working-class poverty and misery. The campaign focused heavily on the plight of those living in the poorest tenement districts of the city, drawing attention locally to the physical conditions of working-class poverty that would capture the attention of less radical reformers in the Progressive Era. George's candidacy frightened the wealthy and party leaders, as unprecedented enthusiasm for an independent labor candidacy developed in working-class neighborhoods of the city. In the end, George came in second to Democrat Abram Hewitt but ahead of Republican candidate Theodore Roosevelt.[47]

The Knights of Labor assemblies of Naugatuck articulated the same radical electoral spirit in the fall of 1886, taking independent political action and running a local ticket with Baldwin heading it as a candidate for town clerk. The ticket swept the Naugatuck elections, and Baldwin attributed the local electoral success to the local Knights' decision to "play a lone hand here, just as it must have to everywhere." At the same time, he lectured readers of *John Swinton's Paper* that only "When labor learns enough to strike at the ballot box in earnest, for a monetary system that will not have in it the sting of usury, then 'the clouds will begin to roll by.'" W. F. Hinckley, an organizer for the Knights, tied the local effort to the same spirit that animated the campaign of Henry George for mayor of New York City, asserting that the Naugatuck Knights were "as a unity in sympathy with the spirit that nominated HENRY GEORGE for Mayor" in New York. Baldwin too saw meaning in the New York contest, calling it "inspiring" and concluding that it "has actually stiffened up my muscles for the real labor contest two years hence."[48]

Though Baldwin perceived a different ultimate cause of working-class misery than George had, focusing on currency rather than land, the moment reflected a willingness of radicals to cooperate, and occasionally in the years to come, that cooperation would prove fertile as Baldwin would clearly incorporate Georgeist themes regarding land monopoly into labor speeches. Yet threats to this common language of reform unity appeared as factions of trade unions, and socialists proved unwilling to subordinate their visions to George's emphasis on a land tax. By the summer of 1887 the New York City coalition that had run George the previous fall collapsed. Though the moment passed in which national independent action by labor seemed viable, Baldwin continued to blend support for labor and radical monetary politics for the rest of his life, and in 1890 he headed an independent labor ticket in Connecticut as its candidate for governor.[49] As a candidate, Henry spoke what Eleanor would write: a broad reform laborite agenda, grounded in the experience of the nineteenth century.

In the late 1880s, organized farmers in the South and on the Great Plains moved beyond support for inflation in their proposal for C. W. Macune's "subtreasury" plan, which called on the federal government to issue notes based on the produce that farmers would store until prices rose in government warehouses, all while calling on the government to nationalize the railroads and the telegraph. The core element of the Omaha Platform of the People's Party, the subtreasury plan was sacrificed in 1896 for the less radical and simpler-to-explain support for the unlimited coinage of silver by the government.[50] In each case, the goal was to inflate the currency and drive down the cost of borrowing capital, which inflationists believed hamstrung the economy and led to high unemployment and low wages.

During this surge of anti-banker politics, this time associated with the People's Party, Baldwin again shows up in public accounts of working-class protests, drawing attention to the power of bankers and corporations to attenuate the rights of citizens. The industrial depression of the 1890s deepened the sense of a crisis of governance, providing a growing sense that corporations were in control of all aspects of American government. For labor officials, the use of the army to put down the nationwide railroad sympathy strike by the American Railway Union (ARU) in support of striking workers at the Pullman Car Company's construction plant demonstrated that the Cleveland administration was hostile to unions. When the federal courts intervened, ordering the union men to leave the trains carrying US mail unimpeded, it introduced in a national event the ability of a judge to arrest and convict union members, in this case ARU president Eugene V. Debs, avoiding the kind of jury trial that often proved resistant to the conviction of local union activists. For radicals, it became increasingly evident that all branches of government had been corrupted by corporate power. The People's Party, despite its origins in the problems of small farmers in the Cotton Belt of the South and in the wheat fields of the Great Plains, extended its critique of corporate banking power to include the travails of industrial workers and posed itself as offering a revival of republican society and governance.[51]

Working with the People's Party, Baldwin addressed a gathering of a few hundred of the local unemployed in the spring of 1894, linking their plight with the contraction of the currency supported by the Democratic Grover Cleveland administration.[52] A few months later,

Baldwin gave a speech praising the unemployed associated with the Coxey's Army movement that had organized to march on Washington in support of a paper currency.[53] The following year, in Hartford, Baldwin addressed a considerably larger crowd, estimated at twenty-five hundred, that was called to express support for the grievances of local street railway workers against the Hartford Street Railway Company, which had discharged union members. Following a procession of three hundred men, representing thirty unions, through the streets of the city, local speakers addressed the rights of working people to act in unions, before Baldwin delivered the meeting's principal address. Baldwin put the local conflict in national context, focusing on the growing problem of corporate power. He called on voters to use their implicit power in the grant of corporation itself to "amend or take them away, if they are not used for the benefit of the people." He denounced the decision of the US Supreme Court in upholding a contempt conviction of American Railway Union leader Eugene Debs for that union's defiance of a court order during the Pullman Strike of 1894, warning that the people "no longer had the right of a trial by jury when a corporation was against them."[54] Baldwin's political vision led him to perceive in the accumulation of economic and political power the working out of a long-standing effort of bankers and other economic elites, step by step, to destroy any semblance of an egalitarian society. Baldwin understood himself as fighting an old fight: that of Jackson against a "monied aristocracy."

Abolitionist Morality and Henry Chalmers Baldwin's Gilded Age Radicalism

If his grasp of social problems was rooted in an old Jacksonian scenario, so much so that he would embrace white supremacist Andrew Johnson as the best working person's friend in the White House, Baldwin's sense of the ability to overcome such evils paradoxically came from the battle against slavery, a matter rooted deeply in the New England landscape and in his family's own history. The abolitionist crusade served as the great example of the moral crusade in which those fighting evil acted selflessly against those who grasped self-interestedly for more and more power over their fellow human beings. While these examples are evident in much of his correspondence with newspapers, they are especially evident in the extended reminiscence that he wrote about Naugatuck in the years before the Civil War.

Though it is unclear exactly when Baldwin wrote the extended "Personal Recollections," we know that thirty-eight chapters were published in the 1880s, when Henry was in his forties and active in Greenback-Labor political circles. Many years after his death, this set, with another twelve chapters that were not originally published, was given by his widow, Millicent Baldwin, to the Naugatuck *News*, which published all fifty in 1927, some forty years after the original publication and about seventy years after the events discussed transpired. In these recollections, Baldwin portrays a nostalgic portrait of the small and relatively harmonious manufacturing village, one that was rent some by the agitation over slavery. Henry used that portrait, much as his sister Eleanor would in later years, to distinguish between the moral foundations of sacrifice that were evident in the abolitionist crusade and the self-interested economic behavior that was currently destroying the fabric of social life in Naugatuck and in the country at large. The "Recollections" were both a piece of nostalgia and a call to action.[55]

They begin with a satirical statement about corporate power that echoes Henry George's emphasis on the evils of land ownership and sets the tone for these published memoirs. Baldwin asserted that the effort of the "masses of mankind" to "procure 'our daily bread'" still benefited from the availability of "air and water," only because they had thus far "escaped the control of corporations, and can be obtained without their consent."[56] In a later installment, Baldwin explicitly referred to George, reflecting on "why it is, when the earth is so large that so few own their own bits of trees, or are free of rent and usury. Henry George was speaking in London the other day and quoted 'The earth is the Lord's.' 'Yes,' shouted an Irishman, 'the land-lords.'"[57] A similar sentiment about the avariciousness of those who would monopolize nature was expressed in his story about his "Aunt Molly," for whom he had cut firewood as a child. After doing his work, she read him the Wordsworth poem "Goody Blake and Harry Gill," in which farmer Gill stops the poor woman Blake from gathering wood on his land to keep her warm in the winter. In anger and frustration, the woman curses Gill that he would remain cold—"His teeth they chatter, chatter still!"—no matter how much wealth he had accumulated. Baldwin recalled that then the story made his "teeth 'chatter, chatter,'" and since then had led him to "feel like pronouncing the prayer of old Goody Blake" on seeing "fallen and rotten wood all about," that the "hundreds of poor families . . . suffering from the cold . . . dare not go to gather this worse than wasting wood, for fear of some avericious [sic] owner."[58]

The question, then, curses notwithstanding, was how those working for progress could find the means to overcome the kind of self-ishness that makes people indifferent to the suffering of others. These were questions that were central to many radicals, Eleanor and Henry included. Henry knew that the clergy should be instrumental in this purpose, but he wrote of them as a class no less self-interested than the rest of humanity. Like a come-outer lambasting an educated but unconverted ministry, Baldwin posed a secular analysis of the clergy's collective lack of scruples. He asserted, "Not one in ten of the clergy-men in this land today believes in the existence of the old orthodox hell, and not more than one half preach it, and four out of every five who do, do so for the sake of favor, bread and butter." For Baldwin, religion in the hands of such a self-seeking ministry was tantamount to superstition, which he claimed "has been the means of enslaving the ignorant many, thus allowing the cunning few by means of a threat of Hell or promise of Heaven, to live in idleness and luxury."[59] His anti-church writings were inspired to remind his readers in the 1880s that clergymen had been just as obtuse in their thinking about justice in the 1850s. He remarked, "It seems strange today to recall the fact that the church as an organization could defend slavery, and that its preachers and bishops had no difficulty in finding and quoting from the Bible, ample authority to justify their cause, precisely the same that they now do to justify another system of slavery, a little more refined but none the less cruel." Such clergymen actively worked against reform, as some made it a practice to preach against "the wicked abolitionists," who they charged sought to "make the slave discontented 'with the lot where it had pleased God to put him.'" Though considerably less devout, Henry wrote in ways that his Wesleyan father, Lucius, would have appreciated.[60]

Reform would need to come from outside the institutions that had accommodated themselves to capitalist power, just as it did to destroy the slave power a generation before. Baldwin argued that it was the self-less individual, who risked reputation and wealth to denounce slavery, who had brought the issue of slavery to a crisis point. "Lloyd Garri-son, Wendell Phillips, Horace Greeley and Charles Sumner," Baldwin reminded his readers:

were denounced right and left as men who should be treated
as public enemies, but in nearly every neighborhood there
was some bold mind not afraid to speak up in defense of
these men, and declare they were simply the vanguard in the
advance march of human progress.

In Naugatuck, the possessor of that bold mind was John L. Bird,
who refused to knuckle down to clerical authority when it would lead
to foolish waste, leading him to violate Sabbatarian strictures against
work on Sunday in order to save his crop from the threat of inclement
weather. Baldwin described his neighbor as confident "in the strength
of his position on the question of slavery," and that he "would calmly
endure any abuse in words" from those who "claimed it a 'divine
institution,'" and respond "with the keen blade of logic pointed with
the doctrine of 'unalienable rights.'"[61] It was Bird, who "with a few
keen words full of logic and humanity" enraged "every proslavery
man in the town into a towering passion," by defending "old John
Brown," who "began the war on slavery in earnest by attacking Harp-
ers' Ferry." Otherwise, Naugatuck had just a handful of men who did
not believe "that the sentence which sent the heroic old man to the
gallows was just."[62]

Similar virtues would be necessary in the battle against industrial
inequality. Again, selfishness, enabled by inequitable law, would have to
be opposed. Baldwin recognized, as did all Greenbackers, that "Money
can be made by law," but he worried that the "worship of money" would
"strangle" American "courage, virtue and honor," a "trinity without
which our republic will become worse than an empty name."[63] In this
paradigm, in which virtue was antagonistic to self-interestedness, the
inequalities of industrial society took on a kind of moral equivalence to
those of slave society. Baldwin asserted, "The greed and avarice of the
slave oligarchy was only equaled by the capitalistic greed of today that
has grown arrogant and tyrannical because it can legally plunder labor
by controlling, as slavery did, the law-making and executive branches
of the government." Like the slave power before it, the "capitalist rob-
bers" were arrogant and "invited attack" because capital "monopolizes
the bounties of nature, confiscates in the name of debts, bonds, interest
and 'sacred legal obligations,' the results of the labor of the millions who
toil." Baldwin concluded his comparison by noting that, like slavery,

which "went out in a red sea of blood," the final reckoning with capitalists "will be fierce and bloody."[64]

For Henry Baldwin, the moral crusade and revolution of his childhood that led to the destruction of the system of slavery remained the
model by which the new inequities of industrial society would have to
be opposed. In this, he brought into the Gilded Age the moralism and
antislavery posture of his father and of select community members like
John Bird. His sister Eleanor would bring similar commitments to her
columns in Portland during the Progressive Era. Monetary radicalism,
in particular, seems to have been a family inheritance.[65]

The New England Origins of Eleanor Florence Baldwin's Ideas

Eleanor worked many similar materials into her writings, though she
came to the same intellectual place by a somewhat different route, one
mediated by gender and birth order. While Henry worked and lived
outside of the family home, he did not leave Naugatuck until he joined
the Fifteenth Connecticut at the age of twenty. By that time in her life,
Eleanor would already be moving from household to household, and
these movements would lead her outside of the village of her birth. In
terms of career preparation, instead of attending Yale University Law
School, Eleanor would attend the New Britain Normal School, which
graduated mostly female students, preparing them for a low-paying
white-collar career teaching in the public schools. And while Henry
engaged assertively in the male-dominated sphere of electoral politics,
Eleanor's engagement with public issues was more personal and unencumbered by any political party, more affected by her adherence to
New Thought spirituality (discussed in chap. 4) than the success of any
electoral coalition.

Eleanor's childhood and adolescence were shaped by the tragedies
that befell the family during the war decade. Five family members died
in these years, culminating with the deaths of her parents, Maria in
1868 and then Lucius in 1870. Three of Eleanor and Henry's siblings
also died, the first of these, Louis Sherwood Baldwin, in uniform in
January 1863. After the war, twenty-year-old Matilda Augusta died in
June of 1866, and Albert Warren followed her to the grave in January
of 1868. For the next thirty years, records find Eleanor residing outside
of Naugatuck, but usually with the family of siblings. For instance, in
1870, the census lists her at the age of sixteen as a domestic servant

in the household of her older sister Esther, who lived with her husband John F. Brown in the city of Lynn, Massachusetts. There Eleanor undoubtedly helped with the couple's four children, who ranged in age from two to nine. By the time that she matriculated at the Normal School in 1878 and as late as 1880, she boarded in nearby Meriden with Lettie and Edmond Bingham, and while Lettie was not a sibling, an older sister, Frances Adelaide, had married into the Bingham family, so there likely was some family connection. From the mid-1880s to the late 1890s, Eleanor sometimes shows up in the records living with her widowed oldest sister, Jerusha, and her daughters in Medford, just outside of Boston, and before that she is known to have stayed with Jerusha and her husband, Thomas Small, in Provincetown. While the death of her aging parents—Lucius was seventy-four when he died—may have forced Eleanor out of Naugatuck and from household to household, family relations continued to structure much of her life.[66]

And so did gender. While there were some male students at the Connecticut Normal School at New Britain, it was primarily young women who attended this publicly funded academy for the training of schoolteachers, and in her graduating class, ten of the twelve who finished the program were female. By the post–Civil War era, public school boards had paid attention to the pleadings of advocates like Catharine Beecher, who argued that moral Protestant women in the classroom would provide the best professional cohort for training the next generation, a growing number of them immigrants from Catholic lands. If they also noted that they could pay those women less than men, it only further opened the field to female employment. Increasingly, teaching was becoming a female profession; if Henry's gender led him toward the ballot box, so it seemed that Eleanor's led her toward the classroom.[67]

The New Britain Normal School was established in 1849 as a free public institution that provided a broad education in relevant subject materials while providing classroom training in the "model school" that was connected to it.[68] Its mission to train teachers was declared repeatedly in annual catalogues, which stated, "None, therefore, are admitted who are not willing to declare their intention of teaching, and the diploma of the school will be given only to those who show fitness and enthusiasm for the work." Students received instruction in elementary mathematics; the physical sciences of astronomy, geology, and chemistry; the life sciences of zoology and botany; history; art; and grammar and composition.[69] Eleanor must have mastered the material reasonably well, as she was selected to deliver an essay, "Errors and Criticism," during the commencement ceremony.[70]

Nonetheless, after finishing the curriculum of the two-year program, Baldwin only briefly entered the classroom, perhaps teaching as little as one sixteen-week term in a grammar school in West Meriden, where she was paid forty-five dollars a month, slightly more than an unskilled man could expect to make, but considerably less than a male in white-collar employment would earn. The basis for a robust independence it was not, but in the segmented labor market, in which women had limited opportunities to sell their labor time and skills, it provided a relatively reasonable subsistence. The New Britain Normal School attempted to track its alumni for a number of years, and in subsequent reports they note that Eleanor had not taught since 1880.[71] Though teaching proved not to be her calling, and there are no clues as to why this was the case (in fact, more than a few of her columns would be devoted to the problems facing educators), the education probably served Eleanor well, leading to her ability to support herself as a single woman through a career in journalism and stenography. Despite the institution's statement of purpose, other women, with intentional foresight or not, did as Baldwin, using the mostly public-funded education provided by the Normal School as the foundation for a career in white-collar work.[72]

For the rest of the nineteenth century, Eleanor Baldwin's life comes in and out of the historical record, appearing in narrow snapshots in census reports and city directories, and then disappearing with little trace. Though we have some idea about whom she lived with during these years, there is no precise evidence of whom she worked for and in what capacity. Yet there are clear, if sporadic, signs of the vision of social justice and moral progress that would be evident in her column in the first decade of the twentieth century. The first appears in *John Swinton's Paper*. In these letters, written in the mid-1880s, Eleanor displayed a commitment to workers and their advocates in the labor movement; unlike Henry's messages, these were devoid of any kind of electoral politics.

Yet there was a strong and acknowledged connection between the two siblings. Eleanor attests to the influence that her elder brother had on her by dedicating to him *Money Talks*, the monetary pamphlet that she would publish in 1915. Looking back, she explained that she had "felt a consuming desire to learn about money" when she was "just a girl at school." But the faculty, "though well equipped for their work," admitted ignorance and could not satisfy her "hunger for knowledge." Instead, she found satisfaction from Henry, who "could and did answer all the questions I asked," setting her "eager young feet on the long trail of inquiry they have ever since followed . . . the ultimate reality of money."[73] Though she would not bring together her thinking about money in any systematic way until the second decade of the twentieth century, she would spend much of her adulthood addressing similar kinds of inequity as her brother had.

But those ideas were more diffuse throughout the family. Eleanor's older sister Celia, who was closer in age to Henry, shared a belief that the source of social oppression lay in inequity of the nation's currency system. In 1896, as Henry canvassed for the Populist Party, Celia wrote to the reform journal *The Arena* to admonish the followers of Henry George for not recognizing that it was money that mired the masses in poverty. "Bankers," she wrote, "produce no wealth. All that they get then is at someone's expense. How do they get it?" she asked, only to provide the answer: "By usury." The Baldwin clan, then, granted its youngest member with a broad sense that the kinds of inequality that were emerging in the industrial landscape violated the promise of a benign natural law.[74]

In the fall of 1886, as Henry was leading the local ticket in Naugatuck and beginning to pay attention to the George campaign in New York City, Eleanor denounced the greed and imposition of male power that she thought was evident in Provincetown, Massachusetts, where she may have been living with members of her sister's family, including Jerusha's son, Joshua T. Small, who ran a bakery and was active in Greenback-Labor and populist circles. Baldwin explained to Swinton and the readers of his newspaper that a new shirt factory had been established in the past year, and since then had revealed itself to be "the true child of ugly, wrinkled Competition." The factory quickly established the means, as she put it, "to filch coppers from many poor girls to make dollars for a few rich men." Baldwin then charged that the chief owner and superintendent was engaged "in the slave-driving line," beginning with the enforcement of new work methods that extended the amount of time to produce a unit of product, but without raising the piece rate. The result was a decline in daily wages of about thirty cents. Moreover, management forced "each girl to pay for the machine" that she used by deducting fifty cents month from her wages, and when in one instance a girl replaced another for a month, Baldwin charged that both girls found fifty-cent reductions in their next paychecks. As bad as conditions were, employers exerted other forms of power over their female work force. Baldwin noted that a second factory, this one producing shoes, had recently started up in Provincetown, but that the owners of the newer factory had colluded with those of the shirt factory by pledging to hire no former shirt factory operatives. Baldwin concluded, "no matter how unbearable matters get, the shirt factory hands have nothing to hope from this new enterprise," and she called for the establishment of a Knights of Labor Assembly in Provincetown to provide a check on the power of local capital.[75]

Less than two months later, Baldwin wrote in support of the "Chicago anarchists" who were convicted for the Haymarket bombing. Pointing out "the elections are over," she urged that attention be refocused on to their plight and called on labor supporters to circulate a petition calling for their pardon from their death sentences. As we have already seen, Henry wrote in support of them, but that would be a year later. In her letter, Eleanor declared that the convictions had been imposed on the anarchists "for daring to tell the truth in public." Moreover, the case cast the state as impeding the improvement of society, of preventing those with moral grounding from acting on it. As she put it, these "seven noble souls and seven well-trained active brains" were working "for the good of their race and their time."[76]

Eight years later, Baldwin again entered public debate, this time to defend the striking railroad workers who acted in support of workers at the Pullman car factory in 1894 in a letter to the Boston *Daily Globe*. She began with an apologetic assertion, as if engaging in a ritual demanded of women who addressed matters outside their sphere. Then she proceeded on two fronts; the first was a direct and pointed question about who should bear the responsibility for the growing strike, as she asked why the railroad workers were "blamed for the refusal of the railroad companies to carry the mails," as "no striker has refused to handle" the mail cars. She charged that the railroad companies had "broken their contract with the government to transport mail," because they chose to affix mail cars to those trains with Pullman cars. In this, Baldwin again took a similar position as her brother, that labor has been pressed by an unholy alliance of corporate leaders and government. The second point was that the violence in Chicago surrounding the strike was also not the responsibility of the strikers, but of the very poor, of those whom she said "herd in the dark dens of all our cities, ground down by brutalizing poverty until every human instinct is crushed out."[77] While Baldwin placed the blame on the urban poor for irrational behavior that was unleashed by the tensions associated with the strike, the comment had other potential meanings, particularly the implicit argument about the effect of depraved environments on human beings, a subject that she would return to often as the editor of a woman's column a decade later.

Those themes were further developed a few years later in a letter Baldwin wrote to the populist *Kansas Agitator* in response to an article that had appeared in the *Globe*. Responding to that paper's reporting that an unemployed worker had committed suicide, Baldwin asserted that the deceased was "but one of many thousands who will this winter find themselves out of work," and in such straits would have to either "enlist in the black banner of crime" or take the more "noble, proud and sensitive" path of passive acceptance of "the fact that there is no place for them in the world and so leave it by the rapid transit of bullet or poison." She used the example to make a broader critique of power, noting that "maintenance of law and order" means simply "that the plundered people shall submit quietly to every variety of legalized spoilation and when at last crowded to the dead line, they must die uncomplainingly and decorously, in no way annoying those law abiding persons who attend the horse shows and grand opera." The *Globe* had done as much as it could in recognizing the event; they could not register protests unless they were willing to "lose advertising patronage and be assailed by their contemporaries as subverters of the public order."[78]

Her concerns about injustice, power, and the social environment led her to criticize the clergy, which she implied should have been attuned to the perpetuation of moral injustice. In the same letter written to the *Agitator*, she declared, "The minister [sic] (with a few noble exceptions) are feeble folk, piping their platitudes under the protection of the plutocratic pillars of their church," even though the land had become "a Golgotha and every hill a Calvary where humanity is crucified." Baldwin responded in other ways to ministerial feebleness, demonstrating that her sense of justice extended to question of gender, specifically the control that a woman exerted over her own body. She had attended a talk delivered in Naugatuck by an older minister, Reverend Robert Coliyer, who was described by the local editor as "gentle, kindly and serious." It was not his manner, however, that led her to respond in the local press. Instead, it was his call on married couples to have more children in response to a declining birth rate. Baldwin said that since "some woman must put her life in pawn, it strikes one as being in questionable taste for a man to publicly urge upon other men the duty of marrying early and rearing children as a life business." She noted that it would be difficult to find "many conscientious and eloquent women lecturers" who would urge the same path on women. Here, a decade before Theodore Roosevelt began to encourage other men to forego sexual self-control and to father more children in an attempt to avoid "race suicide," Baldwin noted with some alarm that such talk had already been directed toward men.[79] The implications for female education and opportunity to use it in substantial ways were at stake in the reverend's appeal, and in her objection Eleanor Baldwin articulated themes that would be presented to the readers of her daily column in Portland.

But the incident furthers our sense of the way that late nineteenth-century progressive attitudes about progress and society could lead the moralist into linking together mass poverty, female opportunity, and the possibility for a more moral civilization. Baldwin rejected Coliyer's assumptions that there was a shortage of children, and suggested that instead of deploying the kind of "clear grit" that the reverend thought was necessary to produce more children, it should be deployed "to make the world a fit place to receive the babies that are born." In a sense, the argument became a litmus test in Baldwin's hand for determining whether a woman should become a mother, for she argued, "Only women of stupid minds and slavish souls (and such are unfit to be mothers)" would be willing to bear sons destined "to be tramps or food for power," or daughters who, like Emmeline in Simon Legree's hands, are to be ravaged by "maws perpetually feeding on innocence, beauty and unrequited toil."[80]

This letter prepares us to appreciate how class and gender were integrated into Baldwin's understanding of society and progress. Reproduction and production were mutually reinforcing categories. If her imagery looked back to Harriet Beecher Stowe's portrait of female vulnerability, it also anticipated Charlotte Perkins Gilman's argument in *Women and Economics* that it was the moral, educated, and fully free woman, liberated from the rigid confines of domesticity and prepared to engage and improve the world, who would ensure progress and help to resolve the tensions unleashed by competitive capitalism by limiting the competitive drive in the economy and increasing the competition among men for procreative opportunities.[81] When Baldwin pretended to apologize for engaging in the male sphere, she addressed the expectations of men, but there is little sense that she came to these subjects as anything but a woman's business. And that perspective would make her an interesting read once she obtained her own column in 1906 with the *Telegram*. Yet as a daily columnist she would be in the position of writing regularly for the mainstream press, dependent as it was on advertising revenues, on the support of businessmen for its survival.

And in so doing she would bring the perspective of the petty bourgeois female who had been born of a struggling farm family and who was acquainted with the household forms of the early Industrial Revolution. Her public education attempted to fit her for the classroom, but instead it provided her an education that would enable a degree of comfort and independence in her later years, and the wherewithal to produce clear and effective prose. She followed a path that was carved out not only by her politician-lawyer brother Henry, but also by her sister Celia, a writer who would become prominent in the suffrage campaigns waged in Colorado.[82] The family adopted a petty bourgeois perspective, expressive of the concern that a class of selfish tyrants unrestrained by traditional moral values had appeared to exploit a growing working class, that would be repeatedly expressed in her columns and throughout the rest of her life. And in examining those columns, we will recognize the way that this female journalist worked to broaden the demographics for Progressive Era radicalism in Portland.

2
A Vision of Progressive Womanhood

> I sing to the countless women
> Who have missed the goal of life,
> Who have ne'er felt baby fingers
> Nor claimed the name of wife;
> But strong in your ways appointed,
> Have lived for the common good,
> And loved till your hearts were opened
> To a measureless motherhood
> —Henry Victor Morgan, "The Song of the Singer"

By the time Eleanor Baldwin arrived in Portland, the women's page had already been established as a staple of the urban newspaper. It was not unrelated to the Gilded Age rise of department stores, which by the 1890s had come to dominate retailing, and in so doing had created a new female commercial space in the middle of cities where female clerks sold a huge array of goods to female customers. These department stores became regular advertisers in the newspapers, and editors recognized that copy attractive to women would make advertising in the paper more appealing to these large retailers.[1] Their ads called on female consumers to leave the home and enter the commercial sphere in the center of the city, necessitating for many Portland women a ride on streetcars run by the Portland Railway, Light and Power Company. Socioeconomic change in and of itself was breaching the boundaries of public and private, of home and the larger community. Hence the woman's page was part and parcel of an overall cultural move toward standardization, mass consumption, and the blending of public and private roles for mothers and wives.

For these reasons the newspaper editor sought a columnist who would be guided by multiple compulsions. The column needed to be readable and compelling enough to be attractive to department store customers; if it did not draw in a substantial female readership, the editor might have to think about hiring a different writer. Many editors were uninterested in what actually appeared on the women's page, though they believed there was a simple formula that would gain female readership. Sarah A. Evans, a suffrage advocate who was broadly active in the network of Portland women's organizations, and who as the president of the Oregon Federation of Woman's Clubs wrote a weekly "Woman's Club" column for the Oregon *Journal*, reported what female journalists were often told by their managing editors if they were disinclined to write about fashion and recipes: "It's just what they want." In a paper delivered before the Oregon Woman's Club, Evans told those who gathered at Clara Colby's apartment in the Selling-Hirsch building that though it was true that the "woman's page is consecrated to this class of journalism," she like many others refused to succumb to this, suggesting that is was their "mission to be . . . the intellectuals, the revolutionists, the revolters, if you please."

Baldwin publicly denied that she faced such restraints, attributing to her editor, John Carroll, a "sagacity" that "far exceeded that of his contemporaries." Baldwin claimed that though he knew that women liked "beauty concoctions and new ideas on cooking and housekeeping and society notes," Carroll wanted a woman's column because he knew that women were "positively famished for mental food and soul uplift." When Baldwin asserted that "The Woman's Point of View" "corresponds so nearly to the demands formulated by Mrs. Evans," she seemed to claim the mantle of "intellectual, revolutionist and the revolter."[2]

Though Baldwin was responsible for a woman's page that appeared in the *Telegram* every Saturday, her primary work went into the composition of a daily column. Baldwin used those columns to provide her readers with "mental food," by which she meant a vision of the world in which women were unleashed from the restraints of the home, unencumbered by the demands of family and a sense that social roles were determined by gender. Moreover, Baldwin asserted that if women pursued their desires and sought to fulfill their own aspirations, society would be better for it. As she did this, she drew on the gendered construction of Victorian morality, by which female influence was associated with moral improvement, and that presumption allowed her, as it did many other reformers, to engage a discourse that

"The Woman's Point of View" logo appeared at the top of every weekday column, beginning in late May 1906. It features a woman with pen in hand, clad in an empire dress, the kind of nonrestrictive clothing that Baldwin and other supporters of dress reform would endorse.

would not necessarily alienate women who did not see themselves as radical. Early twentieth-century feminism perceived in female morality a means of social reconstruction, and Baldwin's columns—whether they addressed the immediate needs of women, socioeconomic problems, or spiritual matters—made women central to the building of a better world.[3]

While meeting what she perceived as the needs of her readers, Baldwin also tended to her own, gaining a source of financial independence. Though we have no clues as to her contractual arrangements with the *Telegram*, other newspaper writers, women included, were paid about seven dollars a column. As Alice Fahs puts it in her history of Progressive Era female journalists, "newspaper work offered a welcome alternative to such occupations as teaching," a relationship that speaks to the choice that Baldwin made to leave the classroom soon after finishing her course of study at the New Britain Normal School.[4] Considering that she produced five columns a week and also wrote and edited a woman's page for the larger Saturday issue, we might calculate that she made close to fifty dollars a week, and while this was not a huge sum, it was about what a journeyman in many well-paying trades might have earned and was clearly the basis for an independent existence. While she wrote autobiographically in some detail about the poverty of conditions that afflicted the young white-collar workingwoman, as a middle-age newspaperwoman, Eleanor Baldwin seems to have enjoyed considerable comfort. Her three-year tenure on the *Telegram* staff was at least one period of economic stability and perhaps of considerable comfort, though there are reasons to believe that before and after she found other forms of employment that allowed her to purchase and sell real estate, both in Portland and in Provincetown, Massachusetts, where she had lived for a time with her sister's family.

She did less to meet the needs of the *Telegram*'s advertisers. The columns rarely addressed the array of goods that were displayed in the newspaper, and near the end of her tenure with the paper, she began to openly criticize retailers and the way that they marketed goods to female consumers. While there were numerous reasons why Baldwin may have lost her column abruptly in April 1909, for she could alienate readers and did so with at least one male reader who paid attention to her columns, her criticisms of consumption during the Christmas shopping season of 1908 challenged the very reasons that editors had created women's pages. Baldwin could be quite the "revolter."

In terms of predilections, Baldwin was not out of step with many of the other women hired to handle the women's pages of the nation's metropolitan newspapers. Fahs points out that the writers of such pages were commonly independent women who sought inclusion into the mainstream of newspaper work. Many of them, as would Baldwin, wrote confidently about female capabilities, and they favored expanded rights for women; some newspaperwomen of Baldwin's age moved beyond the household hints type of writing toward an emphasis on women's progress.[5] But most feminist newspaperwomen were limited, as Sara Evans suggested, by the constraints of the work to which they had been assigned. Moreover, their contributions were remembered in conventional ways. Longtime *Journal* editor Marshall N. Dana, who employed Evans to write that paper's woman's page, discussed women's contributions that revolved around the household and public morality. He reminded his readers that Progressive Era women writers focused on the saloons and prostitution; that Millie Trumbull, the child labor activist who sometimes worked for the newspaper, wrote that American men were, in Dana's words, "deficient in chivalry"; and that women supported "high-class dairying so that butter, cream and milk in the home would be of high-grade quality."[6] Whether or not it was because her editor was as sagacious as she suggested in her column, Eleanor Baldwin's writings are particularly interesting because they do not reflect such constraints; they remind us just how broad women's concerns could be in the era immediately prior to the winning of suffrage.

Women and Progressive Reform

Walking the line between the challenging and the accommodating might today seem like a larger problem than it was. Much feminist language of the period was grounded in Victorian assumptions about female morality and male irresponsibility, and for this reason it is hard to imagine the nineteenth-century woman's rights movement without the context of the broader Victorian culture. The product of largely conservative folk who worried about the Jeffersonian ascension in the early nineteenth century, American Victorianism was a response to the breakdown of communal constraints—particularly on male behavior—that came with industrialization, urbanization, and democratization. These were hallmarks of a modernizing society; the loosening of individuals from village controls had granted new realms of self-determination for men who now moved about from city to city, aided in their movements by steamboats and railroads, which provided the technology for ever faster and more regular transportation. American conservatives had doubted the ability of common men to cast votes responsibly, yet democratic innovation had begun in the postrevolutionary new nation, and it was solidified by new democratic initiatives during the 1820s and 1830s, the period associated with Andrew Jackson's rise to political prominence. But the ability of common men to evade the moral authority of local elites bothered them just as much.[7]

Broad socioeconomic changes that would disrupt traditional communities were put into motion by a complex set of events and processes; among the most important were the improvements in transportation technology that permitted goods and people to move in as little as a day or two across vast distances that would have taken their grandparents' generation more than a month to traverse. Whether they were transported by railroads or steamboats, goods were more certain to find their way to market, sellers more quickly to gain remuneration for their goods, laborers more likely to find employment. What some historians have called the "transportation revolution" changed expectations and helped create a truly capitalist America, one in which physical barriers to the movement of goods and services dissolved in the face of technological advance.[8]

And it had moral consequences. With the breakdown of communal controls and the growth of market connections, per capita alcohol consumption doubled from the levels consumed during the Revolutionary War, a period when Americans were hardly a sober lot. Any examination of nineteenth-century city directories will reveal great numbers of saloons where men spent the paper money in their pockets on drink. And so the saloon became the perfect symbol for urban chaos and immorality: it brought together the unrestrained male, alcohol, and prostitution in an unholy mix. Whereas once men could escape familial responsibility by entering the trans-Atlantic merchant marine labor force, one could now do so simply by moving from neighborhood to neighborhood, or from city to city. Increasingly, people regularly came into contact with others whom they did not recognize. If American social historians have agreed about one thing, it is that Americans in the nineteenth century were geographically mobile.[9]

Rapid changes of these sorts could be anxiety producing, and the anxious made many kinds of resistance to them. Jackson's opposition to the Second Bank of the United States left the nation without a central bank that could put a brake on the note-issuing power of individual bankers, so privately owned banks now operated in an environment with few controls. Banks printed notes, and all who engaged in economic relations accepted them as currency, knowing that the bank cashier's promise to pay the bearer of its notes in gold depended on the holder's ability to travel to the bank and present them, as well as the bank's ability to pay all those who presented the notes at a given time. In a world in which the note from a small bank in the West might circulate in New York, paper money was often scrutinized for signs of counterfeiting or that it had been issued by an overextended bank, and there were no shortages of these, especially during economic downturns. To be involved in the economy was to be immersed in a set of imprecise and hardly transparent relationships. It is no wonder that Whigs and Democrats spent so much political energy on the issues of banking and currency.[10]

If some distrusted the paper money issued by private banks that permitted the exchange of goods, others distrusted the goods that were made in other locales. Among the more interesting of these was Sylvester Graham, a former Congregationalist minister. Among other things, Graham gave lectures and wrote treatises calling on young men to control their sexual impulses and to avoid an animal diet and any kind of alcoholic or stimulating beverage, and he called on all to avoid the hazards presented by commercial bakers who used adulterated, untrustworthy flour in their bread. A forerunner of the organic food movement of the twentieth century, Graham called on women to bake the bread for their families, using only whole-grain flour and love instead of purchasing a commercial product. The set of economic relationships that were characteristic of the emerging national economy generated many sources of fear and anxiety.[11]

If the character of goods and currency was subject to guesswork, the same could be said for the character of men. Women's literature was filled with stories of trust and betrayal, in which young women yielded to men of apparent good character who sought their hand in marriage, only to abandon them, pregnant and ruined. The New York Female Moral Reform Association (NYFMRA), which was formed in response to a report that New York City had seen a huge increase in the number of prostitutes in its streets during this period of urbanization, soon came to battle against male immorality and the sexual double standard. While many Jacksonian Democrats sought to rid the economy of bad paper bills, these women attempted to boycott and criminalize untrustworthy men who unleashed themselves upon pure and moral women. The leaders of the NYMRFA printed in their organizational newspaper stories deriding such men as "Seducers." But their anger led them to take stronger measures; they listed the names of those who were known to visit brothels, and encouraged women to shun such them, keeping them outside of respectable society. And they petitioned the state legislature to make seduction a crime. Many early feminists began their careers in public life in the temperance and moral reform crusades. Less traumatized by the problem of immoral paper money, they turned to the men who abused young women without village controls.[12]

The two most famous women associated with the nineteenth-century woman's rights movement, Elizabeth Cady Stanton and Susan B. Anthony, were both influenced by reform movements that attempted to reimpose morality on young men. Stanton at Seneca Falls denounced the great inequity of denying the vote to intelligent and moral women while the ballot was possessed by "drunkards, idiots, horse-racing, rum-selling rowdies, ignorant foreigners, and silly boys," and called it "too grossly insulting to the dignity of woman to be quietly submitted to." As late as the 1900 convention of the National American

Woman Suffrage Association, Anthony asserted that the opposition to the female vote came from "the gambling house, the brothel, and the saloon," and she told the activists, "if you believe in chastity, if you believe in honesty and integrity, put the ballot in the hands of women." While women's rights activists struggled against much of what was conventional about Victorian (and non-Victorian) assumptions about womanhood, particularly its romantic glorification of the home and the woman's place within it, they often wielded the Victorian image of the moral woman as a means of combating their own second-class citizenship as well as male vice.[13]

More conservative women than Stanton and Anthony could seize this ground as they engaged in reform activities. Many such women turned from efforts to legislate restrictions on male sexual behavior and instead turned to establish institutions, veritable "Homes for the Friendless," where young, pregnant women could find refuge, to give birth and offer their progeny for adoption, before returning home without the physical evidence of ruin. More such women would find their way into the growing Woman's Christian Temperance Union (WCTU); these women were in many regards the intellectual heirs of the temperance and moral reform societies of the antebellum era, arguing that female purity had to be defended from male vice.[14]

While the WCTU grew out of prohibitionist crusades against the saloon during the 1870s, the boundaries between the conservative and the radical were shown to be particularly porous under the leadership of Frances Willard, when the WCTU would come to support female suffrage and a broad reform platform that would eventually put it squarely in the middle of the progressive movement. The woman's rights movement of the turn of the century rejected artificial constraints on women's freedoms, but as a rule it did not reject the notion that women were purer than men.[15] Hence the same ideological structure that had in the antebellum period argued that women were unfit for the amoral rough-and-tumble world of politics and the capitalist marketplace became the basis for an argument that they were in fact needed most in those places. As historian Paula Scott points out, efforts by women to have government engage in the realm of social policy that had previously been handled by women's voluntary associations helped diminish the public/private divide that had separated men's and women's political cultures. As Scott puts it, "'Motherhood' and 'womanhood' were powerful integrating forces that allowed women to cross class, and perhaps even racial, lines."[16]

These same forces operated among activist women in Portland. While many—most notably, Abigail Scott Duniway—insisted that the suffrage movement separate itself from the WCTU and temperance, there remained among many a strong sense of male sin that animated their action. Some of the tensions and competing strains within the woman's suffrage movement that would emerge after the loss of the 1906 suffrage campaign were already exposed when the National American Woman Suffrage Association held its 1905 convention in Portland in conjunction with the Lewis and Clark Exposition and the unveiling of the statue of Sacagawea.[17] Worried that an invasion of eastern women whom she believed were antagonistic to men and ignorant of local conditions, Duniway urged the assembled to work behind the scenes—to engage in what she famously termed the "still hunt"—and not turn the 1906 campaign for suffrage into a spectacle that would awaken and concentrate the liquor industry and others hostile to female voters.

One of the more interesting developments that arose from the Lewis and Clark Exposition was the appearance of the Travelers' Aid Society, which women established to protect young women and girls from predatory males on their visit to Portland and the Fair, leading to the appointment of one of their own as a policewoman. Baldwin's columns expressed the full force of this Victorian sensibility in its most tolerant and radical guise: she supported suffrage and refused to damn men entirely for their proclivity to drink, but she also denounced some men for destroying female purity, and pocketing a profit for doing so. Radical and conservative are relative terms, depending on the issue, and in her depictions of male lust as a great threat to women, Baldwin sometimes spoke a language that was familiar to the women of the WCTU.

That Baldwin would frequently address motherhood is not surprising considered in the broader context of social and cultural history, nor is it less so that she would focus often on women who chose careers and avoided marriage. Her columns, which appeared nearly every day for about three years, covered a wide variety of subjects, and in so doing she replicated the experience of other women's page writers. Alice Fahs emphasizes how newspaperwomen wielded the woman's page as a site in which women could engage and discuss issues that mattered to them; as she puts it, the woman's page became "a way of developing a woman's

reading public, of connecting with other women in communities of conversation that sometimes had a national reach."[18] That is what Baldwin
accomplished in Portland. While the woman's page that appeared in the
Telegram magazine of the expanded Saturday issues often carried articles
about cooking and the day-to-day exigencies of running a household,
the daily columns, which appeared on the paper's editorial page in plain
sight of all the newspaper's readers, covered much more challenging
and overtly political themes. Because of the way that the language of
Victorian gender, particularly regarding female moral concerns, could
transmit both radical and conventional ideas, Baldwin's columns were
capable of being understood in different ways; as David Paul Nord points
out, "journalism is the literature of politics," attempting to create a community of readers, but clearly some of her readers read the columns
differently than others.[19] What is most interesting about the columns
is that in the apparently innocuous and commonplace as well as in the
radical, Baldwin brought forth a consistent vision: that the very sources
of female character, grounded in sympathy and benevolence, were reasons why female influence needed to be felt everywhere: in the home, in
the school, in the economy, and in foreign policy. Progress depended on
women achieving independence and expanding their opportunities in
all aspects of economic and social life.

That vision was sometimes restated in response to criticism, for
though the *Telegram* provided a space for Baldwin to articulate an integrated vision of women's rights and anticapitalist ethics, it did not go
without challenge. In the summer of 1907, a conservative female reader
who identified herself merely as "A Young Lady" asked why such a
"capable woman" as Baldwin would "waste good space and give rise to
theories that have a degenerating tendency for the home and all that is
sacred."[20] The writer defended the cultural embrace of separate spheres,
arguing against any notion that women should maintain a separate
existence as a necessary means of maintaining decency and order. She
lectured Baldwin, "It is a complicated thing, this life of ours, and we easily get off the best paths that lead to surest happiness. Not separated, but
united interests, is the only working creed of happily married people."

Baldwin responded with a defense of the column that came with a
statement of purpose. She granted that "Young Lady is a bright girl and
writes well," but she asserted that she "does not seem to understand
the object of this Woman's Viewpoint column." Though she began by

insisting that she was not out to impose her own views on readers, Baldwin got to the heart of the matter better when she stated that she intended to provide her readers with "the mental attitude of just as many different kinds of people as possible among those who are outside the pale of conventionalism and who are frowned on as enemies to society, as well as those who are supposedly the bulwarks of society." Instead of using the conventional bourgeois labels of the respectable and the unrespectable, Baldwin insisted, "we need to get out of our shells of prejudice and smugness and look at people as Jesus did, solely from the standpoint of our common humanity." She announced, "to comprehend our fellows; to be able through comprehension and sympathy to help both them and ourselves—that is true culture and the highest flower of education."[21]

Then she returned to the question of marriage, and here she engaged "Young Lady" more directly, suggesting that the two may have had more in common than the letter writer had supposed. Whereas the young lady had enlisted divine authority in her defense of the holy bonds of matrimony, Baldwin responded with greater appreciation for the failure of experience to reflect the idealized notion of marriage. She suggested that the writer would agree with her that "chains that are exulted in are not chains," but to ensure that marriage would not be akin to slavery, she asserted, "the love and friendship between married people should be conserved by self-sacrifice, if necessary, on the part of each." In that, Baldwin transformed the Victorian expectation of female self-abnegation into a prescription for an egalitarian marriage in which men and women both subordinated their own desires for their mutual benefit.

And yet the modern reader might find that Baldwin challenged the institution of marriage less than the young lady had thought, and in fact a cursory perusal of the columns might lead to a misperception about the "viewpoint" that was being espoused there; these columns mark for modern readers the porous boundary between the radical and the conventional in her writing. Responding to a request about how to prepare for marriage, Baldwin six months earlier had urged young women approaching their weddings to avoid "fits of anger or periods of the sulks or the blues, no matter what the provocation may be." She warned young brides, "If you are constantly having fits of indigestion, sick headaches and 'nervous attacks' . . . you will be handicapping your husband very heavily in the life race by those foolish things."[22]

Instead, a positive attitude, a dedication to perceiving the signs of her husband's love and dedication rather than seeking out evidence of his neglect, was the proper bearing of a woman whose role it would be to take the money provided by her spouse and use it to "give tone and character . . . to your home life." It would be hard to imagine more conventional advice from mid-Victorian literature.[23]

Child Welfare and the Female Reform Community

The subjects of the columns reflected the larger sphere of female influence in the community: traditional concerns of women for marriage and for the raising of children were frequently articulated, but in a much more public setting than any simple notion of a private woman's sphere would allow. Baldwin's concern for the gentle raising of children, especially the boisterous male child, was repeated on a regular basis. But so was the larger concern about social parenthood and the raising of the next generation. In a column devoted to the "right [of children] to playgrounds away from street corners and saloons," Baldwin asserted the community's role in providing the structures through which parenting would occur. At the same time, she suggested that many "grown people" dislike boys out of ignorance, terming the "live interesting boy" as a "bad boy" and a potential future criminal. She spoke of her own experience as a Sunday school teacher in a large Southern city, with "frightfully active boys" who required "original methods" to hold their attention. And she related the story of an itinerant speaker who spoke of an "utterly depraved" boy who frustrated his own mother so much that she brought him to the police. But in this case the man in authority turned the bad practices—in this case, the carving of "desks at school with his jack knife"—into a productive life course, turning him over to a carpenter who provided "the saving influence of the carpenter and his tools."[24] So it was revealed that good or bad character was a result of the social environment in which the male child was raised. Parenting was a social process.

But it was not just a problem of handling the male child. Children of both sexes needed better parenting, and that ultimately meant less punishment and less gendered restraint. She told her readers:

> It's high time to educate children less from the standpoint of gender and more from that of the all-round human being. As

a matter of fact, there is no sex in moral qualities. The same
need of patience, of course, of a sturdy faith that the right
course is the best course, no matter how much appearances
indicate the contrary, is needed just as much in the education
of one as the other.[25]

Baldwin lectured her readers about the need to be gentle with all
children; she saw enlightened parenting as an element of improvement
in a progressive age. Rejecting the hard obedience that her father had
demanded of his many children, she expressed faith in the natural good-
ness of human beings. In response to a letter writer who said that she
was raising her children strictly, as she had been raised, the columnist
responded by pointing out "the belief about children that still lingers
in the adult mind is that they are naturally vicious, and that by virtue
of superiority and strength, the parent must scold and whip the human
cub into some shape previously decided on." This was an affront to
republican values, Baldwin asserted, charging, "If no nation of grown
persons should submit to be governed in their consent, no more should
grown people arbitrarily compel obedience taught in this world." And
then she summed up: "we owe obedience to no authority under heaven
except our own inner self that sits in judgment on us and forever urges
us to live up to the highest we know."[26]

Progressive Era Oregon was fertile ground for those who thought
that society could no longer permit the family to remain a fully private
institution, and Baldwin gave a lot of attention to the most visible
manifestation of their efforts, the Home Training Association. The HTA
was an affiliate of the State Congress of Mothers, which in itself was a
branch of the national Mothers' Congress, organized in 1897 and out
of which the Parent-Teacher Association, or simply the PTA, would
develop a few years later. The Portland HTA was established in the
middle of the first decade of the century by "a small but earnest band
of mothers" interested in the formation of a "practical club to which
any mothers or teachers in our city might turn for instruction in the
weighty problems of child training." The first vice president of the
HTA, Mrs. R. H. Tate, asserted a broad set of intentions by the women
who formed the organization: "We felt that the term 'mother' would
debar many whom we wished to interest, namely, the fathers, teachers
and women that are in hearty sympathy with the better training of

children, yet having none of their own, whom we call the 'spiritual' mothers." Tate explained that the HTA sought to organize "circles" throughout the city through the "various schools," to help develop "systematic early training in honesty, purity, courage and faithfulness."[27] By that measure the organization had to be judged a success. Within a couple of years, the HTA had spread across the city; where it once held meetings of the entire membership in a committee room in city hall, a few years later it had established circles in fifteen of the city's schools.[28] Working closely with teachers, the HTA provided copy for *The School and the Home*, a newsletter put out by the Teacher's Progress Club of Multnomah County.[29]

As circles appeared throughout the city, their meetings received coverage from Baldwin, who not only reported but also participated in the organization's affairs. Meetings became a means by which information was distributed from women with national connections to those whose worlds were more than filled up by their households and their immediate neighborhood. The agenda for 1906 included a wide range of talks meant to help parents raise their children correctly, including "How Far Should Parents Subordinate Their Lives to Their Children?" Baldwin gave a talk on "How Can Children Be Instructed in the Value of Peace and Patriotism?" The Mt. Tabor Circle organized a similar lineup of talks, from the development of "voice culture" to the nutritional value of "the school lunch."[30]

The HTA expressed many of the philanthropic energies that Progressive Era women developed in their efforts to remake the city, drawing on the notion that expertise provided the answers to many social problems. Baldwin spoke of the need for such expertise when she claimed that the average young woman was untrained to have children, and that she amounted to "one baby taking care of another, with the results that might be expected from that situation." She saw the HTA as the kind of work that would result in a "wiser, kinder, more enlightened, and far happier type" of mother.[31] Judge Frazier of the juvenile court understood the reformist potential of the HTA, and Baldwin paraphrased his plea for the membership of the organization "to work among the poor and the unenlightened." Displaying an optimistic view of child nature, Frazier argued that children were often worse off because of the homes in which they lived. Responding to the judge's tale of a story of a woman who was happy to have her son live in the detention home because he was otherwise a drain on family finances, Baldwin quipped, "it isn't so much child-training that we need as it is grown-up training."[32]

The leaders of this organization were driven by the belief that in an era of greater and greater professionalization and the growing influence of scientific knowledge, the most crucial of institutions—the family—had been left without the guidance of experts. Speakers frequently regaled local circles of the HTA about the scientific character of their endeavor. One such speech, by Mrs. W. G. Hawkins, asserted that despite the general rise of scientific prestige, there was still no institutionalized science of child development, and what she meant was the uncovering of natural laws about the raising of children. Hawkins criticized those who authoritatively made statements like "obedience must be had at any cost" without what she considered scientific grounding. This was a position that Baldwin embraced wholeheartedly, insisting, "No adult has the right to demand 'obedience at any cost' of a child unless he himself is ready to do instant and absolute disobedience to the laws that Nature herself has implanted in the child for his own development."[33] When Mrs. John Stafford of the Oregon State Mothers' Congress addressed the Home Training Circle at Mt. Tabor, she raised the question of credentialing parents. Stafford urged that all institutions of learning from the ninth grade to the university offer courses on enlightened parenting. She remarked that the state requires a certain course of study before licensing a young man to be a pharmacist or to practice law or medicine, but then asked:

> Is it not monstrous . . . that the fate of a new generation
> is dependent upon the chances of unreasoning impulse,
> fancy, joined with the suggestion of ignorant nurses and the
> prejudiced counsel of disinterested friends? If a merchant
> commenced business with no knowledge of arithmetic we
> should exclaim at his folly and expect disastrous results,
> but that parents should begin the difficult task of rearing
> children without ever having given thought to the principles,
> physical, moral and intellectual, which ought to guide them,
> excited neither surprise at the actors nor pity for their
> victims.[34]

The assuredness with which such women articulated the notion that there were scientific laws and principles that should inform parenthood allowed some female reformers to speak in condescending tones to many of the poor, with whom they otherwise held great sympathy. For instance, socialist Florence Kelley advocated the development of "Practical Housekeeping Centers," which she identified as "avowedly a place of teaching." Baldwin approvingly quoted her further:

> The bane of the tenements is the unskilled mother. She it is who feeds the baby foul milk, bananas and beer. She drugs with sleeping draughts the crying victim of the vermin she does not know how to banish. She exhausts him with excessive clothing which she washes so irregularly that he languishes for want of the simplest freshness. It often seems that, of the baby's three enemies, milkman, landlord and unskilled mother, the unskilled mother is the deadliest, because her opportunity for doing him harm is so continuous and her means of attack so varied.[35]

What could be seen as cultural imperialism of Kelley and her Portland admirers should not distract us from their commitment to the improvement of conditions faced by the masses of working people who lived in the overcrowded districts of the cities. It was in that spirit that Millie Trumbull lectured the mothers of the Montavilla Home Training Circle in East Portland about the evils of child labor, relating the story of a young girl working in a can factory who lost three fingers on her left hand. Trumbull mentioned other children who worked in unsafe environments. She told of a boy who was in bed for two days after starting work at a bag factory, with its "choking, irritating dust that gets into small lungs." Trumbull begged the women of Montavilla not to send their children to the factory during vacation "just to keep them off the streets."[36]

There is a long history of ethnic and class antagonism between bourgeois Protestant women engaged in philanthropic work and their less fortunate, often immigrant, sisters whom they sought to help. The gendered construction of morality that tended to portray women as the bearers of virtue, but also the victims of male vice, taught them that the solution to poverty lay in sisterhood. Yet many immigrant and working-class women rejected the intrusiveness visited upon them from middle-class native-born women. A practice of home visitation by church-based charity workers was adopted in the antebellum era as mass immigration from non-Anglo lands coincided with the Second Great Awakening's emphasis on ridding society of evil. Those visitors were careful to ensure that motherhood in the impoverished family was pure and moral before any aid would be dispensed.[37] The women of the Home Training Association who lectured the mothers of Monta-villa may have abandoned the evangelical fervor of earlier reformers of the mid-nineteenth century, but they replaced it with an equally intrusive embrace of science and expertise, one that would increasingly be enforced by the state instead of voluntary religious organizations. Nonetheless, that should not obscure for us the hopefulness with which female reformers took up their mantle of improvement. Women like Baldwin embraced the new methodology of reform because they believed it would lead to a better society.

For Baldwin, real reform required the efforts of both men and women. Reflecting on a letter from a member of the HTA, she laid part of the blame for poor child-raising on "the fact that motherhood is studied as a problem apart from fatherhood, while fatherhood is looked upon as an inconsiderable factor, if, indeed, it is considered a factor at all in the rearing of children." Only the efforts of men and women together could prevent the development of "juvenile monstrosities and hardened little criminals of eight or ten years of age." Baldwin called on fathers to join with their wives in the interest of the future generation, and while domestic education courses were usually reserved for female students, much of Baldwin's columns suggest that men would benefit from them as well.[38]

Baldwin highlighted some of the specific efforts that individuals made to alleviate the conditions of the destitute and to help ensure that poor children would gain some of benefits of a better environment than their homes could provide. In particular, she publicized the endeavors of social worker Valentine Prichard, who ran the People's Institute, a settlement house located just north of the city center at Fourth and Burnside Streets, self-consciously modeled after the efforts of Jane Addams and her colleagues at Hull House in Chicago. The People's Institute provided classes for children, a circulating library, clothes and other necessary goods to needy families, an employment bureau, and a health clinic. Baldwin called it "a lighthouse, a life-saving station and oasis all three," existing amidst the inequality of the city where "cruel want and reckless wanton waste exist within a stone's throw of each other."[39]

In her report of 1909, Prichard described the many volunteers who helped the institute provide its many services as a "well-disciplined army, with every soldier at his or her post, fully realizing the importance of individual responsibility." Those services were required because of the same problems that had led to the formation of the HTA. She claimed there were a "large number of boys in this city who are being woefully neglected," and she pointed out that the "report of the Juvenile Court proves the consequence of this neglect." Speaking to the social causes of juvenile delinquency and the potential of individual reform, Prichard asked her readers, "Are we fulfilling our responsibility in helping to make them worthy citizens?" The volunteers at the People's Institute were engaged in the kind of reform work that they believed was necessary to maintain a republican society.

But Prichard also shared the concern that many women had about the trauma of impoverished girlhood. Though she noted that many neighborhood girls took advantage of the domestic classes at the People's Institute, she worried about those who worked in the city's factories and who were unable to take advantage of the settlement house environment. She proposed that the People's Institute establish a "rest room where they could come for the noon hour and bring their luncheon." Through this they could form them into clubs, and through such means the institute would provide them "an influence that would create a desire for some amusement beside that of the low dance hall and the 10-cent theater, and inspire them to better ways of living." In language that appealed to many of the city's organized women, Prichard asserted, "it is the low, degraded ideas of life that need to be eradicated from the lives of some of these girls."[40]

Portlanders anxious over the free movement of females in a highly mobile society organized to assure that young women would be protected from "low, degraded ideas of life." Baldwin sometimes gave publicity to meetings of the Social Hygiene Society of Portland, which included several prominent Oregonians, including Governor George Chamberlain and reformist mayor Harry Lane. The organization sought to fight the spread of venereal disease while advocating a single standard of sexual

Valentine Prichard founded and
directed the People's Institute,
inspired by Jane Addams's work at
Hull House Chicago, as a settlement
house on the North Side of Portland.
Courtesy of the Oregon Historical
Society, ORHI2167

purity for both men and women. Baldwin applauded the efforts of this
organization, which she said was established "for the purpose of replacing the usual foul and abominable ideals that prevail all too widely upon
matters of sex," with what she termed "sane, clean, natural, sensible
ideals." After regaling readers with an evening's lecture on sexual hygiene and knowledge, she quoted from *The Light*, the newspaper of
the National Purity Federation: "There are 300,000 'fallen' girls and
women in houses of shame in our country. They have been gotten there
through the trickery and wiles of those engaged in the traffic of girls
and the environments resulting from the immoral condition of society.
Their average life is but five years; 60,000 girls dragged down to this
life every day."[41]

It was this kind of trafficking that had motivated local women to
take action when the Lewis and Clark Exposition opened in 1905. A
local branch of the Travelers' Aid Society (TAS), funded in no small
measure by the Travelers' Aid Committee of the national and New York–
based Girls' Friendly Society in America, was established to prevent females traveling to the exposition from being preyed upon by rapacious

Lola Greene Baldwin, America's first female police officer, appears here in old age wearing a badge. No kin relation to the subject of this book, she was associated with the Travelers' Aid Society, which formed to protect young women visiting the Lewis and Clark Exposition from the hazards of predatory males. Courtesy of the *Oregonian*

men. The women lobbied the city council and successfully won the deputizing of Lola Greene Baldwin (no relation to Eleanor), an officer of the TAS. Women like Baldwin tirelessly policed train stations and the fairgrounds, making sure that "white slavers" kept their distance from traveling young women. As the policewoman put it, most of these women "bore no evidence whatever of being fast. They were educated, refined, and would grace any position in life. Some of them had never traveled, and many of them would have been easily led astray." As columnist Baldwin put it:

> It's the nature of wild beasts to hunt for their food, and if they are carnivorous, why so much the worse for the unlucky wight that gets tangled up in the jungle undergrowth where they stalk their prey. Let us do what we can to clear away the tangle, and also, since those who skulk in it may be susceptible of transformation when we let in the light— change both jungle and beast at the same time.[42]

The women who established the Florence Crittenton Home for unwed mothers expressed a similar impulse. The product of New York merchant Charles Nelson Crittenton's grief over the death of his four-year-old daughter and Dr. Kate Waller Barrett, who would lead the organization into the twentieth century, the National Florence Crittenton Mission aimed to convert, save, and rehabilitate prostitutes, but the organization came to increasingly serve unmarried mothers, fearful that pregnancy would ruin their reputations, while the admitting board assumed it was dealing with a one-time indiscretion. By the early twentieth century, there were seventy-three Crittenton homes spread across the United States.[43] Baldwin covered the organization sympathetically, calling on men of wealth to support the institution. She could be condescending toward the girls who sought refuge there, speaking of "some poor, foolish girl in need of its sheltering care," while conveying the ethos of the women who worked for the organization, like Miss Mullen, the "matron" of the home.[44] Mullen told Baldwin that the residents were "not 'bad' girls," but largely country girls who had been raised in "an atmosphere in which there is not a trace of refinement or gentleness." Mrs. Cleveland Rockwell, the president of the organization, explained, "We don't tell them they're sinners; we just ask, 'What can we do for you?'" Baldwin, appealing for financial support so that new facilities could be built, asserted, "Dark, cramped uncomfortable quarters don't help a girl to lift her head, to take heart, to let love and hope and self-respect take the place of hatred and despair and humiliation, when she already feels hunted, disgraced, beaten down in the battle of life by what has befallen her."[45]

The protective approach to independent women expressed an older impulse; in the hands of the Portland Women's Union, it had expanded well beyond unmarried pregnant women in need of refuge, expressing concern with wage-earning young women in general, especially those who had left their families behind to work in Portland. The Women's Union established in 1887 a boarding house that could accommodate about sixty young wage-earning women. The women of this organization expressed little desire to foster female independence; instead, they understood that as an unfortunate fact that required action. Women who took up lodging at the Anna Lewis Hall House, paying a proportion of their wages in rent, had to file an application that included character references and an agreement to obey a strict set of rules, including lights out at eleven o'clock. Dr. Emma J. Welty, who delivered a history of the organization to the membership in 1910, reminded them that they had given a home to those "entering industrial life" who were "unfitted to look out for themselves" in a urban environment "beset with pitfalls for the unwary." Stressing the establishment of a new set of restraints meant to emulate those of the families that the young girls had left, the Women's Union provided room, board, laundry, social activities, education, and curfews. Welty reminded her colleagues what the organization still needed to accomplish by reminding them of the nature of the young and independent woman:

> The young, simple minded, unwary, foolish, thoughtless,
> unguarded, heedless, disobedient, but not evil, women are
> in danger; of what, and by whom, I need not enter into; the
> protected and established women must look to it themselves,
> look to it in a broad way, and stand loyally together while
> so doing, they must go out to stay the engulfing blackness
> which is swallowing our young women, into which no ray of
> light ever penetrates.[46]

If the Portland Women's Union drew a largely fearful vision of female independence, it was not out of line with other efforts to protect young women from the designs of men. Baldwin expressed a set of contradictory sentiments that were not hers alone. Concerned that some men abused women horribly, she praised efforts to provide refuge for girls who may have been "foolish" but who were able to reclaim their lives with the aid of devoted, well-meaning older women. Such efforts built on older Victorian conventions, that male carnality was a threat to female virtue, so special measures needed to be taken to protect the innocent from gross exploitation. In many cases, the answers proved to be institutional, not merely a shoring up of the family. While middle-class reformers could be condescending to those whom they sought to aid, ultimately they sympathized with those who labored under the difficult circumstances to provide food and child care while working to support their families. What is most instructive about the way that Baldwin and others like her approached the subject is that there was no insistence that those who might need protection be cloistered within the home and the family circle. Instead, concerted efforts of organizational women would build the institutions that would make the public sphere safer for the young women to enter the world. For those like Baldwin, the goal of independence was something to be embraced; it was not to be feared. There was too much riding on a broader social role for women to keep them cloistered at the hearth.

The Vote and Influence

That so much successful female influence was grounded in concerns about the family and moral purity had the potential to derail the move toward woman suffrage. For if women were in fact guardians of the public morality and benevolence, then political action might corrupt them and deprive them of this kind of influence. This contradiction within female thought and action had long raised questions for female activists, some of whom despite their concern to be granted sufficient income by their organizations were careful to give the appearance of acting totally without regard to their own self-interest to maintain the image, if not the substance, of female benevolence.[47] In the columns in which Baldwin addressed conflicts among women over the suffrage, the controversy was usually with regard to this question of how female influence would be best wielded.

Baldwin's most direct link to the suffrage movement was Clara Colby, who was mentioned frequently in the column and with whom she shared both an apartment and a religious/spiritual orientation. Colby had moved to Portland in 1904, bringing with her the *Woman's Tribune* that she had been publishing since 1883 and some ambitions to prominence in the Oregon organizational work. She almost immediately ran afoul of Abigail Scott Duniway—which was nothing unusual since Duniway was frequently at odds with the national suffrage leadership over tactics—who read her the riot act, accusing her of meddling where she did not know the lay of the land and thus doing the suffrage movement "infinite harm"; Duniway would associate Colby with efforts to turn the suffrage effort over to the WCTU by the national suffrage leadership. Colby allied herself with Sarah Evans, the president of the Oregon Federation of Woman's Clubs and a part-time newspaperwoman, to seize control of the organization in 1906, but ultimately Duniway outmaneuvered them. Nonetheless, Colby continued to work for suffrage for the rest of her time in Portland. While in Portland, she traveled to Amsterdam and England in support of the International Woman's

Suffrage Alliance and the International Peace Congress.[48] Baldwin provided readers with Colby's account of a suffrage parade through the streets of London. On her return, Baldwin devoted a column to a tea that Colby held, where she told local friends that she had given thirty-seven speeches while she was in England and had met Victoria Woodhull, now married and known as Woodhull-Martin. To emphasize just how powerless women were without the vote in England, Colby told the gathered that a law allowing a man to swear before a magistrate that he had a principled objection to having his children vaccinated did not allow for women to do so, even if the father was too busy at work to make it before the magistrate. It was the lack of power that women held to control their own lives that punctuated Baldwin's discussion of Colby's trip.[49]

Otherwise, columnist Baldwin did not regularly discuss the movement for the ballot, but when she did, she emphasized the same themes that permeated so many of the columns, no matter the subject. She scoffed at arguments that women engaged in public differently than men and that they were more suited to influence behind the scenes. Reacting against such an argument, Baldwin rejoined, "Men and women are very much alike under similar circumstances, and a woman who attempts the futile task of proving her own sex less capable of self-government than men . . . must have some personal score to settle."[50] Though she denied on one occasion that she was a "rabid suffragist," she quickly followed that by saying "no argument worthy the name can be adduced against woman's voting."[51] Baldwin portrayed opposition to equal suffrage as unnatural, a mechanism placed into constitutions to preserve privilege. "There is nothing that so scares men at this very moment," she told her readers, "as an appeal to the laws of the universe as against their own tangled web of statutes and institutions."[52] Though she often spoke of the influence that women like Valentine Prichard and Florence Kelley exerted through social work, she scoffed at any notion that this demonstrated that women did not require the vote. She denounced such arguments and asserted that they were most likely to be made by wealthy women who lacked any real independence and any sense of the importance that legislation and government had on individual women. Her treatment of the campaign for suffrage, while infrequent, reflected her beliefs in the importance of female independence, female capabilities, and gender equality.

And she perceived a relationship between female independence and action in the public sphere and the gaining of full citizenship. These were matters of evolutionary progress, and only retrograde beliefs or intemperate action could impede these developments. Responding to news that advocates of suffrage had been arrested in London, she asked her readers if this was "a case where a flank movement or an indirect attack will be much more effective and attended with far less waste of time and effort than a fight in open field." In this spirit, she addressed the efforts of Margaret Haley, whom Baldwin termed "a peppery little Irish school teacher of Chicago." Haley had responded to news that empty city treasuries, caused in part by the failure of the city to collect taxes from large corporations—the Pullman Company was said to have entirely evaded taxation on its more than a million-dollar local property—by leading a movement to compel the local Board of Equalization to collect corporate taxes. She engaged in the painstaking research into corporate assets necessary to bring the Board of Equalization to court, and won a judgment that local corporations owed the city nearly two million dollars. When the Board of Education again reneged on the contractual promise of a raise for teachers, diverting the money for other purposes, Haley again filed a successful suit that led to the awarding of back salary increases for teachers. Baldwin lauded her actions, which "taught beyond all controversy . . . that a strong woman—a woman with perseverance and courage can do things in politics without waiting for the ballot." Though such efforts would take time, Baldwin posed them as the "surest way to the goal" of obtaining the vote. [53]

Accepting activism without the vote was one thing, but arguing that women did not require the vote was another. Baldwin took bestselling British novelist Marie Corelli to task for arguing that women's influence did not require the power of the vote. Corelli often wrote about mystical and spiritual matters, and she could write about single women as reasonable actors rather than as objects of pity, matters likely to catch Baldwin's attention and that of her readers, but here she denigrated Corelli for romanticizing feminine influence and for opposing woman suffrage. She quoted Corelli, who asserted, "The clever woman sits at home and, like a meadow spider, spreads a pretty web of roses and gold spangled with dew." We may get a better sense of what Baldwin objected to in this passage from Corelli's 1906 novel *The Treasure of Heaven*:

A woman who really loves a man . . . governs him,
unconsciously to herself, by the twin powers of sex and
instinct. She was intended for his help-mate, to guide him in
the right way by her finer forces. If she neglects to cultivate
these finer forces—if she tramples on her own natural
heritage, and seeks to "best" him with his own weapons—
she fails—she must fail—she deserves to fail! But as true wife
and true mother, she is supreme!

This kind of argument elicited from the journalist a denial that
women had a special nature; Corelli's assertion that women's influence
should be wielded surreptitiously instead of publicly at the ballot box
defied Baldwin's general sense of equality and independence. In response, Baldwin asserted, "Women are not—simply because they are
women—spiritually above men, and men—because they are men—are
not on a plane far below women. . . . Sex has nothing to do with it."
She accused Corelli of "doing as much as any writer . . . to foster and
perpetuate this mischievous and absurd distinction," all to denigrate
the efforts of those women who engaged in public activism to secure
the vote. Baldwin accused her of ignoring that "there are women
working for these objects [the suffrage] who lack nothing in feminine
grace or womanly traits and who rank with the best, both socially and
intellectually."[54]

The following fall, Baldwin would take a more characteristic
position, blaming opposition to suffrage on wealthy women who,
like Corelli, entered public life only to use their influence to deny the
masses of women the ballot, a matter that she thought was "deserving
of contempt." Baldwin noted that such women often spoke of the ballot
as "notoriously corrupt," which elicited from the columnist a demand
that women have the same opportunity as men to express their "ignorance, vice, intelligence, and right ideals." Baldwin charged that the
women who spoke this way in public were "almost to a woman, . . .
wealthy dependents upon men, either as daughters or wives. . . . In
short, they are the women who toil not, neither do they spin." Because
of their protected and dependent status, "their very outlook on life is
distorted." And so these "women of wealth and leisure" sought to deny
the independent and workingwoman the ability to more fully influence
their lives.[55]

Women on Their Own and the World's Account

Baldwin took great pleasure in regaling her readers with examples of women who engaged in thought-provoking, dangerous, or important work outside of the home. Her support of suffrage, occasionally expressed, was relatively muted in comparison with the amount of space that she devoted to the growing numbers of women who were making a difference in the world. In many ways, her attention to Valentine Prichard of the People's Institute was of this ilk, and though she shared with many other women the belief that women's efforts in social welfare were necessary to overcome the problems of male avarice, Baldwin paid attention to women who made their mark in other ways. But the overall point remained: that unleashing women to exert their talents could only improve the social world. Simply, there was nothing to be lost by having women leave the home.

On occasion, Baldwin directly attacked the notion that women should be prepared only for motherhood. To the assertion of novelist Amelia S. Barr that a woman "has no right to a career until she has married and had children and gone through suffering and sorrow," Baldwin responded that this was "the rankest nonsense." She charged that Barr and others "attach too much importance to the physical fact of motherhood," and then responded, "True motherhood is neither made nor marred by the mere fact of physical motherhood." Instead, all women should seek to be a "mother in heart," and she defined this in terms of society rather than the family: "Wherever there is suffering to alleviate; injustice to be overcome, loneliness to cheer, homeless and forlorn children, young or old to be cared for, there is a place for a true mother." Progress required this more spiritual motherhood; it was essential "in the development of the world to higher planes of thought."[56] But it did not require the woman to marry and physically bear children.

Baldwin sometimes went further, arguing that the family itself could be a trap for the young single woman. On Christmas Day 1906, she urged her reader to think of herself as a "center of power and influence," and that women needed to develop their talents to "play our small parts worthily." She urged the young woman to "make something of yourself" and develop "some special talent which you possess." Most importantly, she turned the moral expectations of self and family on their heads, admonishing her readers not to "let your decision be weakened and your powers dissipated by responding to the selfish calls for help and self-sacrifice from various members of your family, who may, thoughtlessly, consider you only a convenience for themselves." She warned that should she succumb, the young woman would find herself "hampered and hindered in the race of life, lacking the equipment you meant to acquire, and by so much lessening your usefulness and happiness in the world."[57]

In a possibly autobiographical column, Baldwin wrote knowingly of a lonely working woman, alone with her books and her dingy clothes and living on eight dollars a week in a "little attic room in an Eastern University city." Heated by a coal-oil stove, lighted by a "tiny south window," she could see the homes of families where there was "plenty of Thanksgiving cheer." Baldwin told her readers that the young woman ruefully considered that "she was educated above" her weekly pay of eight dollars a week, and she asked, "Of what use to have a world where education is free and the means to live the educated life beyond reach of the many in the control of the few?" But the point wasn't pure envy; the young woman disdained the women in those homes that she observed from her small attic window, because their lives were characterized by the "perdition of slavery and degradation which was the price of their luxury and immunity from toil." It was a matter of "self-respect," and in a more positive moment she felt assurance within her soul that she had the power within herself to "break the chrysalis of loneliness, and the fetters of $8 a week and expand to better, broader living."[58] Expressions like this explain why the conservative "Young Lady" had found the "The Woman's Point of View" column so threatening.

Baldwin portrayed growing female participation in the public sphere as a major sociological and evolutionary phenomenon, and she celebrated the efforts of individual women to engage the public on the dais or at the workplace. When she asked her readers to contemplate that only fifty years earlier the current "pleasure" of witnessing a "cultivated lovely woman on the platform speaking to an audience" was a risky venture for those who did not want to be "classed with women of no character and no reputation," she linked progress of women into the public sphere with the invention of new machinery: there was a technological imperative driving growing female influence. And while she acknowledged the importance of the sewing machine as a source of female wage labor, opening new realms of factory work to women, Baldwin asserted, "the real entrance of women in business came with the invention of the typewriter," which was "preeminently adapted to the capacity of women." What she termed male innovation and female skill brought forth constant progress, so much so that she suggested that those who think this process would not continue to "be felt in every avenue of human industry, interest and activity," might "need the attention of a skilled oculist."[59]

Baldwin implored younger readers to appreciate that effort and the acquisition of skill to enter some occupations would require sacrifice, but sacrifice for one's own ultimate end. To encourage them, she devoted columns to the lives of women who had become famous through the development of their skills. In an article about violinist Maud Powell, Baldwin emphasized that "hours and hours of study and hard work" made her the virtuoso she had become, and in so doing she had "obliterated sex in her work," which she declared a "distinct gain for her sex and her art."[60] When the Department of Agriculture sought to fill a laboratory helper position, Baldwin publicized the job and asserted, "there is nothing in this work to bar a girl if she has the experience," and she pointed out that the recent "discoverer of radium was a woman chemist—Madam Curie."[61] Baldwin was quick to point out that the *New York Sun* had run an article about a number of women who had recently been admitted to practice before the US Supreme Court.[62] And she praised local innovator Linda Bronson-Salmon for her efforts to improve her clerical work by revising the shorthand she had been taught, by which she had "practically [made] a system for herself, which she copyrights and teaches." In all these instances, Baldwin's intentions were explicit:

> Whenever this page gives the history of an unusual
> occupation that some woman has followed successfully, it is
> with the hope that her example may serve as an inspiration
> to some of the women with their own burdens to bear, or
> perhaps show some one groping for the right rope to grasp,
> just the occupation she can most congenially and so, most
> successfully, adopt as her own.[63]

Female success in unexpected places could be instructive about the false conceptions that had long guided society. When Baldwin wrote about "clever" lion tamer Claire Heliot, she sought to prove not only that practice and application could make a woman the equal or superior of any man, but also that men had constructed a world through false assumptions, positing a hostile and fear-ridden universe instead of a harmonious one. In this instance, Baldwin argued that male lion tamers operated cruelly out of fear and loathing of the animals, which made them much more dangerous. It was their failure "to understand the lion heart" that led so many of them to be "made into mincemeat by their animals." When Heliot explained that she found it difficult to gain "the confidence of these beasts and convincing them that I meant them no harm," Baldwin pointed out that it was "only by infinite patience and unswerving, never-failing kindness that she at last removed that fear." Heliot recalled that when she first fed the lions through the bar, "They would sniff at the meat suspiciously, walk away and growl deep down in their throats, glaring at me, though I spoke kindly to them through the iron bars." With time, the beasts accepted food from Heliot's hands, learning that there was nothing to fear from this kind and brave woman. Baldwin extrapolated further from the lesson, equating much human behavior, particularly the accumulation of vast estates at the expense of others, rooted in the famine-plagued preindustrial past, with the beast's fearful behavior. Assuming that the present era of progress would eventually put social life on a better grounding, she asked, "Is it possible that fear is at the bottom of much of our own troubles too?"[64]

Male fear and loathing characterized the way that humanity misappropriated technology, and yet these new forms of technology perceived in their right light were both signs of progress and opportunities for women to engage themselves. In a column about air flight, Baldwin ruefully charged, "men can never invent anything first hand for general human welfare. Already they see in the flying machine a vast engine for wholesale human murder." Like men who approached lions with an ingrained burst of fear and violence, countries prepared to use the airways for war, when in fact the atmosphere was "beautifully clean and pure." A better model might have been provided by the Philadelphia Aeronautical Recreation Society, which had sixty women among its active membership, and which offered a more benign vision of the airways, which Baldwin claimed were naturally "the atmosphere of purity and truth," and as such, naturally "women's sphere."[65]

Not all women entered this expanded notion of women's sphere on an equal basis; when they entered the world of work, whether it was motivated by the need for self-support or self-expression or some combination of the two, they entered a world characterized by class distinctions. Baldwin was always aware of the distinct problems that working-class women faced as they entered the public economic sphere. Working women grappled with some of the symbolic manifestations of social class that American men had long been keen on overcoming.[66] When "some Portland firms" sought to put caps on their salesgirls and waitresses "as a distinguishing mark of their occupation," Baldwin interpreted the move by employers as reflective of "the caste and servility of the Old World." Arguing that employers sought to put a mark of inferiority upon the "attractive, bright, refined women behind the counters" who were often "the superior in beauty and brains and education of those they serve," she charged that the practice "would be un-American" in that it would "place such a mark of division between those who must work for a living and those who do not." Yet Baldwin did not leave it at that, for it was the intent and meaning of badges of distinction that caught her attention. Whereas she was disdainful of the effort by employers to contain the employees' aspirations and bearing, Baldwin thought that a mark that identified the woman as self-supporting and independent was worth taking on as a badge, not of negative distinction but of assertion and pride; it would distinguish them "everywhere and at all time from the leisure class of women." She told working women to "glory in their independence" and take "pride in their station in life and, further, of their intention to become the comrades and friends of all other working women." That this was the newspaperwoman's penultimate installment of her column may have unleashed her to charge that the retailers, among the most prolific advertisers in the *Telegram*, were promoting an "un-American" practice.[67]

More commonly, Baldwin addressed the immediate problems facing independent women who worked for a living. Nowhere was this more evident than in her efforts to support the building of apartment houses specifically designed for such women. Housing for young working women had long attracted the attention of women from some of the most prominent local families. She framed the need by asserting that there were structural reasons why such a housing stock was direly needed, casting the present as poised between a past filled by restraint and a future in which there would be none. In one column, she gave vent to anticapitalist sentiments, speaking of the growing numbers of "bachelor women" as "a transitory feature of this period of industrial warfare." She explained, "Men are being slaughtered by the thousands every year in the 'peaceful pursuits of industry.'" She claimed that others have estimated an average of "one life sacrificed to every floor laid in the great Gotham skyscrapers," and so "human sacrifices are daily offered on the gilded altar of the great two-headed god, Interest-and-Profit." The result was many women who lacked the opportunity to find a male mate, a condition that would end only "when this cruel war is over," and men were recognized as "more valuable than money." Until that time, the single woman was present in unprecedented numbers, and she was "giving a good account of herself." But she would need housing in the here and now.[68]

When discussing the efforts of the Young Women's Christian Association to find financial backing to build a multistory residential building for the "self-sustaining girl," Baldwin portrayed the problem as something more than mere subsistence; instead, the objective was to provide a comfortable and humane existence. She asked her readers, "Shall we not who live in these times of toil and stress do what we can to prepare the way for that gracious embodiment of womanhood who waits in the future, and may our efforts tend to make life in all ways a more beautiful thing than we ourselves have found it?" The features that she believed the YWCA building would offer included: a laundry, gymnasium, "swimming tank," large assembly halls, dining rooms, and private parlors, "where young ladies can meet and entertain their personal friends."[69] When she appealed to businessmen to support the venture, Baldwin asserted, "the young women of Portland who work in factories, offices, stores, homes and schoolrooms are doing their full share in the upbuilding of this city," and she reasoned that they were contributing enough that the town could "afford them their building, with its comforts and its pleasures and its sense of proprietorship which will make them feel that they are something more than air-plants in this world."[70] In other columns, Baldwin suggested that there might be a cooperative solution to the problems of housing. She imagined that an "organization of all self-supporting women, regardless of occupation, but united on that one common interest of self-support," would be able to "change the present expensive and uncomfortable lives of many working women and give them the surroundings and comfort they need and to which their place in the world entitles them."[71] Unlike the

Portland Women's Union, whose efforts at providing housing for poor women was guided by a sense that women needed to be protected from the public sphere, Baldwin stressed comfort and sociability of women in an expanding public sphere for women.

At the cornerstone-laying ceremony of what the *Oregonian* termed "the first apartment house to be erected in the United States for business and professional women," Reverend J. D. Corby of the First Universal Church and Dr. Benjamin Young of the Taylor-Street Methodist Church officiated. Linna G. Richardson, a nurse who had led the campaign to have the edifice built, handled the trowel, and another nurse, Miss Earle, read a brief statement, which thanked Baldwin, among others, for her support. Dr. Young praised the young nurses who serve faithfully at the side of the sick but then "are forgotten except as they are needed." Baldwin paraphrased Young's comments, which noted that the building was reflective of "loving service," and warned that "the terrible disregard of this loving Christ spirit of service" in the business world and in government had in the past and would in the future suffer the "wrath of the people."[72] Just a few months later, as the building neared completion, Baldwin asked what kind of history the women who lived there would make:

> Will it be a history of women living under one roof happily; living without the careless criticism of each other which women so often indulge in? Will it see a steady growth of the spirit of kindness and loyalty among women? That is what we hope. But more than that: We hope it will become a center for active thinking; we want it to be a radiant center, scattering lavishly and constantly, the light that illumines and broadens. We hope the parlors will be the gathering place of different groups of women, all interested in making life better and broader for themselves and for others, while they keep a watchful eye on the progress of events all over the world, insofar as it affects the destinies of women.[73]

As the project neared completion, Baldwin refused to consider her mission fulfilled; now she turned her attention to the desperate women, those who worked in low-paying positions—"the waitress, or salesgirl, or factory operative—who must look to the indiscriminate lodging-house for a home." She promised that "one of these days," the woman's page of the *Telegram* would provide a picture of a house "that could be built for these earners of small wages," meeting their needs and "still return a fair if small percentage to the man who would invest his money in it."[74] Though such a drawing would never appear, as Baldwin would soon lose her column, the call to remember working-class women reflects the broad-based optimism about progress that Baldwin brought to the page. And it reflected her belief that women's self-activity outside of the home, and the rebuilding of society to accommodate such an expanded women's sphere, was inevitable and evidence of social progress.

Materialism, Consumption, and Womanhood

When Baldwin chastised as un-American the proposal by some retailers and restaurant owners to have their female help wear badges that would distinguish them from customers, she undoubtedly challenged some of those who advertised in the *Telegram*. And because this was her penultimate column, we might surmise that the subject was related to the reasons why she lost her column (though there were other sources of tension in other columns that may explain the same; one of these is discussed in chap. 5). In milder form, she had taken up the interests of workingwomen over those of the retailers since the beginning of her tenure at the newspaper. In August 1906, she had written sympathetically of the difficulties that such women had in clothing themselves. Concerned that "fashion and other periodicals for women utterly ignore" that working-class women had limited means, she pointed out to her readers that it was the socialist press that "recognized the need of the downright poor woman for a little counsel on the dress question." Baldwin asserted that working-class women needed to ignore the strictures of the fashion industry and to recognize that "there's a sort of moral and good sense in adapting one's dress to one's circumstances and to one's work that command instant respect." She urged her readers to live within their means, telling them "there is a whole lot of comfort to be had on a small income if one has the courage to sturdily accept the life that is conveniently possible to be derived from it."[75] Conceding that cultural standards demanded that the workingwoman "look neat and trim and tidy if not actually stylish," Baldwin made it clear that this was easier said than done. She pointed out that the typical working girl "has but one room and one small closet to hold dresses, jackets, house gown, street suit, shoes, rubbers and what not." A rainy day might require that clothes be spread out to dry, or if she was unfortunate enough to sit "next to some tobacco-infected individual," the odor would "surely communicate itself to woolen goods" and these too would have to be hung and aired.[76] Baldwin urged working-class women not to overextend themselves to conform to the dictates of retailers and fashion magazines.

But it was not only women of limited means who Baldwin thought needed liberation from the industry; she saw that fashion was a detriment to female health and well-being in general, and as such it threatened to reveal that society's progress was a charade. Though she rarely deployed the terms of "civilization" and "savagery," she did so here ironically to point out the foolishness of Western presumptions. She told her readers about "a race of savages who lives happily and simply somewhere in the southernmost portion of Patagonia," where they "wore no clothing whatever, but in winter weather greased their bodies" to keep warm. This practice came to an end in what Baldwin called "an evil hour," when a missionary "brought his preconceived opinions to bear upon these poor simple, unlettered but well greased and healthy Patagonians." The result is that they all died "and perhaps went to the missionary's heaven," having "succumbed to the burden of civilized attire and the earth knew them not more."[77]

The story provided a metaphor of simplicity with which to critique the unprogressive nature of the fashion industry, while challenging the artifice of what might be called overly civilized life. Baldwin portrayed Western women as "victims to that artificial and dangerous division of the human body—the waist line." Asserting that "simpler clothing will be worn by women of the future," Baldwin held out for clothing that would be "not less marked with refinement and elegance," but rather compatible with health and well-being. She praised developments in female dress that offered solutions, advising her reader that the "union suit," one-piece underwear that had become popular in the nineteenth century as an alternative to the corset, was a sign that in the realm of dress, progressive developments were possible. Another was the "empire gown," a neoclassical form that simplified female dress, offering women "the beauty of an untrammeled human shape clad in . . . [its] clinging and yet unfettering folds." True progress would lift female bodies from the constraints imposed upon them by the fashion industry only when "women come to regard their bodies as something more than a mere convenience for the display of ravishing toilettes."[78]

It had not always been that way, for contemporary fashion, grounded in the pursuit of profits that Baldwin would always associate with modern industrial capitalism, deviated from timeless and classical models of beauty and form. Baldwin pointed out that while admiration of the "old Greek standards of physical beauty and proportion" had led to the collection of "magnificent fragments . . . of the glory of Greece" and the display of them "in a place we call an art museum," this cultural rectitude remained at some level superficial. She asked her readers to ponder how the models of the statues "attained their beauty and health." The point was that they engaged in the "subordinating [of] clothes to the body instead of making the body fit the clothes." The pride in the body and a belief in its possibilities are what characterized the Greek approach; instead, Baldwin claimed that we hold our bodies "in contempt and shame." And she pointed out that modern clothing had drawn the ire of many others, who saw in it a violation of the classical vision of a healthy body. She quoted a writer in the *Army and Navy Journal* who complained, "A neurasthenic culture and a complex mechanical activity alone are not the energizing forces from which the ideal man and social system can be evolved. A sound man in a sound body are equally essential to a sound character and without this, there cannot be a rational society."[79] Baldwin used the metaphor of athletic contest to denounce fashion in the name of progress and evolution: "As a strong man strips for a race, so the human race in its progress towards its ultimate goal of power and glory must one by one lay aside the seemingly small things that hinder and trouble and distort it, physically."

Baldwin consistently criticized the debilitating impact of female clothing. She wrote contemptuously of "freaks of fashion" that led to unhealthy bodies. She blamed high heels for backaches, and stressed "the vital importance of strong, elastic, healthy feet as a means of movement and progress."[80] In one column, she derided the "tight-fitting coat" she observed worn by a woman on the streetcar, which kept "the lower cells of her lungs in a state of paralysis." In 1908, she bemoaned what she called a craze for the "hipless figure," which led women to try to make their "figures fit their dresses," instead of wearing dresses that fit their bodies, denouncing it as a "physiological absurdity and contradiction," one that would cripple women and "benefit doctors and hospitals."[81] Most constraining of all was the corset, which she held particularly responsible for that "absurd and disgraceful classification of disease—'female weakness.'"

Baldwin therefore perceived the fashion industry as an anti-progressive structure that inhibited the healthy development of female bodies and the further evolution of society. Like other industries, it was in the process of accumulating more power to itself, and she charged that the male magnates who controlled the industry grew "more bold, more autocratic, demanding more and more tribute from their submissive victims." Mesmerized by the expanding world of consumption, women followed their lead "unquestioningly, obediently, with all the devotion of the religious devotee or even worse—the religious fanatic." That meant the acceptance of "every freak, every absurdity, everything hideous, overtrimmed or unhygienic that the hidden autocratic hand of the maker or the dealer points at." Baldwin equated the hold that the fashion industry had over women with that which alcohol had over men, asserting that women "hang like drunken men about the show windows on open days and go home in a state of intoxication—sometimes—that their male kinfolk could hardly outdo at the club or the saloon."[82]

It was hardly exceptional that Baldwin was hostile to the conventions of Victorian fashion; a wide range of women, some of them physicians, had long taken aim at the restrictive garb as unhealthy and as the source of general female debility. One of these physicians, the widely read author Alice Stockham, displayed a Lamarckian sensibility—the idea that mechanism of evolution amounted to the transmission of learned behavioral traits of one generation to subsequent ones—if not a sense of humor when she satirically argued that women should stop wearing the corset *two hundred years* prior to giving birth. Stockham insisted that women exercise more often, even during pregnancy, and that they be "properly clothed" when doing so, "wearing common sense shoes, having the arms free, the dress short and loose," which would allow them to engage in brisk walking "with positive benefit."[83] Likewise, Baldwin suggested that more sensible clothing and an end to the tyranny of restrictive fashion would put an end to "long, dreary illness." While Baldwin was in line with many other feminists in her critique of fashion, her criticism was broader and part of a larger critique of capitalism as an economic system that inhibited progress. Its manipulation of women to wear items that were either unhealthy or immoral prevented them from taking evolutionary steps that would improve society.[84]

The fashion industry also implicated women in a destructive assault on nature. Many considered the use of bird feathers to adorn women's hats as one of the most grievous sins of the fashion industry. The practice was so widespread that historian Jennifer Price writes, "The millinery trade in the 1880s and 1890s cleaned out tern, heron, gull and egret rookeries up and down the Atlantic coast, from Maine to the Florida Keys."[85] Baldwin mocked the use of feathers and other bird parts, what she called "the hodge-podge of 'made' feathers" that adorned female millinery products, as "the greatest offense . . . against good dressing and the artistic sense." Addressing her readers' desire to look smart and neat, Baldwin charged, "They are so ugly, obviously 'made,' so patently for the very shabby object of adding a little more to the expense of the hat without in any way adding to the attractiveness of the wearer, it is a marvel any woman consented to be imposed upon by them."[86]

Baldwin was hardly the only woman taking the fashion industry to task for encouraging the killing of birds at the beginning of the twentieth century. Bourgeois women across the country came together in Audubon Clubs to protest the killing of songbirds and other desirable avian species for the pursuit of profit, and they made appeals to both the industry and to individual women to boycott hats that bore feathers. Though men often served as the officers of these clubs, the actual work of preserving birds was taken on by the largely female membership. Though millinery was only one of the threats faced by winged wildlife, having little to do with the extinction of the once-plentiful passenger pigeon, it did become the focal point of female activism, as it clouded the categories of manhood and womanhood, posing the latter as the destroyer of innocent nature in the name of vanity and fashion. For these reasons, Price argues that "women's bird hats acquired broad moral overtones far more efficiently than game hunting or water pollution" as they "became entangled exquisitely in the fervid middle- and upper-class beliefs in what made men men and women women."[87] Both the Woman's Press Club and the Portland Business Woman's Club, both of which had elected Baldwin to some official position, took up the mantle of bird preservation, the latter hosting an address on "Bird Life" by Dr.

Emma J. Welty. In addition, Baldwin publicized the efforts of Audubon Society members, devoting a column to a lecture from William Finley, the leading advocate for preserving bird habitat in Progressive Era Oregon. Finley served as the second president of the Oregon Audubon Society and was a strong proponent of the establishment of bird refuges to protect breeding grounds. He too joined the assault on the millinery trade, conspicuously destroying a feather-bearing hat worn by a prostitute on the streets of Portland. Baldwin praised his campaign against the "mass murder" of birds for their plumage, which Finley claimed had rendered "the lakes and woods of Southern Oregon and Northern California . . . almost birdless."[88]

Baldwin publicized the supportive efforts of the General Federation of Women's Clubs, which had circulated a pledge to protect the consequently endangered birds, denouncing the "slaughter of these feathered innocents," caused by the "demand of aigrettes for millinery purposes."[89] She condemned the tearing away of aigrettes "from their mother egret in the breeding season" so that "women in love with their own beauty may have a trifle in the shape of an aigrette to enhance their own loveliness." Baldwin hit the point hard, suggesting that it would be reasonable to "suppose the common instinct of motherhood would make this sort of ornament hateful to them and that they would feel disgraced, and branded as barbarians by the wearing of such a palpable evidence of cruelty."[90]

While Baldwin was critical of the way women accepted the killing of birds for fashion, she also denounced the way that bourgeois men took "pleasure in killing birds" for sport. She pointed out that the problem extended to the White House, where President Roosevelt had expressed pride to be "known as a killer of birds . . . for fun—as he makes clear—not for a living"; she thought that the president's example helped explain why boys would "thoughtlessly stone and shoot birds."[91] Baldwin considered bourgeois culture, whether it was expressed through a male penchant for sport and the need to protect animals from plebeian subsistence hunts or the female desire for ornamentation, to be destructive of both women's bodies and the natural environment.

Baldwin's multifaceted pleas to her readers to resist the siren song of the fashion industry inevitably entailed resistance to the advertising appeals of local clothing retailers. Issues of the *Telegram* bore numerous advertisements for bird-enhanced hats by downtown clothing and department stores. Meier and Frank offered women "This season's most attractive models for women and misses—the newest shapes in grand variety and trimmed in satin, ribbons, wings and fancy feathers." A competitor, Old, Wortman & King, promised that women who entered their establishment would find "all new and charming models; tastefully trimmed with ribbons, wings, quills, breasts, etc." Hamburger's "Big New Millinery Store" claimed an inventory of more than a thousand hats with "fancy feathers" as well as "ostrich plumes." Though the ad for Roberts Brothers clothing store declined to explicitly mention hats, it included a drawing of a fashionable woman wearing a hat with a bird resting conspicuously on its crown.[92]

While Baldwin portrayed unnecessary seasonal flourishes as industry's attempt to exploit the desires of the female consumer, one that was particularly destructive to nature, she saw this as part of a broader set of problems associated with the dress and millinery industry. She accused the fashion industry of turning the effort to separate women from their money to "such a science" that every season "the waists and suits bear some distinguishing feature that marks them out so distinctly from the out-of-date creations that the most unobservant observer cannot fail to know when a garment is or is not the seasons' output." Baldwin urged her readers not to be "victimized and led blindfolded into all the schemes for moneymaking at our expense that may be devised by the 'Dress Trust.'" Instead, she urged that women "begin to think a little and boycott some absurdities and let the makers be properly punished by losing money on them."[93] Baldwin's columns under "The Woman's Point of View" and her editorial command of the Saturday women's page hardly succumbed to the dictates of advertisers and the consumerist message that is often associated with the early twentieth-century newspaper. As it did for Sarah Evans and countless other female reporters, the women's column or page offered an opportunity to say something important.

In so doing, Baldwin weighed in on the meaning of the public sphere for women. This was no battle to get women out of the house: the very existence of the department store and the women's column was predicated on the need for women to leave their homes for the commercial heart of the city, and the newspaper advertising that retailers oriented toward women amounted to an invasion of the female-dominated private sphere by commerce and the public sphere. The question had to do with the terms by which women would enter the public sphere. The calls by women's clubs and other progressive women for government to begin to do what private charities had done for decades are reflective of this same dynamic, and Baldwin, in her emphasis on the technological basis for women's broadening world, understood that the days of women being entirely cloistered in the home and neighborhood were disappearing. To patronize the department stores, women needed to find their way downtown, and that meant taking a ride on the developing streetcar systems. Women—wives included—were increasingly in the public sphere; the question was what meaning this changing private-public boundary would have on women and on society.

These were questions that directly bore on the nature of women's lives. Baldwin's appeals to women to maintain their independence and to display it proudly were evident in her calls for female-friendly housing and in her repeated efforts to show that women could do just about any type of job thought to be well within what might be termed the male or public sphere. Yet that did not lead her to ignore what might be considered the traditional subjects that were deemed pertinent to women, whether they be fashion or motherhood. In both cases, however, she portrayed an improving world, one that was dependent on thoughtful and independent female action, whether the individual woman was self-supporting or not.

At the same time, Baldwin understood gender through a prism of class. She explained the opposition that some wealthy women made to suffrage as a matter of their class, that they had, like the women she spied from the attic room that she shared as a struggling white-collar worker in New York City, succumbed to the mentality of the slave, dependent as they were on their husbands' industry for their living. Her criticisms of Marie Corelli were of this ilk. While she may have been closest to Clara Colby among suffrage activists, and Colby struggled financially, many other supporters of suffrage were quite comfortable. Though suffrage in general was not a class-based movement, Baldwin's own emphasis on class, power, and profit-seeking behavior frequently made its way into "The Woman's Point of View."

And that raises some questions. Many newspaperwomen, like Sarah Evans, believed that male editors ignored the women's page as beneath their contempt, and historian Alice Fahs suggests the same, maintaining that the desire to reach women shoppers and the editors' contempt for women convinced them that the woman's page would be filled by harmless fluff. It is worth thinking about Baldwin's defense of John Carroll, the editor of the *Evening Telegram*, as being more enlightened than that. If he held such ideas, he would have been sorely disappointed, since so much of "The Woman's Point of View" reflected on the perversity of capitalism, as we shall see. But it is hard to imagine that he would not have been aware of Baldwin's content, as the column appeared daily on the editorial page, a choice ultimately made by Carroll. While the weekend woman's page was segregated in the Saturday magazine of the *Telegram*, on other days "The Woman's Point of View" was hiding in plain sight. More likely, Carroll understood that Baldwin's themes were welcome in the larger community, and in that way "The Woman's Point of View" helps expand our understanding of the nature of radicalism in Progressive Era Portland.

3

The Radical Assault on Capitalism

> Pioneers for Human Freedom—
> Pioneers! O Pioneers . . .
> Priests and kings his power beguiling,
> Reaping gold from children's tears;
> Blind his eyes and deaf his ears
> To all else than golden profit.
> See ye not? O Pioneers!
> —Henry Victor Morgan, "Pioneers"

Though the fashion industry's relationship with its female customers served as an obvious subject for a column addressed to women readers, those installments in which Baldwin attacked its profit seeking at the expense of women's health and nature's balance were hardly exceptional. It was the impact on women that made the industry unique, and for that reason many women writers, especially feminists, understood dress reform as a means of establishing female independence. Yet Baldwin handled the fashion industry's disfiguring of female bodies and its destruction of bird populations in ways that were akin to her treatment of other industries. The criticisms of the fashion industry that appeared in "The Woman's Point of View" reflected the general position of the columnist, who routinely portrayed a social world that was in the process of being destroyed by profit-obsessed capitalists and that was in dire need of redemption. In her daily newspaper column, Baldwin regularly presented ideas that she and others in her family had expressed during the Gilded Age, ideas that she would continue to articulate in the more radical *Oregon Labor Press* in the decade that followed. John Carroll, editor of the *Telegram*, hired her to write a column written specifically for women that for three years consistently assaulted capitalism and capitalists for putting money before people and that called for the overthrow of that system.

The path that Baldwin took from her childhood abolitionist origins to her adult concerns with the inequities of the emerging corporate order had been trod by women of an older generation. Among the more prominent, Mary Livermore had identified women's rise to political consciousness not with the struggles for suffrage associated with the Declaration of Sentiments, ratified by the Seneca Falls Convention of 1848, but rather with the emergency associated with the war. There were reasons for Livermore to write in this vein. The war had immediately brought more and more Northern women out of their homes into charitable and organizational work in support of the Union Army. Many served as nurses in army hospitals, heeding Dorothea Dix's call for women to bring maternal concern to help the healing process of wounded men. Others worked to raise money and material for the support of men in the army. After the war, many would refuse to return to the domestic hearth, instead finding new organizational roles in the urbanizing society of the postwar era. As they increased their activities in the public sphere, and as they witnessed the growing numbers of women employed in wage labor, it became apparent to them that women could not always rely on men to support and protect them. Many would come to advocate expanding rights for women, including the right to vote. They would celebrate women's right to labor and to gain independent control over their own lives. Livermore's public life moved in this direction, and it eventually led her in the direction of socialism.

Many women like Livermore whose civic participation led them to advance the interests of their sex were struck by the impact of industrialization, which accelerated in the years after the war. As factories and sprawling cities replaced the closely knit towns of their memories, these women were shocked by the kinds of poverty that spread across the industrial landscape. As Mari Jo Buhle says of this cohort of women activists, "They were shocked by the squalor of the slums and the failure of civic institutions to provide for that growing class of citizens, the poor, especially the underpaid women forced to labor under unhealthy conditions."[1] For women like Baldwin who grew up in an era of small-scale production only to see their hometowns transformed into factory cities, the transformation of society and the economy was self-evident.

In carrying this tradition into the twentieth century and onto the pages of a daily newspaper, Baldwin broadened the discursive community that engaged in radical, anticorporate politics in Progressive Era Portland. Robert Johnston has examined this form of radicalism in the city and has located it in a broad alliance of the labor movement and the middle class, one that seized on the tools of direct democracy—primarily the initiative and referendum—to attempt to restructure the economy in a more equitable direction. He portrayed in the political support for physician Henry Lane, or in that for William S. U'Ren's versions of the single tax, the basis for a radical politics that challenged the prerogatives of capital. In this world of democrats with a small "d," virtue was associated with labor, not capital, and the impoverishment of the masses was seen as a sign of a perversion of natural law that understood labor as the creator of all wealth and deserving of its reward.[2] On a few occasions, Baldwin addressed direct democracy, reasoning, "if the people have the power to elect representatives to administer their power they have the power to retain that power and administer it direct."[3] Her support for the single tax, which was never close to her heart or her head, was expressed in a column that noted opposition to the measure among farmers belonging to the Grange in eastern Oregon, except for the "one man who defended it very ably," who asserted that "it was rich men's money that was being employed to kill it."[4] But though these particular issues were rarely discussed, anticorporate politics infused many of "The Woman's Point of View" columns.

Johnston's work hints as to the manner in which this popular democratic movement had some grounding in gender politics. It was evident in U'Ren's most democratic of proposals, a 1920 measure that would have replaced geographical, district-based legislative districts with occupational ones based on the proportion that a given occupation made up of the entire population; this plan would create a nearly lawyerless legislature, a body to be dominated by productive people. But Johnston noted that when U'Ren saw fit to include the occupation of "housewife," it would make adult, married women, who had just gained the suffrage, the largest occupational grouping, and therefore the largest single bloc in the legislature. In making this proposal, U'Ren, a longtime supporter of women's suffrage and of temperance, blended his contempt for what he perceived as the chicanery of corporate leaders and their hired lawyers who dominated the legislature with his belief in female morality. His proportional representation scheme reflected a combination of Victorian morality with an anticorporate agenda, and though it appeared on the ballot several years after Baldwin quit writing her column, it had been mentioned in radical circles for years.

Baldwin's own commitment to radical democracy and its attendant anticorporate politics were grounded in a sense of loss, one that she expressed in a piece about her hometown, Naugatuck, that focused on environmental degradation as a metaphor for the fall associated with rise of industrial capitalism and the potential redemption of civilization from its thrall. Her writing style reflected her own lifespan, detailing the changing impact of the environment from the days in which "handiwork [was] done in a home to the small factory owned and operated by one man, to the factory owned and operated by a firm, and now by a trust, for one of the two of the large trusts that have their grips on the little valley and its working force of inhabitants." She wrote broadly of the "white man" and his impact on the land as he worked to "harness the beautiful brown water and make it work," with "less sagacity than the beaver, whose industry he rivaled." White men cut down the "friendly trees" that shaded it, and the result was a river that "nursed its anger at the stupidity of the white man," drying up in the summer and becoming a raging torrent in the winter. Now bearing the town's sewage, this "once pure and useful stream of water" had become "murderous-looking and worse-smelling." Nearly three centuries of European settlement had created a constantly worsening depraved environment, but Baldwin held out hope that in the future "that beautiful river will be good-tempered and sane and sensible and clean, and the trees will grow again, and man become too decent to pollute and despoil one of God's loveliest gifts to him, the running stream."[5] In Baldwin's hands, it was not only birds that were slaughtered for the profit of some, but also the entire earth was rendered less hospitable by the rise of industrial capitalism.

This chapter explores the degree to which Baldwin established an anticorporate political discourse in the woman's column that provides evidence of the broadening of such a politics beyond the realm of the male-dominated Portland Central Labor Council. Because she wrote for a newspaper that tended to aim at middle- and working-class readers of both political parties (though the paper was officially a Republican Party paper, the editor, John Carroll, was a Democrat), Baldwin's three-year run provides us with a broader sense of the intersections between the political press, women's culture, and labor radicalism. Baldwin's own commitments are clearer. The letters she wrote as a younger woman defending workers against capitalists foreshadow her work as a columnist, but also her later career when she would write for the *Oregon Labor Press*, the organ of the Oregon trade-union movement, which was among the strongest supporters of U'Ren's radical agenda. While her thematic coverage for the woman's column was much more diverse than it would be when she wrote for the *Labor Press*, there was no softening of her anticapitalist message in the columns that appeared in the *Telegram*; in fact, it was a regular feature of her writing.

Corporations and the Health and Welfare of the Family

Where the fashion industry's profit seeking was associated with the destruction of nature and women's bodies, a subject raised by other women, whether they were Audubon Society types or feminists or both, Baldwin portrayed capitalism in general as hazardous to the health and vitality of working-class families. As a women's column, "The Woman's Point of View" focused on the impact of economic developments on the family, and it extrapolated from those issues reasons why women should be generally informed and engaged in the battle to restrain capitalist power. At the heart of the problem, the health and welfare of their families depended on it.

During the furor over unsanitary meatpacking occasioned by the publication of Upton Sinclair's *The Jungle* in 1906, Baldwin joined the fray by charging that the oligopolistic meatpackers were morally indifferent to the health of their customers. She juxtaposed the impact of capitalist decision making on the ordinary family with those headed by elite men who commanded capital and power. Asking her readers if "Armour and Swift and their families eat freely of this sort of meat," Baldwin asserted that the public had a right to know the answer; as she put it, "they really ought to be called to the witness stand and made to testify on this point."[6] Responding to an editorial on the regulation of milk supplies in the New York *Journal*, Baldwin pointed out that the good of families required the regulation of corporate forces. The "trust principle," she pointed out, referring to the consolidation of economic power, "threatens not only the lives of the little children old enough to work, but also that of the baby in the cradle"; in fact, diseased milk threatened "the sanctity of the home." Baldwin pointed out that the defense of the home required female activism, and she asserted that such women "cannot be accused of being out of their sphere if they inform themselves about these trusts and join hands with the men and the organizations that are working to break their power."[7]

The columnist portrayed corporate irresponsibility as a pervasive and dangerous feature of the social environment, and the historical evidence backs her up. Historian John Fabian Witt estimates that one worker in fifty was killed or disabled for at least four weeks each year because of a work-related accident, and in the anthracite coal mines of eastern Pennsylvania, the figures were much worse: 6 percent of the workforce was killed, another 6 percent permanently crippled, and yet another 6 percent was seriously but temporarily disabled.[8] Baldwin pointed out that while workers suffered industrial accidents, leading to maiming and death, companies responded by seeking means of minimizing their responsibility, and in so doing they were aided by legal doctrines that rejected any notion of causation that might lead plaintiffs to the capitalist's pockets. The first workers' compensation laws were only then being established by legislatures, and it was still common for the families of workers who were injured or killed on the job to suffer devastating losses. When lawsuits were filed, corporate attorneys often relied on legal devices such as the fellow servant doctrine, which placed the blame for accidents on the workers themselves, absolving companies of any responsibility. The subject raised questions about justice as well as the moral character of the corporate leaders who hid behind such defenses.[9]

Recounting the tragic death of an engineer on an eastern railroad who had been killed because of a defective boiler, Baldwin drew a portrait of corporate greed that had ensnared the deceased and his family. In this particularly pathos-ridden case, the engineer had known beforehand that the boiler was defective and had written a letter to that effect, only to be told that he must run the train as it was or lose his job. Fearful of losing his wages and his ability to support his family, the engineer lost his life when the boiler exploded. Of the corporation's management Baldwin charged, "they knew, too, that it was cheaper for them to run the old machine till it gave out than it was to take if off" for repairs. The widow was left without any settlement while, as Baldwin pointed out, the railroad continued to pay "fat dividends" to its stockholders. In lieu of taking responsibility, the company declared that the "blowing up of the engine was an 'act of God,'" which negated their responsibility to either the widow or the children.[10] This was no unusual breach of morality; Baldwin contended that attorneys for the "railroads and other corporations" routinely responded to damage suits "brought by some maimed and crippled individual" in this way, stressing that the corporations sought "to get off scot-free and pay no damages."[11]

Baldwin framed such discussions within the broader parameters of a woman's column, integrating her emphasis on female independence with her disdain for corporate power. In addressing the case of the engineer and the company's refusal to fix the engine, she suggested that if "a woman" would mismanage a house "as this letter of an engineer shows the most ordinary railroad matters are mismanaged, we should pity her husband for having so miserably incompetent a person as queen of his home, and we might charge it up to feminine incapacity."[12] In response to a case in which a corporate lawyer exchanged funeral expenses for the widow's waiver of a right to sue the company, Baldwin suggested that this made a mockery of any notion that men were the natural "protectors of women." Male corporate greed raised serious questions about any call for separate spheres.[13]

Baldwin provided extended coverage of similar local incidents, and with it a treatment that broadened the thematic content of the column, juxtaposing corporate irresponsibility against the union's commitments to its members. A twenty-four-year-old iron worker, J. E. Hustler, engaged in riveting on the new Portland and Seattle Railroad bridge across the Willamette, had fallen twenty-five feet onto a steel girder, crushing his skull. Baldwin spoke of the bravery of the young man, describing Hustler as a "soldier of the common good," who "braved danger . . . roosting on a slim, cold piece of iron, 25 feet or more above safety." She emphasized that Hustler could not rely on anyone but the union in the harsh industrial environment that capitalists had constructed. It was the Structural Iron Workers' Union that would send Hustler's body to his family in Canada, paying the costs of transportation and for a member who accompanied the remains. Preaching the gospel of unionization, Baldwin explained to her readers, "the union is the only organization in all the world that recognizes the existence of the working man or exerts any influence to protect that existence and to make it tolerable." She rhetorically asked her readers if they knew of "some corporation that insisted on paying the funeral expenses of employes killed in its service," answering that "you know and I know, that we may expect something like that of a corporation when all the Bengal tigers live on peanuts." The editor of the *Bridgemen's Magazine* saw fit to reprint the column, praising its "beautiful thoughts," and commented that it was remarkable because "such statements do not generally appear in the columns of the daily press."[14]

Industrial accidents like these allowed Baldwin to make categorical denunciations of corporations, casting the corporate form itself as a legal contrivance meant to enhance the firm's ability to gather wealth at the expense of the community. She described the corporation as "nothing but men banded together to acquire wealth," as a legal device that protected morally indifferent, greedy men from the consequences of their own actions. Like many other writers during the Progressive Era who exposed corporate malfeasance, she sought to draw general principles from the numerous incidents with which her readers were familiar that would reveal the moral content of corporate law. To say that a corporation "has broken the laws," Baldwin explained, is really to say, "some men have broken the laws and are therefore criminals." If a corporation "killed a hundred persons in a year because it is too stingy to provide safeguards to life," it followed that the men who comprise it "are murderers" who use the corporate form to enable them to "escape detection and responsibility." Baldwin called on her readers to take the clothing of corporate legitimacy and "strip it off."[15] The problem would only be solved when "a sentiment" was "aroused among women to the righteousness of properly safeguarding the men whose work is sorely needed," to protect them from "the rapacity and niggardliness of great corporations."[16]

Baldwin consistently hit the theme of corporate irresponsibility, and she did so in numerous and varied contexts. For instance, it was deployed to help convince her readers that they had an interest in the city charter then being debated by the city council. At one point she warned that if the charter did not name a specific agency to collect taxes from a corporate entity, corporate lawyers would argue that, "under the provisions of the charter," the people could not collect the taxes legally levied against the firm. Both Baldwin and her readers, aware of Margaret Haley's strenuous efforts to force Chicago corporations to pay their taxes so that the public schools could be supported, understood this as a potential problem. But more grippingly, she argued that a well-written charter might provide less legal ground for corporations seeking to avoid the payment of damages to those whom they harmed. In this vein, she told the story of a young boy who waved his hand out of a window and touched a live wire that killed him; it was the coroner's report that nobody was responsible for the death on which the tale turned. Baldwin asked her readers to be outraged that a utility company could run a live wire without "anything whatever to indicate its presence" and not be held responsible. By mockingly concluding, "It's a wonder they didn't say he came to his death by 'an Act of God,'" Baldwin reminded her readers how corporations routinely evaded responsibility to the community.[17]

Similar problems pervaded modern society, as Baldwin linked corporate irresponsibility to a transformed set of social ethics that ultimately permitted the acceptance of great poverty. The conditions to which working-class families were subjected were frequently addressed. For instance, she quoted Maxim Gorky's descriptions of children on the Lower East Side of New York who "pick out from the garbage boxes on the curbstones pieces of bread, and devour it, together with the mold and the dirt, there in the street in the stinging dust and choking air." She urged her readers to ponder the contrast between "the dogs of the rich," who "wear sable collars and dainty shoes," and the impoverished children of the Lower East Side, and called on them to "do what one person may to change the current of public opinion until these ridiculous and cruel extremes shall not be."[18] Manufacturers who employed child labor or landlords in New York City "who evict women and children in the dead of winter" acted like "cannibals," but the point was extended to anyone who exploited his or her own position, such as the "woman who grudges the girl who works in her kitchen any leisure, any happiness," terming such a woman a "cannibal, living off the life that belongs to another." Similarly, she condemned the "thoughtlessness" of bourgeois women who supported foreign missions but gave little thought to abruptly canceling with the poorer women who cleaned their homes because their plans had changed and keeping the appointment would now be inconvenient, forgetting that domestic servants "eke out a living" to support their children and pay the rent.[19]

Baldwin's commitment to child welfare in all its aspects led her into different terrain. Responding to the appeals of President Roosevelt to have more children and thereby avoid what he termed "race suicide," she insisted, "Race suicide consists not so much in the children that are not born as it does in the conditions that are forced upon the luckless millions who are." Echoing her hostile response to the Reverend Collyer in Naugatuck nearly fifteen years earlier, she suggested that Roosevelt stop pressuring those "who hesitate to bring children into this industrial inferno" and instead apply it "toward those who are responsible for the inferno itself."[20] She compared poverty to a disease, and while scientists searched for the cures to physical ailments, she assured her readers that poverty too was ultimately "curable." The problem was in the aim: "we have been taught to believe that this disease is incurable; that always there must be people who suffer from it; we have quoted Christ in support of the perpetuation of this terror, 'The poor ye have always with you.'" The cure was available in the world of thought: transform thinking, and people will come to recognize that "no little child need henceforth be killed or maimed by the disease of poverty and it will be only a question of time when that disease which is entirely within human control shall disappear."[21]

Class inequities bore on the health and welfare of the next generation of working-class children. Baldwin lectured her readers that "the attempt to provide for babies anywhere in this world on any other basis than that of absolute equality of supply of love and care and intelligence, and money, is a pitiful farce and a shameful wrong to the children."[22] Baldwin addressed child mortality in the slum districts of New York and Chicago, calling for "a search for the fundamental cause of the stifling poverty that chokes out the life of these babies who have made an unsuccessful attempt to live in this world." Instead of radical change, she suggested that reformers must "be content with palliative measures" that aim "to snatch a few little ones from the black maelstrom of city conditions." Similar problems, she asserted, had appeared in Portland, where "the inevitable question of rent is . . . precisely what it is in these larger cities, thus compelling families to live in places wholly inimical to healthful infant life." She questioned the priorities of women who donated their time to support fairs and festivals that celebrated the city, when they could have been more morally engaged by working to put pressure on government to improve living conditions, concluding that "a city with both roses and babies flourishing in their perfection would be a matter for the world to ring with."[23]

The Rose Festival, then in its infancy, came under specific criticism when Baldwin turned to the question of working-class housing, a subject that broadened her expressions of concern for the construction of apartment units for independent females. She suggested that the kind of collective effort necessary to put on the "Rose Show" could be turned to the development of better housing, asking "how much prouder" residents would be "if they could truly say that nowhere in Portland were human beings living under conditions that effectually prevented the maintenance of good health or self-respect."[24] Deploring the class divisions of New York and the resulting conditions, which she likened to "the murderer of the innocents," Baldwin asked about the choices that Portland would make in the future:

> Is Portland going to be a place for moneyed men and stock
> gamblers, where little children die for land and fresh air
> or grow up to fill jails and refuges and insane asylums and
> almshouses, or is Portland going to be city of the New Time
> in which the chief business shall be the culture of the child
> for the sake of the magnificent harvest of sane and wise and
> kind and strong manhood and womanhood?[25]

When it was announced that some of the Portland Fire Department horses would be retired and put out to pasture to be maintained by the city, Baldwin used the occasion to juxtapose the conditions faced by working people with those soon-to-be retired working animals. Claiming that both were "beasts of burden," Baldwin opined that pensions would be an appropriate reward for the "man who works all his life for the poor privilege of keeping himself above ground for three score years and ten."[26] When a one-hundred-year-old woman who had long worked as a domestic servant died at the poor farm, Baldwin told her readers that though "we say it is no crime to be poor, but as sure as you live, there is very little difference in the treatment accorded the very poor and that meted out to the criminal."[27]

As bad as living conditions were for the poor, it was the use of child labor that most directly connected capitalists to the inadequacies of child welfare. Baldwin insisted that child labor be understood as "part of a system of evils" that would require a more radical approach for reforms to have any "lasting benefit."[28] When she discussed Edwin Markham's 1907 essay on the subject, she focused on his explanation that competition forced employers to hire children to be able to make a 3 percent profit, leading Baldwin to conclude that capitalism and its quest to provide investors with a constant and steady return demanded that children "be devoured," and that if the people mobilized to stop it, she mockingly warned it might "disturb that supersensitive, shrinking and timid thing—Capital."[29] A month later, she accentuated the point by discussing the case of a child killed by a railroad in New Jersey, in which a judge awarded the family two dollars in damages. Baldwin assured her readers that the parents were poor, "and of no account in the eyes of a judge, who measured all values by the 3 per cent standard" and she called on "humane people to band together to protect the child from the insanity of greed and the mania of profit."[30]

Capitalists who defended the practice of child labor were particularly held out as symbols of what was perversely wrong in modern society. In September 1907, Baldwin criticized a leading member of the National Association of Manufacturers, J. W. Van Cleave of St. Louis, for standing up after a dinner at the Waldorf Astoria and giving a speech that "excused and palliated the crimes of his associates against women and children and charged . . . ignorance and mendacity to those who are working for the betterment of these same women and children who work under dangerous and disease-breeding conditions." Ironically labeling it a "humanitarian and truly patriot address," Baldwin asked if Van Cleave would wake his own wife at "5 in the morning, wake up the two or three little Vans, dress and feed them and take them off to a day nursery while she went to some factory and began her day's work at the sharp sound of the 7 o'clock whistle." After two days of this routine, Baldwin suggested that Mr. Van Cleave "would discover that there was something besides 'ignorance' and 'extravagance' and 'mendacity' back of the representations of such women as compose the Consumers' League and the reports of men like Edwin Markham regarding the conditions of the children and women who work!" Noting that Van Cleave identified merely as a "capitalist," she sarcastically asked, "What more can a man be?"[31]

Sometimes Baldwin's discussion of child labor revealed how her economic orientation could transcend the Victorian moral assumptions about the evils of the practice. On hearing of efforts to prevent children from performing on the theatrical stage, removing them from a sphere always associated with the tint of immorality, Baldwin scoffed. Instead, she said that the point of activism was to "stand between the child who is overworked, underfed and badly clothed and the rapacity of some child-eating corporation or business enterprise." To make clear what she meant by the child who needed protection, she referred to the textile mills of New England where, "I have been told, small boys wade naked in the big bleaching vats in the chemicals used to whiten the cloth." The issue, as it so often was for Baldwin, was economic power: she asserted that the child actors would be accorded "good care and humane treatment" because of their "money value" as well as their capacity to "add the brightest and purest feature of modern drama."[32]

Poverty and Morality

Much of Baldwin's attention to poverty can be understood as an attempt to detach cultural linkages between class status, economic crisis, and moral behavior. Considerable gendered discourse of the Victorian Era associated poverty with male improvidence, an explanation that fueled much activism in the temperance movement. While Baldwin maintained a moralistic understanding of poverty, she equated immorality not with the behaviors of the impoverished but with the greed of the wealthy, and she thereby turned the class understanding of poverty and immorality on its head, stressing that it was the capitalist's immoral designs that led to mass poverty, not the moral failings of those in need. To convey this, Baldwin wrote in ways that played on conventional expectations, revealing how language could obscure inequities.

The Oregon Land Fraud Trials, in which well-placed and wealthy men sought through illegal means to accumulate wide swaths of the federal and public domain, offered Baldwin an opportunity to rearrange moral categories. The scandal was just unfolding when Baldwin began writing her column. She responded with a claim of intent to examine "society" at the local jail, noting that the word tends to be deployed regarding the "leisure class." Baldwin made her readers aware of how respectability, though associated with morality, often was a marker of class privilege rather than a reliable signal of social virtue. Her subject, now in residence at the jail, was the corrupt surveyor Stephen A. Douglas Puter, a former state senator who had played a leading role both in the development of the land scandals and then later in the trials after he provided a thorough confession. The ring in which Puter had played such a prominent role had corruptly accumulated federal lands, often by bribing "dummy entrymen," that were expected to be purchased

Stephen A. Douglas Puter, depicted here in his prison cell working on his book *Looters of the Public Domain*, played a prominent role in the Oregon Land Fraud Trials and in revealing the extent of the corruption. Courtesy of the Oregon Historical Society, ORHI61630

back by the federal government for the formation of new federal forest reserves, or to be used in exchanges between railroad companies and the federal government. Puter had bribed both officials in the land office and higher-ups, including the US senator from Oregon, George Mitchell. Describing Puter as "an intelligent and agreeable man," Baldwin sardonically asserted, "it is gratifying to learn that the man who robbed Uncle Sam so long and cleverly does not drink." It was men who had all the trappings of respectability who had engaged in corrupt land monopolist practices that deprived hard-working people of an opportunity to set themselves up on the land as independent producers.[33]

Baldwin challenged her readers to come to know the poor as human beings, and promised that if they did, they would realize that bourgeois conceptions of poverty and depravity were inadequate. She asked them to "leave the shopping district, detach yourself from the beautiful part of the city where the homes of the affluent and refined are and go down among the unemployment agencies on Burnside street and near the waterfront in other places." She asked them to "Look at their faces. See the lack of hope and spirit upon them." Then she asked the woman reader to "imagine your boy of 18 or 20 landing in Portland with, say $5 in his pocket to last him until he gets a job." Without any resources, he would save money by "going into a saloon for a glass of beer and a free lunch." She added, "there are hundreds of other mothers' boys doing that every day in the year." And many of them would be arrested eventually for vagrancy and "sentenced to the rockpile," which she said is "what we call it, when we arrest a man for his poverty." Those not arrested were subject to abuse, like that inflicted upon a soldier by a "wolf in a private employment agency who took the last cent" he had "and sent him off away out in the country to take that job that existed only in the imagination of the wolf." The soldier "tramped" back to Portland, "penniless and heartsick and footsore."[34]

Baldwin often used her column to generate sympathy among her female readers for workingmen. When local Unitarian minister Harrison D. Barrett, a fellow New Englander, wrote to "The Woman's Point of View" to complain about the lack of chivalrous behavior displayed by men toward women in the Northwest, an opportunity presented itself. Noting that men engaged in smoking in front of ladies and that they competed for streetcar space with women, Barnett called on men to "give their elder brothers and their wives, sisters and sweethearts places of preferment in the streetcars." Baldwin rose to the challenge, asserting that women were able to walk alone on the streets of Portland at night, which drew on the larger theme in the columns of female independence while asserting that Portland men did maintain the most meaningful forms of chivalry. More importantly, Baldwin responded by again inveighing against the middle-class inability to empathize with workingmen: "I should not wish any man who had worked for 10 hours at hard labor of some sort and had dropped into a seat for a little rest to feel obliged to give up his seat to a strong woman who is provided for, and does nothing harder than haunt bargain counters."[35]

One of the places where she clearly stood aloof from many, though not all, women's rights activists was in the way she discussed alcohol and saloon culture. Though she assumed that all readers of her column were "believers in temperance," she distinguished herself from the "zealous reformers" of the Anti-Saloon League of Oregon by questioning whether they had "the right to say that other persons shall not drink beer . . . if they really want it." Here, as elsewhere, she was less apt to turn a discussion of the harmful effects of alcohol into a diatribe against evil; she accused the anti-saloon reformers of focusing too much on the effects of alcohol and too little on the reasons people actually indulged in the drinking of it.[36] Instead, she stressed that alcohol existed within a social context, one that was often depraved by economic power and industrial misery, which is what she meant when she asserted that the thirst for alcohol "has been inextricably woven and interwoven by a sort of devilish cunning into every strain of our social and business and industrial life."[37]

Without a doubt, Baldwin perceived alcohol and saloon culture as a "curse," but its most negative effect was not its role in creating poverty but rather its ability to cloud the mind and make people accept the systematic evils that afflicted the poor. She considered a citizenry composed of people "befuddled with alcohol" as just the kind that would "permit a steel corporation to kill men; to permit government by railroads; to be unable to see that most girls would rather live in comfort as prostitutes than to starve to death on hard work and inadequate wages." Reform and transformation required that the "menace of drink" be removed so that voters would be "clear headed." And for those reasons, Baldwin refused to rest with calls for the "elimination of the saloon," charging that there needed to be alternatives that provided "the rest and warmth and light and opportunity for association many men find in saloons, and find nowhere else."[38] In a column noting the birthday of Frances Willard, the former leader of the Woman's Christian Temperance Union (WCTU), Baldwin exclaimed, "she saw that the question of the use of intoxicants cannot be considered by itself; it is too closely interlinked with a thousand other problems." Again she implored her readers to recognize that the "drink problem" had to be studied in conjunction with "industrial and economic problems," and that "it is not enough to see that drink makes poverty; it is even more necessary to see that poverty makes drunkenness."[39]

"It's foolish to say that there is nothing good about the saloon," Baldwin asserted; her point was that temperance reformers needed to be mindful of what services it provided to its customers and then to supply them in another way. She pointed out, "the workingman can drop in and find a place where he knows he is perfectly welcome," stressing the sociability of the saloon, the music, the cheap beer, and the food for those who generally lived miserable lives. She queried, "Do any of the people who hate the saloon provide attractions of this sort for the men they want to see stay away from the saloons?" Rather than stress an appetite for alcohol, Baldwin asserted that drinking beer was the cost of partaking in the sociability offered by the saloon.[40]

Her emphasis on the context in which drinking was engaged was reinforced in a column that she wrote about an experiment in Gothenburg, Sweden, where concern about the rise in pauperism led an investigatory committee to the saloon. The committee expressed alarm over the degree to which "liquor men were in business with the pawnbroker," together taking the lion's share of the wages of workingmen. The community response was the formation of a company that aimed to take over the entire liquor business of the city, slowly buying up licenses and taking over the places of business when leases and licenses expired. The result was a monopolistic public-private venture in which shareholders were paid 6 percent interest while excess profits were deposited in the town treasury. Baldwin stressed that this cooperative company set out to make all pubs "clean, light and airy," and it served only "pure liquor" and "good wholesome food" as the diminishment of the profit incentive led to the abandonment of adulterating booze with "poisons." Baldwin concluded that the experiment "reduced the evils resulting from saloons," turning them into "decent, comfortable resorts" while adding "thousands of kroners to the public moneys."[41] For her readers, Baldwin seemed to suggest that stronger food and drug laws, rather than moralistic condemnation of the drinker, were the proper solutions to the problem of the saloon.

The assault on the saloon was always mediated for Baldwin by her beliefs in the harshness of capitalist society. She continued to express these concerns after losing her column. Within a week of the passage of Oregon's statewide Prohibition law in November 1914, Baldwin wrote a letter to the editor of the *Telegram*, challenging him and "the good women who hustled and got the saloon voted out of business" to understand that their work had only begun and that it would not be finished until there should be "a string of bright, clean coffee houses to take their places, where good, wholesome food could be had at reasonable prices; where games and reading matter and warmth and light, and if possible, a bath, could be had." No defender of the saloon—she termed it a false friend of the workingman and had given attention in her column to prohibitionists, both male and female—Baldwin stressed the evils perpetrated on working-class men, women, and children by the sheer circumstance of poverty more than she did the evils of drink. Her commitment to the position did not waver in the years after losing her column.[42]

The Moral Content of Economic Life

The readers of the column received a vision of immorality that centered on self-interest and the economy. There was something conventional about Baldwin's approach, for which there had been important precedents. Harriet Beecher Stowe had continually made economic activity the source of so much male evil in her denunciation of slavery. In *Uncle Tom's Cabin*, men who struggled for economic advantage engaged in constant competition as they unleashed their self-interest and their passions on others, particularly black enslaved women. For Stowe, it was only the homey influences of the God-fearing woman that could temper this otherwise male force, which was so destructive of morality. Whether she was defending the workingman's inclination to visit the saloon or his need to get some rest on the streetcar, Baldwin rearranged some of the old tropes of mid-Victorian literature, suggesting that it was not maleness and economic activity in themselves that were so destructive, but rather the economic inequalities that led some more powerful men to seek their own self-interest to the detriment of the community. Economic morality was the overriding social problem; overcoming it would require replacing the ethos and practices of industrial capitalism with a more mutualistic approach to social relations.

As it was, the community, so long as it remained unorganized, would suffer as a result of the self-interest of those with economic power. Baldwin warned that the high cost of living in Portland would hinder the movement of productive people to the area, for such folks asked questions about the ratio of wages to rents. And if unanswered, she warned that community efforts like the Rose Festival, "so far as inducing people to come to Portland to live . . . will be as sounding brass and tinkling cymbal." She asserted that Portlanders paid "extortionate prices" for dairy products, fruits, vegetables, and grains despite living in "one of the most productive areas in the world." Suggesting male malfeasance and exploitation—she equated current pricing to "robbery"—Baldwin suggested an "association of women" be formed to inquire into the cost of provisions to overcome the actions of the "thoroughly organized" wholesalers and retailers. In calling for consumer

organization, she pointed out that in the modern economy the unorganized consumers of Portland were "absolutely helpless in the hands of
effectively organized dealers."[43]

Baldwin showed her readers that the ethos of the capitalist marketplace invaded all aspects of social life. In response to an article that celebrated the importance of the paycheck as the measure of an individual,
Baldwin castigated the author, asserting, "Men are already trampling
on each other like frightened cattle in a maddened stampede for money,
without another word being said to intensify their madness." Beginning
with the proposition that conditions "have forced 99 per cent of the men
in this world to humbly ask for the other 1 per cent the opportunity to
draw a pay envelope," she advised her readers, so long as they "are fit
to stand on two feet and not walk on all fours, never measure yourself
by your pay envelope, be it small or great." Work, as necessary as it is
for survival, should be done as "the highest expression of that person's
love and gratitude for the beautiful world he is in and for the combined
comforts and luxuries that fall about him like fragrant flowers from the
same loving activity of others, many of whom he never sees or knows,
but who, nevertheless, minister to him as he to them."[44]

Baldwin brought similar counsel to the question of marriage. Com-
menting on an article that urged women to refuse to marry any man "too
improvident" to have assured himself at least a twelve-hundred-dollar
annual income, Baldwin contemptuously asserted that the writer had
provided "the lowest figure at which you are permitted to sell yourself
in marriage." Abhorrence of both slavery and the pecuniary orientation
of capitalist culture led her to call on the "dear girl" to think first and
foremost whether she loves the prospective husband without thinking
about the man's earning potential. She reminded her reader that poverty is "the crime of civilization," and not a reflection of the character of
the young man. It was more important that family life should rise above
crass materialism, and she argued that husband and wife needed to be
kindred spirits, sharing "confidence and a spirit of bravery and courage
that makes them feel they two, should to shoulder, are a match for the
world, the flesh and the devil."[45]

On occasion, Baldwin addressed the Arts and Crafts movement as
a means of reducing the impact of materialism on the home. Arriving
out of England in the romanticism of John Ruskin and the romantic
socialism of William Morris, the Arts and Crafts movement responded

to mechanization and the factory by seeking to harmonize labor and art through a revival of traditional craftwork. In Morris's hands, the movement articulated a belief that artistic transformation could help transform the conditions of the working class, but many also appreciated the movement solely on aesthetic grounding and as such could easily be accommodated to the commercial marketplace.[46] Baldwin wrote approvingly of the English socialist William Morris, describing him as "one of those rare spirits, born to wealth, and who yet understand the disadvantages of the poor," and she wrote that his ultimate aim was to rid the world of "wickedness, greed, oppression, [and] injustice." Much of Baldwin's appreciation for Morris was based on aesthetics, as she praised him for teaching that furniture that is "good and substantial, which best meets the demands of use upon it, is the most beautiful."[47] On the Saturday woman's page, Baldwin quoted Morris on the need to "win back art again to our daily labor, win back art, that is to say, the pleasures of life to the people." And on the same page she quoted Ruskin, that "Life without labor is guilt; labor without art is brutality."[48] Similarly, she characterized Morris's effort to transform the goods that filled bourgeois dwellings as being guided by the principle that when "beauty has done its perfect work, wickedness, greed, oppression, injustice, will spread their black wings and fly away."[49] In 1910, Baldwin delivered a talk at a socialist meeting on Morris's poetry.[50] Baldwin read *The Craftsman*, the American Arts and Crafts monthly edited by furniture manufacturer Gustav Stickley, and praised discussion there about transforming women's clothing according to the same principles. "Dress," she commented, "illustrates the arts and crafts idea as well as anything—perhaps better."[51] Years later, Baldwin wrote an article for *The Craftsman*, praising a couple who over the course of many years built their own craftsman home by "listening to one's own ideals."[52]

But Baldwin could be critical of the Arts and Crafts society in Portland. A correspondent to "The Woman's Point of View" complained that a lecture on "Basketry" was open only to "members and invited guests," which led the writer to conclude that the society was "founded, not in the interest of true art, which is universal, but simply as a bit of dilettantism tending the self-exaltation of the few members." Baldwin agreed and suggested that the members of the Arts and Crafts Society "follow the very admirable example set by the Audubon Society, which invited the public to its meetings through the press and welcomes them when they attend." Baldwin considered the goals of the Arts and Crafts Society relevant to the public good, asserting that it should "refine and elevate the mass of people to a higher comprehension of what is true and beautiful, and teach them to despise nothing intrinsically useful, but rather to see the beauty which, by reason of its use, it should possess."[53]

Though she was concerned about reducing the effect of crass materialism on the home, it was the indifference to human suffering in the very institutions that should be most concerned that most roused Baldwin's ire. Her sensibilities were violated by the increasingly anonymous city, not because men disappeared into the culture of the saloon there, but because the so-called best people ignored the plight of their fellow human beings. One story about the "insensibility" to human suffering hailed from Boston, where the toney Trinity Church, attended by "the most refined and well-bred, well-fed and elaborately clothed Christians," had its service interrupted by a "shivering band of overcoatless unemployed" who numbered three hundred and who sought refuge from the "savage, searing wind of the Back Bay." Baldwin pointed out that once there, they saw on the stained glass "Christ and his 12 working men." They were led by political theorist and activist Morrison I. Swift, who suggested that the rector "preach a sermon on the duty of the City of Boston to the unemployed, and asked that the day's collection be turned over to these men." But the church leaders rejected the proposal, as they were determined to make sure that the collection went to "Foreign Missions!" Baldwin thought "words fail to describe the action" of the rector, whose inflexibility—he had said that he would accommodate the unemployed men's demands the following week—prevented the church from "making the slightest pretension to a living faith in Jesus Christ." And she concluded by suggesting that this indifference is the reason "that the mention of the church so often brings to the surface a ripple of derisive laughter in a meeting of working men."[54]

Local clergyman W. C. Sheppard of Vancouver defended the Trinity rector, noting that the minister had already prepared a sermon and had promised to address the problem of unemployment, a matter that he suggested required "careful study," while "courteously" welcoming the three hundred unemployed to sit on the cushioned pews of the church. Sheppard expressed "indignation" at Baldwin for her intemperate attack while blaming her for widening whatever breach that might exist "between the church and the workingmen." Undeterred, Baldwin expanded her criticism of the church. She asserted that the millions of "men, women and children—existing in the direst poverty" were sufficient reasons for churchmen, "had they been so inclined," to study unemployment instead of waiting until they "marched up to the very altar asking for relief." More to the point, Baldwin said the time was past when "churchmen or cities or even nations can expect commendation for merely helping the poor. The demand of today is for the complete annihilation of the conditions that make chronic want and misery possible among millions of human beings in a country of fabulous wealth."[55] That ministers needed to be lectured about this only demonstrated the degree to which capitalist values of selfishness had spread across the intellectual landscape.

In that spirit, Baldwin held up to her readers the efforts of those who transcended personal selfish desire and the pursuit of monetary reward. On reviewing a history of the United States, written by Elroy M. Avery, she stressed Avery's claim to have worked on this book for nearly twenty years. Baldwin compared his craftsmanship favorably with that of "literary prostitutes," and commended him for his "conscientious care," which she deemed particularly unusual in "these days of Mammon domination and money madness."[56] Similarly, in her discussion of violin virtuoso Maud Powell, Baldwin emphasized the painstaking preparations that the artist must make before being ready to perform. But she used it to make a more general comment about the way one should approach work, predicting, "the day is coming when not a soul on all the round world will have to 'work for a living' because the living will be so assured and secure that noble incentives will take its place." In this better world, people will look back on the "scramble for bread and butter," so evident in contemporary industrial society, as "half savage and dehumanizing."[57]

Similar attitudes were evident in the fiction that Baldwin highlighted. In one instance, Baldwin trained her attention on a short story written by Elizabeth Newport Hepburn, a writer and poet with suffragist sympathies. The tale, "The Lighting of the Candle," tells the story of a "loving home life" in which the wife insists that her husband follow his own artistic inclinations instead of putting out lesser work for the popular presses. Baldwin considered the piece "prophetic of the day that is coming when men and women will not permit everything in life to be measured by the standards of a mercenary market system."[58]

Though she could associate the problems of crass materialism with male power, she provided examples of women who sold themselves like male lawyers did to corporations. While demanding that there be "equality of opportunity for people of both sexes," Baldwin asked whether anyone "has the right to sell his brains to anybody that wants to buy, for any purpose whatever?" The subject was a woman speechwriter who was engaged in "brain prostitution," which Baldwin considered "far more immoral and far more dangerous to republican institutions than the other sort." Like others who worked merely for money and less for art and craft, the speechwriter and the lawyer symbolized the crisis of the republic. Instead of providing the public with "the truth about trusts," the hired speechwriter poisons the "sources of information which should be kept as pure and clean as our water supply."[59]

As Baldwin made her assaults on the economic system, she sometimes took more direct aim at the emerging world of consumption, characterized by the rise of department stores that advertised in daily newspapers like the *Telegram*. She criticized middle-class women who engaged in a "stampede" to buy goods on a "bargain day." She described well-dressed women "who could have paid $30 for a waist if they had wanted to; and yet they were scrambling like madwomen over that bargain counter of $5 waists." Baldwin lectured her readers that bargain hunting only assured that wages for women in textile mills would remain low, and she recommended that they pick up a copy of Edward Bellamy's *Looking Backward* "to read his wonderful description of a shopping tour as it might be and as no doubt it some time will be."[60]

Baldwin was critical of the world of installment buying, which she thought ensnared unwary consumers, rendering them slaves to capital. Noting that debtors were no longer locked up in dank prisons, she saw that they were seduced by "the siren song of 'a little down and a little a week,'" which imposed new and different forms of dependency on creditors. She sympathized with the man who "is beset on all sides by persons and firms and emblazoned advertisements urging him to run in debt for this or that" while "the sum total of the debt is craftily concealed beneath the small weekly payment demanded." Considering the allurements of the emerging consumer marketplace, Baldwin suggested that the state grant poor and indebted families a form of urban homestead exemption to protect the material necessities of domestic life. Seizure of the home for nonpayment of debt amounted to what Baldwin considered an incorrect view of property, which she asserted belonged "to the man who puts his life into it, to the woman who saved and toiled with him."[61]

In general, the columns presented a view of consumption that contradicted the newspaper's mission to sell advertising copy. In the fall of 1907, she called on her readers to be thoughtful in the selection of gifts, while providing an appeal to not be overcome by materialism, which she suggested was antithetical to the "spirit of Christmas." The emphasis on buying was "vulgarizing" the holiday, leading consumers to forget its religious significance, which would be better served by developing concern for slum dwellers.[62] A year later, Baldwin took a much stronger stand against materialism and crass consumerism. She agreed with the approach taken by the WCTU and the Consumers' League calling on shoppers to not shop the last ten days prior to Christmas to alleviate the pressure put on working people in the stores by the hordes descending on the stores. As Lucia Faxon Additon of the Oregon WCTU put it, "Christmas, that hallowed time, the anniversary of the nativity of Christ, has become a season of cruelty to scores of working people." Baldwin added that it was a terrible thing that Christ, whom she described as "the man who despised material wealth," should be "cruelly misrepresented" by making his birthday a "mad orgy of things, things, things—often needless things, often silly things of no use to the receiver." She cast the giving of the five-hundred-dollar jewel as an absurd commemoration of "the birth of a poor carpenter who . . . plainly declared that his kingdom was not of this world!"[63]

A few months later, she intensified her assault on materialism. Charging that the person whose life revolves solely around physical wants and the gratification of them has a "dead soul," Baldwin argued that this was generally characteristic of the "comfortable" class, which explained their lack of sympathy for the "torture the struggle for existence inflicts upon so many less favored." Instead of inquiring into "the cause of all this misery," they are "too steeped in mere animal gratification and comfort to wish to be told the remedy." They jammed the summer resorts, both men and women indulging in "racy gossip." Arguing that their activities put them outside the bounds of progressive evolution, Baldwin concluded that "the elimination of this class is as inevitable as that the sun shines." The column closes with a telling portrait of Marie Antoinette:

> In a time when life was at its tensest, this child of pleasure, this beautiful creature with a dead soul in her body, played in her round of physical delights about the mouth of the lion's den. Had she tried to cultivate a soul; had she tried to understand the terrible proletariat; had she sought from the first to develop the soul in herself and bring it in touch with this irresistible power of outraged humanity, the history of fair France might have been different. . . . America has thousands of Marie Antoinettes today—beautiful bodies without souls, without comprehension.[64]

Baldwin emphasized through the use of allegory the corrupting influence of great economic power. In one of these, Baldwin suggested that her depth of understanding had significantly grown since she was a young woman. Readers learned that she had earlier worked in a publishing house in New York City, where she had read manuscripts, read proofs, and written book reviews. It was in that role that she came across a manuscript that she had rejected, in part because of "it lacked literary quality" but also "for its horror which I have never seen paralleled in any work of fiction." But in retrospect, Baldwin appreciated its emphasis on the concentration of power in the hands of a "king of finance and commerce," while "the millions were reduced to the most terrible industrial slavery."

In her retelling of the story, the masses of this society experienced "the maiming and killing of men in mines and factories, and then the forcing of inadequate settlement upon their widows and orphans by sharp and utterly unscrupulous agents, so the corporations responsible might escape the penalty for their indifference to human life." The story turned on the development of a flesh-eating microbe that afflicted the son of the "King of Finance and Commerce," who set out to have scientist serfs cure the lad. After the cure had been administered and divulged to the "great man," they were killed slowly by electricity as the "king of commerce had decreed that no person should remain alive whom he could feel under the slightest obligation." Believing that the story had great allegorical merit, she claimed that "if I had now to pass judgment upon it I think I would say—print it."[65]

Whereas it was conventional for a female readership to be immersed in a literature that hailed female morality and self-sacrifice while juxtaposing it against male amorality and self-interest, Baldwin's columns reexamined these categories from an unrelentingly anticapitalist perspective. They asked readers to relocate the source of immorality away from the general category of men or alcohol and toward the self-absorbed members of the bourgeoisie, both male and female. While she held that women had great potential for moving society in a less selfish and more egalitarian future, which could be furthered by allowing them greater access to both economic and political power, for the moment men undeniably held more power and therefore more capacity for corruption. Though she frequently emphasized the gendered source of evil in ways that are reminiscent of Stowe's epic work on slavery, it was the corrupting influence of economic power and how it fostered inequality that was the source of most social evils.

Remedy in Thought: The Study of Political Economy

In an allegory of her own, Baldwin drew a portrait of a world in which a giant, known as the Beaver, was "exceedingly simple-minded, and so near-sighted that he was in reality ruled and all his great wealth dominated by a very small and insignificant Elf that the giant could have flattened to the thickness of a postage stamp by just one small pinch of his enormous thumb and finger." The giant was "a cunning mechanic," and he made fabulous things, but there were no roads that would allow him to exchange his produce. Though he could have built his own roads, the "very small and very weak and helpless" Elf convinced the Beaver "that he and he alone could build roads through his fair farming and wealthy mineral lands," but he waited until they were so badly needed that the "simple-minded and near-sighted giant would give him a large part of all the things that went over the roads for what the Elf called freight and passenger rates." But when the giant had a fall and was knocked on his head, "it knocked an idea into his head," that he could just as easily build a road himself. When the Elf learned of this, he realized, "The game of sham royalty is up. . . . Now the Beaver has found this out, he'll see me as I am," and he "made all speed to leave the land of the Beaver giant who had an idea knocked into his head." Baldwin concluded with a postscript, telling her readers that the first part of this story is true, and she left it to them "to decide just where the writer's imagination has tampered with the facts."[66]

The story presumes a couple of matters essential for understanding Baldwin's approach to political economy. The first is that the role of capital, as represented by the Elf, was unnecessary, that it was the labor of the Beaver that created the real and tangible value in the community, and in that she follows closely the long tradition of the radical enlightenment that had animated labor and farm radicals for decades. The second is that the Beaver's subjugation to the Elf was based on trickery and illusions rather than need; once the Beaver realized that the role of his oppressor was superfluous, that he had been bowing his head to a "sham royalty," the Elf realized that the jig was up, and he left the Beaver giant and his kind to their own devices. Embedded in the allegory is an optimistic sensibility about historical change that locates the agency for progress within the mind. Learning to think through the nature of power and wealth was the means by which the new transcendent order would appear.

In that spirit, Baldwin consistently urged her readers to engage in the study of political economy, beginning in September 1906 when she called on women's clubs to do so. The implication was twofold: social improvement required the education of female minds, but so did the condition of individual women who could not afford to be ignorant of the forces of economic life. She pointed out that the working woman who saved mightily "by self-denial and hard work" needed to have confidence that her deposited savings would not be "squandered on some scarlet woman by an irresponsible bank president or cashier"; instead, she urged that women recognize the potential benefits of governmentally run banking institutions. Whether they were concerned about society or about their own prospects, women needed to inquire into the nature of economic life. She urged women to critique assertions about the prosperous economy, questioning how "a nation can be truthfully called prosperous" when part of the nation is "greedy and idle" while the rest "go half starved and do all the work."[67]

A couple of months later, she responded to a correspondent who complained that she lived "in a dull place," and she praised "The Woman's Point of View" for providing a view into a busier world "of which we have small part." Baldwin suggested that the women of this rural area establish a reading circle, and she recommended that that they should start with books that address "the unequal distribution of good things in this world." Perhaps recalling the travails of her own father, whose apples had sometimes spoiled without sale, Baldwin told her readers that during "one phenomenal apple year in New England . . . apples rotted in great heaps on the ground," though "in New York City, not more than four or five hours' ride from those fragrant orchards there were thousands of little children that could have been made healthy and happy on an apple diet." Pointing out that American productivity had been developed to "a marvelous extent," Baldwin asserted that it was time to study how goods could get into the hands of "all who need, especially those who continually adding by their scantily paid labor to this tremendous aggregate of wealth in which they have no share." Rural women should subscribe to magazines that take up these issues, and read and talk about the ideas that they engage. Baldwin promised, "If you ponder long enough and earnestly enough over any knotty problem, sooner or later it will clear up in your mind."[68]

In her own efforts to "clear" things up, Baldwin put forth the long-standing basis for much American radicalism, the labor theory of value, an enlightenment conception that had informed those writers hallowed by bourgeois economists like Adam Smith, but which had been taken by labor radicals in the early nineteenth century as a means of questioning the authority and legitimacy of capitalists.[69] Socialists and followers of Henry George continued to speak in this vernacular, and Baldwin brought it to her female readership, distinguishing between the realities of labor and the imagined reality of capital. In one column, she defined labor as a "true [and] fundamental" thing, while defining capital as something that "exists only in a blurred and delirious mind." Cataloguing for her readers the concrete earth, forces of nature, and human labor, all of which had a clear-cut impact on life, capital alone remained an abstraction and perhaps a fiction, as it had in her story of the Beaver giant and the Elf king. She concluded her catalogue of real things by noting that she could not find capital there, and then suggested that it could only be found "in the palace of privilege."[70] Capital's primacy was a figment of a corrupt imagination.

Georgian or socialist influence appeared in other columns as Baldwin pushed her readers to think through the relations of capital and labor. Henry George had started with the assumption that land, and nature in general, had been a gift from God to all people, and that labor was the source of legitimate property. In a discussion of the Standard Oil Company's monopoly over gasoline supplies, Baldwin echoed those themes, treating the oil and gasoline as if they belonged to all humanity. She asserted, "there isn't anybody who isn't dead or drunk or delirious who doesn't know that God put the sources of gasoline in the ground for the benefit of all people of this county." From that grounding, she portrayed the Rockefeller Company as engaged in the theft of the people's property, and asserted that mere regulation was insufficient: "Having foolishly allowed the sources of gasoline to be monopolized by a trust, we must now resort to such partial remedies as we can devise."[71]

At other times, Baldwin openly challenged private ownership of industries that were based on raw, natural materials. In the aftermath of the Monongah mine disaster of 1907, in which 361 West Virginian coal miners were killed by explosions, Baldwin blamed the "inhuman greed of the mine owners," and argued that the mines should be owned by the government. Denying that the mining companies had a right to own these resources, she denied that a government takeover would amount to confiscation because the mines were "the people's natural wealth." But first and foremost, government ownership would avoid a repeat of "the terrible slaughter in the coal mines of within the last month." Baldwin suggested to her readership that a female-dominated government would tell the directors of mining corporations:

> Gentlemen, you have enormously enriched yourselves at
> the expense of the whole people; you have starved and
> murdered your employes; you have charged the people, who
> have permitted you to work these mines for your own profit,
> extortionate rates; in every way you have proved yourself
> grossly incompetent to administer so great and so vital a
> public trust, and the people now take over these properties
> and give you the privilege, if you desire, of earning for the
> first time in your lives a manly, honest livelihood by working
> in these mines under safe and sanitary conditions as will at
> once be instituted.[72]

Though she never identified herself as a "socialist" in the columns, Baldwin occasionally wrote descriptions of what had transpired at socialist meetings, beginning when she attended one in January 1907 on the East Side of Portland. While she addressed the socialists as a group apart, she accepted the invitation to join their Woman's Economic Study Club. Baldwin explained that the group included non-socialist women whose interest in economics grew out of a growing realization that "economics is something that extends its influence into every home, and that the humble home is even more interested in the character of this influence than the homes of the wealthy."[73]

Contact with the socialist women's group led Baldwin to cover talks provided by Nina Wood, a regional socialist lecturer and writer recently arrived in Portland by way of Seattle. During a streetcar workers strike, Wood addressed a crowd at Alisky Hall, where she told the gathered the problems of a family of several children who were dependent on their mother's weekly wage of less than seven dollars. The eldest daughter had to take charge of the household until she broke down and was taken away to the hospital. Baldwin concluded that this was a form of child labor "that we can't legislate against," one that "no juggling of statutes will remedy." Instead, she told her readers, "we must get down to the root of the trouble at last."[74]

Wood's lectures and writings focused specifically on the impact of capitalism on families, in ways that would have been familiar to the readers of "The Woman's Point of View." While addressing a gathering at the socialist lecture and reading room about the trauma of poverty and child labor, Wood spoke of the overcrowding of families sleeping in cramped quarters in shifts, of the youngest children put to work sewing buttons, and she implored her listeners to find "some connection between your own heart and those other hearts submerged in such misery."[75] In a socialist tract, *Crimes of the Profit Furnace*, Wood developed these themes further, identifying the "outrage, rapine and murder of Capital," and warning that "Capital holds the sinking bow of the ship of state against the fruitful banks of competition and says to Labor, to you who toil: 'Thou shalt beat thy child and use any and all other force which shall seem to thee most meet for her nurture [sic].'" Like Baldwin had, Wood responded to Theodore Roosevelt's calls on Americans to have more children and avoid "race suicide" by focusing on poverty and unemployment, which she argued prevent working-class men and women from starting families. Advocating "provisional" divorce, necessary under the economic conditions created by capitalism, Wood echoed the utopian themes addressed by socialists and free lovers of the nineteenth century, arguing that all problems would be resolved by the rise of a "co-operative system of government and industries." She argued that one needed "no other proof than pure reason based upon the nature-law of home and family-life" to see that family life would be "larger, stronger, sweeter, wiser, more useful, more beautiful, more happy."[76]

Baldwin also applauded the gathering of West Side women on Wednesday evenings in the Multnomah County Library to listen to Dr. C. H. Chapman, a former president of the University of Oregon, on economic subjects. Chapman brought to the gathering a Georgian understanding of land values, arguing that it was the labor of an individual who helped raise the value of land owned by idle neighbors. Chapman pointed out that the idle neighbor paid fewer taxes because the industrious fellow was "punished for building a house and making several parsnips and onions and roses where nothing grew before." But that neighbor, he told his female audience, will pocket the fruit of the industrious farmer's labor when he sells the land.[77]

On the last woman's page that she edited, Baldwin printed a paper that she had earlier delivered to the Oregon Women's Press Club. Here, on her way out, she provided a clear statement of what she had been driving at in the past three years. She provided two models of divinity, the god of "things as they ought to be," and a more devilish one, the god of "things as he wants you to think they are." It is the enthrallment to this god that explains why the masses of humanity struggle needlessly to make a decent living. Key to this god's imprisonment of humanity is "overproduction," a rhetorical and ideological falsehood meant to cloud the reality of underconsumption. Also key was the belief that each carries his own load, whereas Baldwin pointed out that all carried "the same load" that the entire world is "staggering under." Then she explained:

> Your load or mine is heavier because little children are dying
> in factories; it is heavier by the weight of every hungry or
> shivering victim of under-consumption; it is heavier by every
> poor coal miner digging coal for 30 cents a ton for which you,
> if you burn coal, pay $8 or $9. Every man, woman or child
> who is kept away from a chance to live on the land because

somebody has the right to condemn them to landlessness, only serves to make your load and mine heavier. And I am glad that it does, because it teaches us anew that all men are brothers. We cannot rise very high with men and women and children lying and dying in the depths of degradation which this false god of things as he wants us to think they are is so anxious to perpetuate.

Baldwin admonished her readers to recognize that their portion of the overall burden of humanity "demands that you interest yourself in politics, in economics, until you know just what it is that makes this burden and just how you and all us can be rid of it."[78]

And then she signed off: she acknowledged her belief that women hungered for enlightenment, and that her readers "could not be put off with silly chaff, meant to deaden the mind, and not to stimulate it to life," as so many male editors of newspapers had assumed. She urged them to "keep right on thinking, observing, drawing all your own conclusions" as they attend to "these problems of mind and matter and industry and economics that daily grow more pressing."

In "The Woman's Point of View" columns and in her own personal life, Baldwin made female political and economic study a foremost concern. For over ten years, Baldwin participated in the proceedings of various groups, and she was instrumental in forming the Women's Political Study Group, which met in the main library in Portland. It was there that she first articulated the ideas that would get full expression in her monetary tract, *Money Talks*. But her participation was broader than that. In the years following the termination of her relationship with the *Telegram*, Baldwin spoke at the Women's Political Equality League, which held its meetings at an auditorium provided by the Olds, Wortman & King's department store. There she asserted that gaining suffrage was merely the first step that women needed to take. Responding to an antisuffragist speech by Miss I. T. Martin, who asserted that women were unfit for handling affairs of state, Baldwin countered, "When women are enfranchised I hope they will begin to think about these things, about the currency, the railroads and child labor, and see how we can improve some of these questions." The ultimate goal, she asserted, was "a world in which men and women shall work together for human welfare. . . . It is the evolution of things." She continued to speak to these issues, delivering at the Woman's Press Club a review during World War I of the film *The Food Gamblers*, a denunciation of speculators blamed for keeping food prices high. Five years earlier, Baldwin had addressed these themes at a meeting of the Mutualist Society, in which she praised a cooperative in the East Side neighborhood of Albina for both reducing the cost of living and providing citizens with a "common purpose."[79]

Baldwin expressed a broad radicalism that transcended the internecine squabbles of socialists, Georgists, and trade unionists. She was ecumenical in her analyses, willing to praise insights that worked to undermine the legitimacy of capital's authority no matter the source. It was the inequality and the poverty that had resulted from industrialization that received the bulk of her attention, and she asked how long the "civilized world" would "remain disgracefully and stupidly supine" in the thrall of what socialist science fiction writer H. G. Wells termed "an industrial system that builds up large estates for the few at the expense of the earnings of the many." Calling Wells a "writer of daring imagination," she described his work as anticipating "in thought what slow-following humanity will one day realize." Like the Beaver giant, who accepted the Elf king's domination with hardly a thought, Baldwin asserted, "it brands us as economically idiotic." It was in the realm of thought, she believed, that significant and enduring change would emerge. [80]

4

The Certainty of Progress

NEW THOUGHT AND THE NEW AGE

> Sooner or later the mind of the civilized world is
> going to crystallize and concentrate on this thought:
> Poverty must go. Men and women and children shall
> not longer be sacrificed under the crushing wheels
> of the car of mammon. A world purpose like that is
> destiny. Nothing can stand before it—no institution,
> no system, no matter how revered nor how firmly
> entrenched, will be more than a cobweb before the
> might of that purpose, once it is formed.
> —Eleanor Baldwin, "The Woman's Point of View"

That Baldwin urged women to study political economy, that she suggested that thinking mattered, was nothing extraordinary for the era. While industrialization might have been the most apparent transformation that remade the Gilded Age landscape, tremendous changes in the development of the mind were occurring at roughly the same time. Universities and advanced study created specialized fields of knowledge, and the practitioners of these newly created disciplines often understood themselves to possess scientifically grounded knowledge about the social as well as the physical worlds around them. Many reformers, armed with knowledge of the social sciences, tried to articulate principles that would allow for the solution of social problems. Whether in the field of labor economics like John Commons, who would argue for the acceptance of moderate trade unionism and the regularization of collective bargaining; in forestry like Gifford Pinchot, who would strive to organize the nation's forests so that they would be preserved as both a source of wild nature and of sustained productivity; or in bacteriology like Louis Pasteur, whose work promised the eradication of diseases and the possibility of constructing a healthier urban environment, science, study, improvement, and reform seemed to march hand in hand toward a better future. In the early twentieth century, it was reasonable on both sides of the Atlantic to believe that civilization would continue to progress.

But when Baldwin emphasized the role of thought in bringing about a better social world, she meant something more than the accretion of knowledge in the newly established university disciplines and the development of a cadre of experts who would deploy it in an effort to fine-tune society. Instead, Baldwin's emphasis on thought required the participation of the democratic masses. Baldwin meant that thought would have material force in itself, that the collective mind held the power to shape the material world in all its manifestations, and therefore the implementation of the properly disciplined mind was the means by which revolutionary change would occur. In effect, there were resonances of Edward Bellamy's utopian novel *Looking Backward*, which had posited evolutionary forces that somewhat naturally overcame the inequality and injustice of capitalist society, for Baldwin never spoke of revolutionary force as a means of overturning capitalism, or class conflict as a means for progress. Instead of imagining that economic forces—particularly the monopolization of industry that was, unbeknownst to most observers, leading toward complete monopolization and then nationalization and an end to malignant competition as Bellamy had—Baldwin suggested that material change would come from nonmaterial sources. Change would come from thinking, from the alignment of the collective mind away from competition and toward a more cooperative commonwealth that would banish poverty and want. As such, Baldwin's writings, from the columns in the *Telegram* to her currency and banking treatise *Money Talks*, stand as an attempt to play a critical role in the reorientation of mind away from selfishness.

At the same time, Baldwin, like other New Thoughters such as Elizabeth Towne, attempted to orient human behavior away from the kind of Victorian selflessness that was expected of women, and in so doing she rejected the harsh code of Methodist religiosity.[1] Recalling her father's strict moral code, Baldwin told her readers that she had been raised in a religious environment "where the devil and God were feared with surprising impartiality," but that she had come to the conclusion "that our only devil is our ignorance of how to get the most and the best out of life." Failure to do that would result in a "certain disjointed and nerveless will that is content to fall far short of the best we know and might do."[2] Revealing an antipathy to evangelical excess, Baldwin blamed a murder by a female "Holy Roller" on the way that such religious traditions closed down "the natural and proper outlets of expression," and she referred to the internal needs of the individual as a "stream" whose current could be changed but not dissipated.[3] This extreme incident highlighted a more general problem: Baldwin asserted that too much self-denial was the source of great illness among women, leading some to be committed to asylums. "It is a false and vicious idea of her duty that makes a woman wear herself into insanity working for others, even her own husband and children," she charged. She warned that this "parroty gospel of doing for others" required careful scrutiny, for it was responsible for having "mutilated and marred hundreds of generous souls." Instead, she lectured her female readers, "your first duty is to yourself."[4] In the hands of Eleanor Baldwin, New Thought could break down the conventions of Victorian repression of the female self while reinvigorating critiques of economic selfishness. If in the hands of others this eventually became a prosperity gospel, the early movement was something more complex.

Baldwin was not alone in the New Thought community in transforming the assumptions about economics, gender, and selfishness. The minister with whom she was most closely tied, Victor Henry Morgan, was a socialist his entire life—though he, like Baldwin, could celebrate human desire as manifestations of the human soul[5]—and other prominent socialists, like Berkeley Mayor J. Stitt Wilson, were active in New Thought circles. For socialists and other radicals, New Thought could be linked to the produceristic radicalism that motivated followers of Henry George and socialists alike just as much as it could be hitched to the consumer goods therapeutic ethos of capitalism. As Dan McKanan has argued, "New Thought leaders typically espoused an evolutionary worldview that distinguished itself from social Darwinism by suggesting that 'feminine' cooperation rather than 'masculine' competition was the source of human progress."[6] Baldwin and others like her sought to wield the power of mind to heal society just as much as they did the self.

New Thought was the third of the Portland communities to which Baldwin was attached. It was a small but thriving one that had at one time included prominent New Thought writer and publisher Elizabeth Towne, who was born and raised in Portland, where she began to publish the *Nautilus*, only to move to Holyoke, Massachusetts, after getting married. Upon returning to Portland in 1909 to give a talk, Towne addressed the nature of the growing New Thought community there. Before she left at the end of the prior century, Towne claimed that her periodical had fewer than a thousand subscribers, and she estimated that only twenty were Portland residents. On returning to Portland in 1909, Towne wrote of the growing interest that met her return as she spoke to eight hundred men and women who gathered at the Women of the Woodcraft Hall for a meeting arranged by Victor Henry Morgan and Thaddeus Minard, who with his wife, Mina, ran the New Thought center Home of Truth out of their home.[7] Baldwin gave frequent notice to Towne's articles, and during the second decade of the twentieth century she would publish her currency treatise with the Elizabeth Towne Company.

Others devoted to New Thought produced periodical literature in Portland during Baldwin's active period there. Fellow women's rights activist and newspaperwoman Clara Colby, who published the *Woman's Tribune*, was active in the New Thought community. But the most significant of the local female New Thought editors was Lucy Rose Mallory, the daughter of the founder of Roseburg, Oregon, and the wife of a prominent attorney and politician, Rufus Mallory, who soon moved the couple to Portland. From the Mallory Hotel, Mallory published on a mostly monthly basis, beginning in 1887, the *World's Advance-Thought*, a metaphysical journal devoted to spiritualism and New Thought, one that attracted attention as far away as Russia, where it made an impression on Leo Tolstoy. In its earlier years, Mallory included a broad reform agenda, and coverage of populist and labor issues was common, but with time the paper increasingly emphasized metaphysical themes to the exclusion of all others.[8] Of the more exclusively metaphysical version, Baldwin declared it "a magazine so fine and strong and exalted in spirit and intent as to lead that class of publications called 'New Thought.'"[9] Mallory's spiritualist circle included prominent women activists, including Baldwin, Abigail Scott Duniway, and child labor activist Millie Trumbull.[10] This was no mere happenstance meeting of spiritually inclined women; Mallory embraced suffrage and condemned female legal inferiority as reducing marriage to the relationship between

Elizabeth Towne, a Portland native who moved to western Massachusetts, edited and published the *Nautilus*, a New Thought magazine. Towne published Baldwin's *Money Talks* and would be among the New Thought leaders who emphasized the need for women to seek their own ambitions and fulfill their own needs. Courtesy of the *Oregonian*

a "chattel slave" and "man, her keeper."[11] Mallory often published pertinent columns by Baldwin, and Baldwin often ran columns that focused on Mallory's writing. That all the New Thought publications that Baldwin highly regarded did not take on the themes of anticapitalism, and certainly not to the extent that Baldwin's column had, demonstrates that the tradition was broad enough to allow for distinct interpretations and emphases.

New Thought infused most if not all aspects of Baldwin's progressive vision, providing it with its moral edge as well as its ultimate optimism about the inevitability of change. Bringing together reformers like William S. U'Ren, Millie Trumbull, Eleanor Baldwin, Clara Colby, and Abigail Scott Duniway, spiritualism and New Thought provide insight into the nature of progressive reform in Portland and elsewhere.[12] New Thought provided a degree of theological certainty of progress, especially for those adherents who focused more on the social than the self. For them, New Thought informed what Alan Dawley calls the "social conscience" of the progressive left.[13] This chapter examines the basic premises of New Thought as articulated by its Portland cadre, and examines the ways that it informed Baldwin on some key issues. Some of them were spiritual and personal, as was the case with Baldwin's embrace of vegetarianism and her opposition to all forms of cruelty to animals. But most were socially oriented, like her rejection of harsh punishments of criminals; instead, she stressed the social and cultural causes of crime and the potential for rehabilitation. Her approach to crime was not that different than her approach to the unruly male student, discussed in chapter 2. The point was that negative, antisocial behavior never expressed an evil essence of the perpetrator that needed to be quashed, but rather the wrong-headed and unspiritual thinking that was dominant in society. Perhaps most importantly for the development of Baldwin's own thinking, New Thought provided the grounding for her most systematic attempt to grapple with the problem of currency and bankers, the booklet *Money Talks*.

The Power of Thought

Mallory's monthly journal is our best source for the nature and breadth of New Thought in Portland. The second page of each issue provided readers with a timetable showing the precise time in a series of other locations when the hour reached noon in Portland on the twenty-seventh of each month. Mallory provided this to publicize and enable what she termed the "world-soul communion idea," in which "all who love their fellow-men, REGARDLESS OF RACE AND CREED" and who desired the "blessings of universal peace and higher spiritual light" were encouraged to think the same thought at the same time. Grounded in the experience of telepathy and clairvoyance, demonstrations of which had long been a part of the sideshow world of American healing since the early days of mesmerism and magnetism, the "world communion" turned attention to reform, seeking to exorcise "any world-wide error" by virtue of what Baldwin called "thousands of persons uniting at the same hour all over the world to turn the light of the higher intelligence upon it."[14]

The belief that this could have an effect on human affairs was grounded in changes in both faith and science. New Thoughters cast aside the anthropomorphic God for a belief in the divinity of all life. Baldwin told her readers that she had rejected the literal biblical definitions of God with which she had grown up, that conception of the deity as possessing "human characteristics—with enemies and hates and revenges—with even sex, to be spoken of as him," and asserted that a superior concept was that of "Absolute being," which was "manifest to our physical and spiritual sense" and which united all life. Her favorite minister, Henry Victor Morgan, explained to his readers in *The Practical Christian*, "God is forever incarnating in human form and thus giving Himself into the lives of men."[15] With that divine power in each person, the potential for re-creating the world in a more divine light became manifest with changes in thought. In this way, Jesus had been the first to recognize the full extent of this; Jesus, then, was transformed into the first great metaphysical adept.

To explain what it meant to access such spiritual force, Baldwin deployed technological analogies to explain how the all-important ether, that invisible substance that was believed to allow the transmission of matter through space, provided a spiritual conduit for those who sought it and how humanity had slowly come to acknowledge it. She pointed out that early telegraphs were believed to require a second wire to complete the circuit, but then "It was learned that the earth itself competed the circuit and the second wire was discontinued." As a result of Guglielmo Marconi's discoveries of the 1890s, it was revealed that communication could proceed wirelessly; it could move anywhere invisibly. This more recent breakthrough, Baldwin asserted, meant that "Everything is in vibration, everything is plastic, fluid to vibrations at a higher rate than its own." The spiritual implications for humanity were enormous. Baldwin asserted:

> [If the individual] persisted in the practice of clearing his
> mind of its usual rubbish and listening for something better,
> begin first to see his life in its true light, and it would,
> in a way that he could not explain, become, by degrees,
> distasteful to him and he would begin to change it, simply
> because he had been putting himself in contact with and
> making himself receptive to a rate of vibration above his
> own, and he would gradually feel a wish to conform to that
> higher. That is one of the real, the genuine ways to cultivate a
> taste for integrity and righteousness.[16]

Baldwin brought to her readership Mallory's coverage of French physician Hippolyte Baraduc's widely publicized photographic evidence of spirits and what might be termed "thought particles." Baraduc had taken photos of the recently deceased corpses of his son and, later, his wife, which showed abnormalities of light seemingly emanating from the bodies; he believed that he had seen apparitions and had captured them on film. Mallory addressed a different set of photos that seemed to distinguish sources and movement of light associated with "thoughts of healing and prayer" from those that were "violent thoughts." Mallory concluded the photos offered empirical evidence that "thoughts are spiritual entities of the invisible world and are as real on that plane of existence as are physical entities on this plane."[17] In Baraduc's photographic experiments the affinities between spiritualism and other forms of metaphysical religion that had played out in the United States were reproduced in France.[18] For Baldwin, this was evidence of the way that "slow-footed science" lagged behind truth only to later verify "the dreams of the fleeter imagination."[19]

Like so many others in the metaphysical community, Mallory stressed the existence of the ether in which the earth and all planetary bodies were "built up in and sustained."[20] To provide a stronger scientific basis for these assertions, Mallory printed articles written by astronomer and occultist Edgar Lucien Larkin to ground the New Thought embrace of the ether as the conduit by which thoughts could connect through clairvoyance and attraction. Larkin began with recent discoveries in the rapidly developing world of particle physics, and concluded that physicists were in the process of reviving aspects of the older, mechanical corpuscular theory of matter. "Nothing exists but corpuscles. These are made of pure electricity," he began, and then, deploying this set of physical laws, Larkin expanded into the realm of metaphysics and the paranormal: "All discoveries in electrical, chemical and physical laboratories, everywhere, proclaim with loud voices that mind, thought, soul, consciousness, life, all are one continuous motion of corpuscles." Thought, in Larkin's hands, became the "flow of corpuscles into and out of brain-cells." Referring to Baraduc's experiments, Larkin asserted, "The camera cannot make a mistake." These corpuscular thoughts were understood by Larkin to be made of electricity, and electricity, he lectured, was a "fluid" that traveled in a "current of separate corpuscles." The point is that modern science seemed to be providing the framework for a modern metaphysics in which the thoughts of human beings entered a vast ethereal universe, where they sought each other and developed stronger currents.[21]

These were a set of assumptions that Baldwin returned to time and again. In discussing the telling of a story by which a journalist clairvoyantly came to know of her close friend's death, Baldwin quoted Lillian Whiting with regard to her understanding that "the ethereal world" is to be characterized "by a vibration of eight hundred trillions per second," beyond the human ear's ability to hear, and which science was only beginning to understand.[22] Baldwin likened the flow of such vibrations in the ether to a "great ocean of thought" in which "wholesome streams moving their serene way undisturbed by the whirling currents of unrest and folly; and there are countless eddies and whirlpools of broken and aimless thoughts, all the time seeking their own and resisting and being repelled by all that is unlike themselves."[23] Thought was a fluid, and it was bound together in the ether by the so-called laws of attraction; if they could be concentrated, then, the pure and progressive thought would overturn atavistic impulses toward violence and greed.

While praising Mallory's world-soul communion idea, Baldwin explained: "If you think a thought with sufficient intensity it is projected out into the world of forces just as really and just as materially as if you had turned on an electric current; it will seek by the unerring law of attraction like thoughts in the world of forces, and no counter currents of force can keep them apart." And to ensure that her readers did not lose faith from apparent failed applications of the world-soul communion, Baldwin asserted that every time the process is repeated, "they add strength to that force, just on the principle that constant vibrations of a given number to the second tend to pull down a structure like a bridge." Baldwin asked her readers if they were wasting and scattering their thought on "a thousand trifles of daily life," instead of "learning to control, concentrate, and direct it until you sense a power within you." One needed to practice the right thoughts, not just the right behaviors.[24]

Individual and Public Health

While metaphysical writers perceived a blending of faith and science in the world of particle physics, they could be hostile to other forms of science, particularly when articulated by the mainstream medical community. We have already seen that Baldwin, like so many other activist women of her era, took the fashion industry to task for its malignant impact on female health. Rather than medicalize female ailments, as neurologist George Beard and other male physicians had, Baldwin like many other women, including physician and author Alice Stockham, understood female neurasthenia or "hysteria" as having cultural causes, not the least of which were the impositions of fashion. Though the fashion industry was subject to charges that selfishness and the search for profits overrode concerns about health, Baldwin did not consider greed as the sole problem causing illness, though it was not entirely unrelated. Instead, it was how individuals thought that mattered most, and in this Baldwin drew on the mind-cure elements of metaphysical religion. In an era of growing medical authority, a result of distinct improvements in the understanding of communicable diseases, New Thought advocates retained the mid-nineteenth century's emphasis on the balance and linkage between mind and body, which led them to frequently disparage the advances made by the medical establishment.

Baldwin lectured her readers about the relationship between thought and health. For instance, Baldwin argued that the expectation that rheumatism was "inevitable" made a comfortable home for the disease, and she counseled her readers to "refuse to give it any quarter." She called on readers to engage in exercise so not to "let muscular rheumatism make a doormat of you." And she generalized, asserting that many held "a fixed belief in the fatality of certain diseases," but that "there is nothing now standing in the way of the health and happiness of humanity that humanity has not in itself the power to remove."[25] The relationship between mind and body was further explicated through a story of an Englishwoman who had five teeth extracted without suffering any pain, despite the attending dentists learning afterward that the anesthetic had, unbeknownst to them, not been administered. Baldwin concluded that the "idea" that it had "was so strong in her mind that she passed into insensibility entirely by hypnotic suggestion." Extrapolating from such instances, Baldwin told her readers that such thoughts, with similar power, were ever present in their lives, and that with effort "to get the benefit of that power," her readers could study their own minds, casting out negative thinking and seizing control of their lives.[26]

Sin, like disease, was subject to the human will, and she asserted in critical response to a hellfire and damnation sermon that the proper way "to convert a sinner is to get him on the trail of health and happiness secured only by cheerful obedience to the laws written in his own body and soul by the one unerring Law Maker." Death as well was portrayed as something that the human mind accepted and brought on, so Baldwin asserted that it, "like illness and old age, marks just our mastery of that wondrous kingdom of matter and spirit." It was not an "inevitable thing," she told her readers, whom she called on to "shake off your old fears and beliefs" and to "come bravely up on the mount of faith and hope into the sunshine," where they will be rewarded with a vision of the "march of human progress."[27] In so doing they would enter a promised land "in which 'the inhabitants shall never say I am sick.'"[28] She summarized: "All the elements for healing and health that you individually require, are potential in your very own self and no-where else."[29] Elsewhere she asserted that "for every human ill there is a remedy, and . . . only our blindness causes us to suffer."[30]

The spiritually adept individual, then, would suffer less illness, and because so much suffering seemed to be manifestations of the unthinking acceptance of fashion, the mind-cure movement, which stressed the spiritual connections to good health—so much so that itinerant New Thought preachers like Baldwin's favorite, Henry Victor Morgan, made health and spirit the basis of his ministry—provided a path from the feminist rejection of bodily harming fashion to a broader command over one's own body. In a sense, New Thought reflects the democratization of the mesmerist and spiritualist traditions, which required clairvoyant adepts to access spiritual forces and power. New Thought preachers stressed the ability of individuals to take control of the most critical elements of one's physical life.

And that ran counter to aspects of the era's emphasis on disciplinary learning and expertise, though New Thought practitioners believed that their religious practice required careful study. It was from their grounding in what they sometimes called "Divine Science" (to differentiate themselves from Eddy's monopolization of the term "Christian Science") that New Thought writers critiqued the authority of medical professionals. In praising Christian Science, Baldwin contrasted its practitioners' success with a disparaging portrayal of the physicians' "own feeble attempts to assuage human sorrow and cure human ills." Baldwin claimed it was the science of true faith that mattered, and she asserted that Christian Scientists merely applied "what Jesus said so long ago, that the body is the obedient servant of the mind and the spirit; that it obeys them and cannot choose but do so in answer to the living word spoken with conviction." When the New Thought editor of the national reform–minded *Arena* magazine, B. O. Flower, defended Christian Science by citing cases of tuberculosis and cancer healed by its adherents, Baldwin concluded that her readers should "Never be afraid to reach out in it [the pervasive spirit of God] for the health and strength and aid you yourself need at any time in your life, for more likely than not it is right at hand if you but open your eyes to see."[31] Yet her praise for Christian Science was limited to its rejection of the regular medical community; otherwise, she castigated Christian Scientists for their emphasis on their own health and their turn away from the world of matter. She thought the "prevailing note to be one of personal selfishness." She reminded her readers, "Jesus not only raised the dead and healed the sick, but protested against the mammon worship of his day."[32] For Baldwin, New Thought was not only about mind cure; it was also first and foremost a religion of social protest.

Physicians were often condemned for their own selfishness, for trying to develop a monopoly over the care of individuals, and certain medical practices in particular drew the fire of New Thought writers and activists. The use of animals for research purposes violated what Mallory called the "divinity of all things," and it brought forceful responses from New Thought writers. Baldwin interpreted some advances in medicine as moving "in the direction of more obedience to natural law, with less drugging and less surgery." She denied that animal research, which involved "cutting up rats, experimenting with antitoxins, or studying various brands and tribes of bacteria," was an effective means of combatting illness. Baldwin asserted, "A rat will never aid materially in reducing the ills of mankind. There is but one escape from them, and that is obedience to the fundamental laws of health," which can be "attained at any time without blood-letting." In this she quoted Dr. Robert Bell, a cancer specialist at Glasgow Hospital for Women, who labeled cancer as "nature's protest against overindulgence of the appetite and the persistent neglect or disobedience to those hygienic laws."[33]

In making this argument, Baldwin tapped into a long-standing American tradition of alternative medicine that hailed back to Sylvester Graham and the early Industrial Revolution and had turned proper diet and exercise into the only important matters determining human health, minus the emphasis on the destructive physical impact on the rest of the body by an unleashed libido. As she put it in a column criti-cal of playwright Henrik Ibsen, human pain and suffering "is due to no radical defect, to no cruelty inherent in Nature herself," but rather to "ignorance" of the divine "harmony with nature."[34] In the same month, Lucy Mallory declared, "It is unsafe to entrust your body to a doctor who studies disease, instead of health, and who tortures animals to try and find out remedies for human diseases."[35] The critique of animal research reflected both a sense of the divine nature of all life, one that was reaffirmed by both Mallory's and Baldwin's thorough embrace of vegetarianism, and also a rejection of the authority of the medical pro-fession, even in the wake of the recent bacteriological revolution.[36]

Baldwin proposed that New Thought provided an alternative to the killing and torture of animals that would eventually move medi-cal practice further along the lines of natural law. She noted that the development of the x-ray, invented merely a decade before, or the use of a "well-developed clairvoyant" that allowed a better grasp of human anatomy and physiology than could vivisection of an animal, since the x-ray would discover the body's "natural condition." Asserting on the basis of French experimentation that there was "no doubt any longer about the value of clairvoyant sight," Baldwin suggested that medical research move toward "the development of a few clairvoyants for the purpose of investigation along the lines now pursued over a trail of blood and misery by the vivisectionists."[37] It would be the spiritually developed mind that promised the most in the diagnosis of disease and the healing of the body.

Nowhere was the challenge to medical authority more politically significant than in the brewing battle over the requirement imposed by school boards that children enrolling in the public schools be vac-cinated for smallpox. Growing success with epidemics, particularly in the crowded slum districts in New York City, had granted both medical practitioners and public health advocates great prestige, and this was manifest by the implementation of public health measures by public school boards. Massachusetts had been the first state to impose a vac-cination mandate on children entering public school in 1855, and by the turn of the century, several states had made entrance into the pub-lic schools dependent on proof of immunization. Neither Oregon nor Portland had enacted such a legal mandate in the nineteenth century, but by 1914 health officers did have the discretion to require children to be vaccinated before returning to school in September. The protest movement that the decision generated would reach a peak in an initiative campaign to ban compulsory vaccination throughout the state in 1916. Robert Johnston has written about Lora Little's activism in opposing such mandates and has argued that anti-vaccination sentiment flourished in the same social and cultural milieu as other forms of Progressive Era radicalism.[38]

The opposition to vaccination was characteristic of New Thought medical thinking. Robert Johnston notes that B. O. Flower of the *Arena* termed the medical profession "probably the most dangerous-monopoly seeking class in our land to-day," and declared the fight against compulsory vaccination emblematic of the broader Progressive Era "conflict between privilege and the people in the healing art."[39] Portlanders associated with the New Thought tradition in Portland registered discomfort with vaccination. Lucy Mallory happily quoted George Bernard Shaw's claim that "vaccination is really nothing short of attempted murder," and she scoffed at claims by the physicians who gathered at a recent American Medical Association (AMA) meeting that their objective was "to educate the public upon the Science of Health and Right Living." She saw something much less altruistic at work, claiming that their real goal was to establish "a Medical Monopoly that would compel the people to submit to their dictation."[40] Baldwin pointed out that school-mandated vaccination violated the rights of parents who disagreed but nonetheless were "taxed to support" them. She suggested that defenders of compulsory vaccination take into account those who had been "maimed and invalided," manifesting the "bad results of vaccination."[41] Woman's rights advocate Clara Colby suggested a model to her circle of Portland activists for overcoming the imposition of compulsory vaccination laws by relaying how anti-vaccinationists in one English town had deployed methods of civil disobedience to "get a bad law off the books." They flooded the jails to the extent "that the officers of the law complained to the Magistrate that they had no room for any more," forcing an amending of the measure so that "any man could swear before a Magistrate that he had conscientious scruples about vaccination and get absolved."[42]

The adoption of direct democracy offered other tools for the overcoming of what many saw as public health impositions on individual liberty. Robert Johnston has discussed Lora Little's campaign to overturn such local efforts with a statewide initiative in 1916, but Lucy Mallory

had supported Little's efforts against medical authority for years. In one
instance, Little wrote to correct what she perceived to be a misrepresen-
tation of her views by Mallory. She denied that she objected to the idea
that "we all carry micro-organisms," but maintained that "we should
all make it a point to deny that a healthy person can convey disease to
another" and that therefore "the healthy man and woman must be and
remain immune from health-board interference." She warned Mallory
and her readers that the AMA was expanding its control over society,
charging that "the medical politicians" in Maryland sought through
strict medical licensure laws that would give "licensed M.D.'s in that
state absolute control of the lives of all citizens."[43] Countering such aspirations by regular physicians, Little sold a booklet for twenty-five cents
titled *The Wealth That Is Yours*. Mallory praised it as "an enlightened
presentation of the Power of Thought" that would benefit readers who
previously had not "realized the source within themselves of health and
happiness or woe and disease."[44]

Though Little strongly advocated for a renewal of women's commitment to the home—she frequently mocked the rise of women's clubs,
in part because of their cooperation with medical authorities—thereby
deviating from the New Thought community's embrace of women's
rights and certainly from Baldwin's emphasis on female independence,
her critique of AMA-style medicine grabbed their interest because it
emphasized the ability of the individual to choose health over disease
without the intervention of the male physician.[45] In her column in the
Mt. Scott Herald, an east Portland weekly, Little warned her readers
that a system of "State Medicine" was being imposed on citizens. This
collaboration between public health officials and the AMA was dedicated to making "business for health officers whose chief function is
meddling with nature." Mocking the imprecision of developing medical
thought about the means by which "germs" were spread from person
to person, she predicted that the medical establishment would defend
the "germ theory" at all costs, warning that it would be the grounding
for a future that imposed "universal medical inspection."[46] In an idiosyncratic vision, Little brought together a combination of Grahamite
distrust of "manufactured" or adulterated foods, a belief in the virtues
of the female-administered home, and a belief in the self-healing prop-
erties of the divinely created body that was in part congruent with the
beliefs and practices of the New Thought movement.

Though the evidence is ambiguous whether Little held New Thought religious beliefs, New Thought writers, by challenging the altruism and knowledge of regular physicians, clearly helped prepare the ground for Little's ultimately failed attempt to assault the public health dictum that children attending the public schools needed to be vaccinated. If this challenge to authority and expertise was truly what Robert Johnston calls a "populism of the body," the writings of Baldwin and Mallory helped bridge various eccentricities into a larger radical public capable of mounting constant challenges to institutional forms of power.

Crime and Too Much Punishment

The rejection of institutionalized power was not limited to the medical kind. Baldwin routinely turned the most basic forms of authority—that of the parent over the child and the state over the criminal—into matters that violated the individual's free will and inhibited social progress, and she thereby rejected the claims of parents or the state of the right to impose harsh punishment on children or criminals. Believing that circumstances often dictated behavior, Baldwin emphasized the need to change the environment in which the offender engaged in destructive behavior and deemphasized punishment.

As we have seen in chapter 2, Baldwin paid a great deal of attention, in numerous columns, to that mostly female organization devoted to raising the standard of parenting, the Home Training Association. One of the themes that Baldwin emphasized in these discussions was discipline. At one meeting, held in city hall, the HTA held a parents' night to discuss the proposition that "punishment is not necessary in the development of children."[47] A few months later, Baldwin admonished parents for "mindlessly" disciplining their sons, and while she of course meant corporal punishment, she was interested in less harsh forms of child rearing as well. She warned parents, "Don't be a Herod and slaughter the innocents with foolish, unthinking commands and restrictions that will only distort and dwarf and do violence to that wonderful, divine thing—the soul of a child."[48]

It was inevitable that Baldwin would receive critical feedback on this subject from those who believed that parental discipline was a necessity for the development of a civilized child. One respondent, a mother, wrote, "Anyone who has a family knows that it is serious matter to hinder the mental growth of the child through want of proper amusements, but how cruel it is to let a child grow up unpruned like a wild thistle. Why I love my child too much to spare the rod." The mother warned that the "willful" child will "stamp his tiny foot and is naughty generally, and positively rebels against 'persuasion' and 'suggestion'" and she averred, "from birth the child should be under rule and government."[49] The language of the state was deployed to fix the proper relationships within the home.

And that relationship was key to Baldwin, who rather than seek recourse in social science literature referred to nineteenth-century language about citizenship to ground her opposition to parental discipline. Recognizing that parenting could be difficult, and using language like "nervous exasperation," Baldwin suggested that it was good for the "convenience" of parents to "exact implicit obedience from children," but it had other troubling ramifications. Whether it was achieved through harsh words or bodily blows, it was the implicitness of the obedience that was so destructive to both child and society; she called its inculcation "about the worst thing that can befall him." She then explained that it trained the child either to "hunger and thirst to exact obedience from others," or to "look about for some one to whom he can be obedient." Rather than socialize the future citizen for a free society, parental discipline of the child prepared the child to develop into either "the tyrant" or "the slave."[50]

As she opposed coercion of children, she opposed the brutal treatment of adults who broke the law. Baldwin was among those who were horrified when a Portland judge implemented a state law that called for the whipping of men who beat their wives. The law had been passed by the state legislature at the request of Governor George Chamberlain, and that made Oregon the third and the last state in the Union to pass such a law. Baldwin called on the authorities to recognize their duty "to make" the wife beater "a better man than they find him" and "not to stoop to his level in a spirit of revenge." Betterment, not punishment, fit the criminal if not the crime, and Baldwin refused to accept that such corporal discipline could amount to any good. It could only degrade the entire community, while it "befouls the psychological currents in which we all move." Whipping, she asserted, "pollutes the mental atmosphere."[51]

A year later, when Judge Cleland meted out fifteen lashes to a Russian immigrant who beat his wife, Baldwin went with Nina Wood, the socialist writer and lecturer, to examine the man who administered the punishment. Deputy Sheriff Beatty was "an earnest, capable young man," Baldwin reported to her readers, and he was convinced that the Russian, who had tied his wife to a chair before beating her "with the buckle-end of a strap," was a brute who had attacked a frail woman. But Baldwin considered Deputy Beatty to be a man of limited vision, unaware of the causes that had turned "the man from a lover who could woo this woman in his clumsy peasant fashion into the savage who took pleasure in beating her," which Baldwin thought were of "far more importance to society to get at . . . than it was to get 15 lashes on the man's back."[52] As Baldwin continued to mount opposition to the practice, she expanded her analysis to her overall position on any kind of forcible correction: she argued that wife beating itself had once been justified by men who believed that it was necessary to keep their wives in order, and they made the "same arguments for wife-beating that both men and women now use to justify the whipping of children."[53]

Baldwin thought the practice was barbaric, a relic of an earlier and unprogressive age, and many other Oregonians agreed. Historian David Peterson Del Mar has discussed the law as a reflection of the bourgeois male's insecurities in an era when women were demanding the vote and legal equality. Del Mar points out that while organizations devoted to women's rights ignored the law, those opposing suffrage used the law to demonstrate that men were capable of protecting the interests of women.[54] Baldwin had not ignored the law, however, and her rejection of it went against the editorial position of the *Telegram*, which supported it. At times her criticisms were biting, like when she suggested that the punitive fare be varied by some other atavistic punishments, like "slicing off an ear now and then, or cutting out a tongue, or branding him with a red-hot iron."[55] But perhaps her most unkind suggestion was her final remark on the subject, in which she pointedly suggested its cultural value:

> A good thing for the Rose fiesta would be an attractive whipping-post float. This peculiar Rose city institution should be given all possible prominence in any literature scattered through the land to induce self-respecting people to come here and settle, as it would at once impress them with a sense of our high moral tone and our humane sentiments toward the erring and dehumanized.[56]

The whipping-post law was regarded by its opponents in the legislature as a relic of an earlier age, out of step with a progressive civilization, but Baldwin distinguished it from other forms of criminality and punishment only to a limited extent. Rather than a mere barbaric throwback, the whipping-post law was just a more extreme version of everything that was wrong with the criminal justice system. As a rule, Baldwin objected to most forms of punishment, and she rejected any notion that a bad character was stamped on any individual. She rarely perceived a "criminal," or worse, the existence of a criminal class, always emphasizing that the perpetrator of a given crime was a self in the making who had been conditioned by a harsh environment.

Baldwin objected to characterizations of "hardened criminals" by the press. In one instance, she mocked the labeling of a nineteen-year-old "boy" as a "finished and hardened criminal," claiming, "You can't have a hardened anything at 19."[57] When a photo of such an unhappy fellow appeared in the press, Baldwin read the face in ways that countered the narrative: She found in it "a good Roman nose and a good chin," and while the expression of the eyes "is not all that could be wished," she found a "strong, well-proportioned American face." She asked her readers to imagine that in better circumstances it was the face of a "typical, nervy, wideawake [sic] American business man."[58] In another instance, she described a criminal as "swift, alert, and what is sometimes called 'nervy,'" celebrating his effort to resist arrest, which demonstrated that "he loves liberty."[59] Baldwin made similar use of the criminal history of stagecoach robber Bill Miner, as she praised his possession of "qualities essential to plan and execute an escape from jail" as "good stuff."[60] To label the convict as "bad" or as a "hardened criminal" was to see the individual as fixed and hopeless, incapable of being reformed through a reorientation of mind, and it made punishment and incarceration reasonable social choices. Instead, Baldwin rejected any sense that there was a "criminal" personality. She explained, again using the telegraph metaphor, "I believe the wires between God and any human soul are never all down and out of working order," and that the human heart ultimately remained open to good influences.[61] Such persons could be molded, remade. And it made a mockery of punishment and imprisonment.

Her understanding of crime as conditioned by inequality and poverty furthered her objection to the notion of the hardened criminal.

Baldwin pointed out that the use of "bad" and "criminal" were applied "with so much more ease to persons in pitiful and defenseless poverty than we do to those who are higher up financially and socially, and so are able to command both law and court."[62] Baldwin extended the point that Del Mar has made about the whipping-post law, applying it to law and punishment in general. She furthered her charges of systematic class bias, suggesting that the label of "hardened criminal" would not be attributed to one who had "stolen in a way to meet public approval instead of in a way to bring him under public condemnation."[63] Harsh punishment was reserved for those who came from the wrong side of the tracks, and Baldwin reminded her readers, "the poor sinners of the Standard Oil combine have been saved by the kindness of United States Attorney-General [William Henry] Moody from the terrors of imprisonment."[64] In another instance, she said that discussions of crime and punishment rarely take into account "the men who own our railroads, who fix the rate of wages and the price of everything we eat and wear and who have a proprietary interest in our ramshackle Governmental machinery."[65] Crime and punishment were the stuff of class power.

Baldwin's perception of class bias in criminal justice led her to comment on the criminal behavior of contractors who had engaged in a massive grafting scheme to defraud the citizens of Pennsylvania while building the state capitol. Such men, she declared, "were not poor men outlawed, hunted, cold and hungry, they are rich men or well-to-do men," who "took advantage of the confidence the foolish people placed in them, to steal and rob right and left." She compared these men to the "burglar" who lacks the public respect of the better class of criminal, but who "takes the chances of his precarious calling when he robs a house or breaks open a safe"; Baldwin saw the burglar as "a manlier man than these pulpy, cowardly thieves who, without the pressure of want, violated the confidence of all the people of a great state."[66] The criminal justice system was inequitable in ways that reflected the great social divisions that had emerged in the corporate economy.

But it was also perverse in the way that it threatened future progress. Punishment, as much as crime itself, prevented the full elaboration of progress because it unleashed the brutality of the state and repressed the mind and energy of individuals. So long as "punishment and revenge" motivated society's treatment of "the criminal classes," Baldwin warned it would "reap the terrible harvest of its own ignorance in ever increasing crime."[67] Moreover, she suggested that it was impossible to determine what a criminal deserved, for though he "sinned against society," it must be "accurately ascertained what is the extent of society's sin against him."[68] The imposition of punishment and incarceration, brutalizing the body, or stealing the fruits of labor were all wasteful of human potential. Baldwin paraphrased a correspondent's claim in pointing out the thoughtlessness of criminal justice:

> We are just as prodigal in our waste of human life as we are of our forests, those dumb friends of ours which stand between us and extinction by desert; just as wasteful of it as we are of the coal in the ground and of the best there is hope and aspiration in the human heart. By all means save the life of any murderer and put it to good use for himself and others.[69]

The belief that the individual heart was plastic meant that there were alternatives. Addressing the problem of the nineteen-year-old "hardened criminal," Baldwin idealized a more sensitive response. She suggested that the "sympathizing hand on his shoulder" and "sympathizing glance" into "the hard, defiant eyes" would remind him that "he was a desolate boy in terrible trouble." Instead, the boy was undoubtedly bound for a long prison term, which Baldwin asserted placed the responsibility "for the sort of man that comes out of prison at the end of that term of imprisonment" on the state. In prison, the boy would be "known by a number," and he would be put to work but would not enjoy the benefits of that labor, leading Baldwin to call the state "a thief." Over the course of the convict's term, he would experience a "psychological atmosphere that reeks of the worst humanity can conceive." The effect was that the state would reap the results.[70]

Her thinking about those criminals reflected a belief that human beings possessed energy flows that needed to be released, preferably in healthy directions. Just as she had warned against the harmful effects of the repression of desire, she now used the metaphor of the Colorado River's flooding of the Imperial Valley to form the Salton Sea to discuss proper social engineering. By moving the river, human beings had "turned what was a mighty power for good into the wrong place." Human beings, she asserted, possess a "personal force," but it too was often channeled into the wrong place; society is "supremely silly about this misplaced human energy for we can think of nothing better to do with it than to bottle it up tight."[71] A healthier society would recognize that, rather than emphasize the "suppression of vice," which she called a "dangerous business," it should take a lesson from Luther Burbank's work with plant hybridization: "transmute" the negative traits of vice "into helpful, hopeful and beautiful human traits."[72] Baldwin's New Thought–influenced views on desire and human energy structured her thinking about crime, imprisonment, and punishment.

Baldwin expressed a modern liberalism that celebrated individualism while recognizing the environmental determinations of any individual's ability to overcome obstacles. She reflected a confident progressive understanding of the relationship between the state and society. This confidence was strengthened by the optimism generated by her New Thought outlook, which emphasized flows of thought energy and the ability of individuals collectively to transform matter. Her calls for greater sympathy for the convict reflected a belief in the inequity of the criminal justice system while exposing her belief that thoughts mattered and that punitive ones would harm society and prevent it from progressing.

The Real Source of Money

Early in 1914, Baldwin and a small group of like-minded people, most likely female members of the New Thought community, began to meet in a public library in Portland, determined "upon getting at the bottom of the Money Question." Baldwin had long pushed her friends and readers to study political economy, and in this case the focus was on something that was a longtime concern of hers, one that she shared with her brother Henry in Naugatuck, Connecticut; her nephew Joshua T. Small in Provincetown, Massachusetts; and her older sister Celia, who now lived in Denver. Greenback-Labor commitments were a family inheritance. They brought a devotion to inflationary monetary policy as a form of extricating the poor from debt, stimulating employment, and wresting the money supply out of the hands of bankers and putting it into the hands of the federal government. Greenback-Laborites had been concerned about growing inequality in the 1870s; in the wake of the turn-of-the-century corporate merger movement, the tendency toward inequality had intensified. In 1914, Baldwin explained that the small group studying the subject had been motivated by what they "saw all about them":

> people marrying men or women they did not love—for
> money; they saw bright men prostituting their brains writing
> lies to deceive all the rest of us—for money; everywhere,
> all the time, men were dying for lack of—money; were
> committing murder of others or of themselves, for—money.
> Everywhere in all classes they discovered an appeasable
> hunger for—money.[73]

Through this means, Baldwin began to draw together the Green-back-Labor tradition of her family with the New Thought spirituality that she had adopted sometime since and had made such an important part of her public writings in Portland. This revision of radical monetarism emphasized money not as a means of exchange—something that she would lecture trade unionists about in the years that followed—but rather as a "spontaneously created social force or energy," generated by the collective energies of the members of society.[74]

Like many liberal political economists of the time, she scoffed at the notion that "overproduction" could explain economic downturns in a world in which "there is never an instant of time that millions of these human units in the greatest centers of civilization and culture on the globe, are not in dire need of food, clothing and shelter." Instead, she pointed out that the problem was underconsumption by the masses, caused by the unequal power relations that concentrated wealth in the hands of the few "while the vast majority" of people "are either clinging desperately to the border line of decency and respectability, or have made the black plunge into positive squalor and destitution."[75] Her study group reasoned, "since money alone was lacking, it must have some intimate relation to this terrible maladjustment and misery, always increasing in spite of all the wealth produced."[76] It was from these observations about inequality amid plenty, themes that Baldwin had addressed frequently in "The Woman's Point of View," that she identified for the group what needed to be done; they had to figure out how to harmonize "the needs and productivity of society as a whole, to the needs and product of each unit of that society."[77]

New Thought principles provided the solution. Baldwin began with the assertion that the solution would come from the realm of ideas, and that the natural law understanding of money had lain dormant "in the Universal Mind, waiting its chance to germinate in some human segment of that mind, then to materialize in form. Always it is the Idea that moves the world."[78] Soon thereafter, she explained that the "great Universal Mind" is "in all and through all. There is nowhere it is not."[79] Rediscovery of the real source of money, which lay in thought, and the application of natural law principles would inevitably "move the world" toward reform and the abolition of poverty.

The crucial idea was that money was not a medium of exchange, which could take a variety of forms—such manifestations could be gold or silver coin, the promissory notes of a bank, or the notes issued by the federal government—but rather was a force. In this, Baldwin broke little ground. Social theorists had long spoken of social behavior in terms of forces, including the influential American Henry C. Carey, who had argued in the mid-nineteenth century that American abundance would provide for a harmony of interests between capital and labor. Carey, who believed that Greenbackism and a governmentally controlled fiat currency would foster such harmony, had been influenced by Newton's "great law of molecular gravitation" and would argue that individuals were subject to the law of social gravitation, which "as everywhere else in the material world, in the direct ratio of the mass, and in the inverse one of the distance." As Adrian Johns notes, Carey did not speak meta-phorically; such societal force was understood to be real, and power emanated from the "artful guidance of a circulation of force through its various forms." For Carey, electricity proved to be model of the kinds of forces that flowed through the natural and social worlds.[80]

Baldwin defined money as a real and material force. She defined "force" as something that "effects displacement in matter," but she added that it "is acting just as powerfully and just as continuously upon the mind as it is upon what we call matter, for our minds are constantly in action. Thought is the action of the mind and as there is no action where there is no force, we may truthfully define force as that which effects changes in mind or matter."[81] This money force, Baldwin asserted, was specifically generated by the labor of human society, by "all of them together; one just as much as the other," which made it the property of "all of human society; to each individual of that society."[82] In focusing her readers on money as a force generated by human beings through their productive activity, Baldwin wedded nineteenth-century producerist ideology, which had insisted on labor as the basis of all wealth, to New Thought belief in the primacy of mind over matter.

It was Baldwin's constant assertion that the money force needed to be conceptualized apart from the various legal tenders that flowed through the economy. What people mistook for money were mere "transmitters" of the money force. Transmitters of that force were variable and socially determined. At one point, to get this across, she said, "There is no limit to the kinds of transmitters that may be employed for this money force to express itself through."[83] The problem is that these transmitters did not fulfill the dictates of natural law; each was a "most imperfect and defective conductor," and they were in use because "we do not yet know just what the function of this force is."[84] As a result of this ignorance, transmitters of the money force could be "calculated to keep the mass of the people in slavish misery to a single group, as at present." That malignant transmitter, then, was capable of destroying the very society that had created the money force. [85] In declaring that "a supply for every need is the unvarying rule of nature," Baldwin established that ignorance of natural law, which allowed society to accept banker control over money, was the root cause of social inequality and mass misery.[86]

It was here that her investigation allowed her to express the Greenback-Labor convictions that she had brought with her from her youth in ways that would address the problem of poverty in the early twentieth century. She wrote that instead of being controlled by a few financiers, the proper form of money needed to be universal, controlled by all and not a small coterie of bankers, "since the force called money is created by all individuals."[87] A perfect form of money, or what she often termed a "liberator" of money/energy would flow naturally where it was needed, to those who lacked access to money and who were in dire need of the essentials of life. It would "establish and maintain equilibrium between the needs and producing capacity of each individual and the mass of individuals, or society."[88] By transforming "money" into a force that was generated by human labor, Baldwin attempted to revitalize the "labor theory of value," which radicals had long used to critique low wages and the accumulation of great wealth by those who produced nothing.

Fulfillment of the dictates of natural law led Baldwin to anticipate the growth of the kind of state apparatus that would appear under the New Deal, for she had to clarify how these "transmitters" of the money force would find their way into the hands of all members of society. In exchange for "money," she explained, the unemployed would have to render service to society, and it was that which called forth the vision of a great state. Baldwin imagined enormous public works projects as the means of facilitating the flow of money where it was needed. Referring to public works measures that would control rivers throughout the drier regions of the country through the newly created Reclamation Service, Baldwin foresaw the kinds of federal action that would finally be put into place during the Great Depression some twenty years later. She argued that society had "a sacred obligation" to do this.[89]

Instead, she charged that society was saddled with a form of money that bankers had imposed as a means of extorting interest payments through the mechanism of debt. Operating under an artificial scarcity of money, which naturally should be set at the same level as the produce of the society, bankers were able to impose debt on members of society, who labored and surrendered the fruit of their labor to meet their interest payments.[90] Under this system, Baldwin pointed out that "those who cannot afford to pay the bankers' price for money" must go without, and she explained, "for a man to have no money is" to "be put in the criminal class."[91] Bankers provided no service to society, impeding the movement of money rather than facilitating it, and they used their great wealth and power to ridicule and silence those "who wanted to help improve the situation." In their pursuit of intellectual hegemony, bankers and financiers hired "prostitute writers" to "falsify, vilify, ridicule, deride" those who sought to reform the financial system of the country.[92]

The artificial shortage of money would be relieved by a replacement of the current monetary system with something that Baldwin and others like John Raymond Cummings, from whom Baldwin borrowed, called "natural money," where productivity determined the amount of currency, and where that currency flowed to where it was needed most. The first task of a government, once it had adopted what she termed the "true transmitter" of the money force, would be to "provide work for all unemployed, moneyless men." The adoption of a true form of money "would be to cure once for all, the evil of unemployment or enforced idleness, because it can reach society only through service performed by individuals for the whole of society, through its organized activities, the government." With the proper understanding of money guiding policy, Baldwin perceived a blissfully productive future where debt was abolished, bringing "prosperity for all, beyond anything the world has seen."[93]

Though Baldwin was out of step with developing liberal economics, she was not entirely ignored. Within a year of Elizabeth Towne's publication of *Money Talks*, a variety of periodicals gave it positive review. The *Journal of Education* warned readers, "If you want a conventional discussion of money, you do not want to read Eleanor Baldwin's book." Instead, the reviewer declared, it provided a "New Thought view of money," and readers would find it to be "a thriller" and a "real tonic."[94] The work was reviewed in *American Education*, which welcomed the "New Thought on money," and commended Baldwin for her "original and startling and most practical conclusions in regard to the nature and use of money."[95] The *American Poultry Advocate* highly recommended it as "the New Thought on money," one that readers would find "will repay careful study," and it averred, "it should be in the daily study of every man and woman, that they may know how to vote."[96] The Georgia populist Tom Watson called *Money Talks* a "splendid and illuminating monograph," one that overcame the materialist explanations of money in which Adam Smith and socialists alike had engaged. Baldwin, Watson pointed out, teaches that money is "an abstraction, an invisible influence, working by imperceptible methods, but producing, marvelous results, some of them psychic and undefinable."[97] In the *Efficiency Magazine and Sales Manager*, reviewer John Wenzel thought it "interesting" that it offered "a remarkable and concise exposition of what money is, and what is its function."[98]

Baldwin hit a chord with reviewers from magazines intended for lower-middle-class readers, whether they were petty producers or white-collar workers. But she continued to work with the local labor movement, to press her ideas upon the readers of the *Oregon Labor Press*, where her language became more strident. In 1917, she accused columnist Herbert Kaufman, whose writing appeared in the *Oregonian*, of being a shill for the financial industry. "They use such to coax sheep into the slaughter house," she said of the effect of his writing, "so that an unsuspecting reading public, will inadvertently swallow his capitalist rot." Kaufman had claimed that the United States was entering a period of high wages and prices "due to the shrinking dollar." Baldwin pointed out to her trade-unionist readership, "It is easy to see that the 'shrinking dollar' is planned in the interest of the money-holding class—the creditor class and against the interest of the producing class, who under it, must consume less and less of what they produce." Baldwin took the opportunity to focus attention on her idealist conception of money, arguing:

> under a scientific financial system designed to benefit ALL
> equally, the increase in the purchasing power of money,
> keeping pace with the increased product of the workers,
> would automatically return to them that increase, and the
> only ones to lose out would be the parasite class who now
> live in luxury and power because of the actual reversal of the
> scientific money operation.[99]

Three years later, she wrote an open letter to Samuel Gompers, who in a call for public control of the extension of credit had asserted, "credit capital is not money." Baldwin took this as an opportunity to put her ideas before the readers of the *Oregon Labor Press*, pointing out that the long-term president of the American Federation of Labor had made "the fatal error [of assuming] that everybody knows what money is." But the response revealed that she, like many others who had strongly opposed the war prior to US entry, had seen in the wartime experience aspects of a better and more egalitarian society. The war provided an instance of the federal government helping to organize the productive apparatus, as a public good, and unemployment virtually disappeared. For many, the war made possible what was known as "industrial democracy."[100] Baldwin wrote of the experience as the moment when "we, the people, rendered a tremendous amount of service to ourselves through the agency of our government or business agency." Moreover, Baldwin asserted that the effort had been self-sustaining, not requiring indebtedness. Nonetheless, debt did ensue, which Baldwin declared was a result "purely [of] fiat, created for the benefit of the parasite, the profiteer, the usurer." She argued that this potentially more democratic postwar environment offered the possibility of a world without bankers. Baldwin asked her readers to "take inventory," and to imagine what kind of economy could be constructed:

> We have first the earth with its incalculable wealth in the
> raw; we have humanity; we have the product of its hands and
> brains worked up from the earth's illimitable storehouse and

we have the omnipotent social energy—money—generated
by and within the social organism. You see in this wonderful
economy there are no "stocks and bonds."

In such a world, capital is "nothing more, nor less than the special
privilege granted to a few to run the world in debt through the medium
of the interest-bearing security in the shape of stocks and bonds. There
is no place for debt, hence no place for capital or capitalists in a sensible, scientifically managed world."[101] Ironically, the war had presented
the possibility of a thought-induced transformation of society. Like so
many others interested in postwar "Reconstruction," Baldwin perceived
an opportunity to change the world.

Yet the world was moving in a different direction, and as much
as Baldwin had innovated in applying New Thought solutions to older
Greenback-Labor problems, she remained immersed in the older political discourse of nineteenth-century radicalism. Through her brother
Henry, who had helped her form her early ideas about currency and the
stifling effect that bankers could have on economic life and working-
class standards of living, she had developed a lifelong interest in the
problems of social class and economic power. Now, nearly thirty years
after Henry's death, Baldwin had produced an analysis that remained
grounded in the "labor theory of value." A long-standing source of
radicalism in Great Britain and the United States, the labor theory of
value grew out of the thinking of political economists like John Locke
and Adam Smith, who had framed labor as the source of all property
and value. There was something legitimizing about capitalist relations
in these analyses, as they grounded wealth in labor and not privilege,
and they persisted in the world of political economy into the nineteenth
century. But they also inspired radicals since the days of Thomas Paine
and throughout the nineteenth century, leading workingmen to demand
that the "laborer" receive the value of his or her labor. Baldwin's conception of money was rooted in the labor theory of value, identifying
it as the product of the collective labor of society, and only such a form
of money that would reward those who engaged in that labor would be
legitimate. There was much in Baldwin's contribution that reflected the
era of her childhood.

But the developing discipline of economics was moving away from
the labor theory of value and instead focused increasingly on marginal

utility as the basis for understanding the value of a given commodity. It was not the labor embedded within the goods that determined their value, but rather the added benefit that goods gave to consumers. The idea was that consumers allocate their resources to satisfy their desires and make choices in doing so, and it was at the point at which a given good satisfied a desire, and money was therefore allocated to the satisfaction of other desires, that value was established. By focusing attention away from labor and production and toward the fulfillment of desire, economists moved their discipline to be able to address the questions of a mass consumer society. More progressive economists, like Simon Patten of the University of Pennsylvania, used this shift in disciplinary attention to address the questions of poverty, arguing for a political economy of abundance. These new liberals (as opposed to the older "classical" laissez-faire liberals of the eighteenth and nineteenth centuries) offered the intellectual basis for the kind of modern liberalism that took shape in the New Deal coalition and that more fully developed in the aftermath of World War II. This was a world that Eleanor Baldwin never entered.[102]

Nonetheless, the world was shifting in ways that could not be ignored. Much of Western optimism, of which American progressivism was a variant, was wiped away by the carnage of the First World War. The massive deployment of force and engagement in killing by the most "civilized" nations of the world destroyed any sense that progress was inevitable. At the same time, it opened up new possibilities. The October Revolution in Russia brought the Bolsheviks to power, an event that demanded interpretation and response in cities across the globe. At the same time, a revitalized Ku Klux Klan appeared on the scene in the United States, and some older populists like Tom Watson would play important roles in exacerbating racial and religious tensions that were both central to the Klan's growing influence in Oregon and elsewhere. Though Baldwin would never embrace the economists' world of marginal utility, she would inevitably respond to the challenges of the postwar environment. Her open letter to Samuel Gompers in 1920 provides one response to the new era. There were others.

5

The World of War, Bolsheviks, and the Klan

> What about the American murders, robberies,
> lynchings, burnings at the stake in this country? . . .
> How about the corrupt bosses of our big cities, and
> the no less corrupt little voters who keep them in
> power? How about the big steals and the little steals
> on every hand? How about the ridiculous fashions and
> the cinched waists of the women in high places, and
> the squalor and filth and hopelessness of the people
> in darkest New York and London? How about the
> Mormonism? How about the trusts? How about the
> slaughter house? How about tainted beef and tainted
> money? How about the filth behind our typhoid and
> yellow fever epidemics? How about the corruption and
> eruption in our city of Brotherly Love? How about the
> rest of the evils that cry to heaven from every corner of
> our country?
>
> Are bound feet more heathenish than bound livers
> and lungs? Is American corruption less corrupt than
> East Indian? Our evils are different, that's all.
> —Elizabeth Towne, "The Point of View"

In "The Woman's Point of View," Eleanor Baldwin had articulated a progressive vision of the future predicated on the prior experience of abolition of slavery as an indicator of the potential of social improvement.
The revolution of Southern social relations became a source of optimism
about a future eradication of capitalist exploitation that she believed
was equally bound for extinction. Her departure from the harsh moralism of her father's Methodism for the optimistic New Thought world
of spirituality provided a sense of confidence that human will, exerted

through the activity of the mind, would lead to a better future. In this, Baldwin was not out of step with her times; many Europeans and Americans believed that society was inevitably progressing toward a more brilliant future; they just disagreed about what that future entailed. But the devastating impact of World War I suggested to many that the Western world was not as civilized as progressives had thought, and for some it elicited what one historian has called "the end of American innocence."[1] The October 1917 revolution in Russia brought to power the Bolsheviks, who quickly accepted the harsh terms of the Brest-Litovsk treaty imposed on them by the Germans, events that suggested the war would bear ill fruit for the future. But not to all, as many workers responded to the call by socialist leaders to form the Council of Workers, Soldiers and Sailors of Portland and vicinity, inspired by the example set by workers in Russia. Baldwin, like many within the Portland union movement, particularly those in the metal trades, perceived in the Bolshevik Revolution a source of optimism and progress amid the tragedy and destruction of the war; it did not signify the end of progress but rather one means toward its fulfillment.[2]

This was demonstrated in correspondence with the *Oregon Labor Press* that Baldwin wrote a few years after the war. In a letter to the editor, she compared "Bolshevists" to early Christians, and lectured her readers that attention to the Bible "may give some timid souls courage" to think about the meaning of the former term "instead of having fits whenever it is mentioned." She reminded them that in Acts 24:5, St. Paul was denounced by Tertullus as a "mover of sedition among the Jews throughout the world, and a ringleader of the sect of the Nazarenes," and she then suggested that similar things might be said today about "some 'red' leader, or perhaps nothing more criminal than a union workman slandered by an employers [sic] association." She extended the analogy between the early Christian experience and the present by quoting Acts 19:24, which referred to the resistance to Paul's teaching in Ephesus that was mounted by Demetrius, a "silversmith, which made silver shrines for [the goddess] Diana." Baldwin asked her readers to ponder the possibility that "the faith of the Nazarene was hated very largely, if not wholly, for business reasons," and she suggested that the vitriolic use of the word "Bolshevik" was rooted in the fear of "bankers and usurers and stock and bond juggler of the present day" because it threatened their profits. The point was that "in those stirring times, to be recognized as a 'Nazarene,' was every bit as scandalous as to be called a 'Bolshevist' today." Finally, the letter brought forth the more recent historical experience of abolitionism. Baldwin posed that "not so long ago" the word "'abolitionist' was a term of obloquy and reproach" attached to "anybody who wouldn't understand how perfectly right it was for men with white skins to own and buy and sell men with black, or near-black, skins." History was filled, Baldwin asserted, with instances in which those with vested interests reviled ideas based on natural law that promised human dignity and liberation. In this, an older family narrative about slavery and industrial capitalism, one that Baldwin had frequently articulated, was extended to include the Russian Revolution of October 1917 in the history of human liberation.[3]

In another instance, Baldwin commended the editor of the *Oregon Labor Press* for printing Lincoln Steffens's defense of the Bolsheviks, calling it "a valuable public service," while denouncing the support that Portland Mayor George Baker, whom she derided as "our masterful mayor," gave for police and FBI harassment of local reds. When the *Evening Tribune* criticized the *Labor Press* for publishing the piece, calling Steffens's lecture an attack on religion, Baldwin was moved to clarify her understanding of the cultural world that was swirling around her. In this, she entered waters that were troubled and that would threaten the unity of the labor movement. She urged the editor (and the readers) of the *Labor Press* to "wake up to the difference between prelatism, priestism, clericism—in short—ecclesiasticism and religion." In Baldwin's hands, the Marxist slogan, "Religion is the Opium of the People," became a mere careless choice of words that obscured its true intention. Baldwin could not imagine the Bolsheviks, whom she perceived as promoters of progress and liberation, as hostile to religion, which she asserted was "a divine thing as native to the soul as love, truth, aspiration." She clarified for the readers of the *Labor Press* what the Bolsheviks must have meant: "For any set of men to be authorized and paid by the state to decide what 'religion' is and then be empowered to exact material pay for their alleged spiritual product from all the rest of the world, is the opium of the people as in very truth it is."[4] To Baldwin, the Bolsheviks approached religion in the same way that James Madison and Thomas Jefferson had: theirs was a declaration of the separation of church and state.

The letter finished with a condemnation of ecclesiasticism, which clarified precisely what position Baldwin would take in the religious and cultural conflict that was breaking out in Portland in the early 1920s. Her defense concluded with a barely veiled condemnation of the Catholic Church, as she contrasted the "divine" impulse of religion with "ecclesiasticism," which she explained was "a corrupt, man-made institution commercializing the sacredest impulses of the soul." Alluding to the Catholic clergy and other church officials, she denounced "dangerous parasites whose sworn mission in life is to increase the power of their organization through the enginery they have perfected for the exploitation of the doped millions." Any effort for "real progress" or "industrial peace" required that the "tremendous mechanism of ecclesiasticism is forced out into the open to stand or fall on its own merits, stripped of its benevolent disguise, protected by which it degrades, despoils, disrupts the world."[5] In Baldwin's mind, the Bolsheviks had become a source of human liberation, while the Catholic Church remained the great source of reaction and bondage.

The association of the Catholic Church with aristocracy and reaction was hardly an invention of Baldwin's. The history of Anglo-American Protestantism has been periodically marked by waves of anti-Catholicism. Rooted in the events of the English Reformation of the sixteenth century, this tradition posits a conspiracy of the Vatican to turn back the tide of history and freedom to reimpose the constraints of a hierarchical society. In the hands of some American Protestants in the antebellum era, like Samuel Morse, the Irish were considered means by which the Catholic hierarchy sought to overturn the democratic and free social arrangements of nineteenth-century America. The Know-Nothing movement associated with the American Party of the 1850s was an anxious reaction to the millions of immigrants, mostly Irish and German Catholics, who were coming to American shores after the potato blight of the 1840s. In the 1890s, as new waves of immigration from southern and eastern Europe seemed to challenge the cultural hegemony of Protestant America, a new wave of anti-Catholic anxiety emerged, most notably in the form of the American Protestant Association. In the wake of the First World War, the Ku Klux Klan, which was particularly strong in Oregon, took up the mantle of Protestant guardianship of the American way. An instrument of white supremacy—historians like Eckard Toy among others have demonstrated that the Klan in Oregon could terrorize nonwhite communities—the Oregon KKK made its mark mostly in the fight against Catholic influence, which was manifest in the support that the organization gave to electoral efforts to close down private, mostly Catholic, schools in Oregon.[6]

That Baldwin rejected the Red Scare while joining the social and cultural forces that brought the Klan to brief prominence makes her unusual, an apparent contradiction, but it does not make her unique. Historians have recognized that local socialist "gadfly" Tom Burns also expressed support for the KKK in the 1920s, and there is evidence that he had earlier associated Catholicism with the acquiescence of working people. During the Portland cannery workers' strike of 1913, Burns had been a member of the "press committee," which had spoken disparagingly of progressive Catholic priest Edwin O'Hara, terming him "His Oilyness" for allegedly advising "his parishoners to quit picketing and go back to work," and warning them that failure to return to work would land them in hell." The report went on to describe these striking women as formerly "staunch Catholics" who now dragged "their rosary beads in the mud."[7] This statement suggests how a commitment to worker freedom could lead to an assault on the Catholic hierarchy. Baldwin's commitment to New Thought did not lead her to anti-Catholicism and the Klan, but the way that she blended its anti-institutionalism with a commitment to worker rights suggests that she and Burns understood the structure of the Catholic Church similarly. In other words, it may have been an outgrowth of their progressivism, which was inclined to oppose those forces that seemed to impede the blossoming of human freedom and progress. Burns, however, was an independent storekeeper who spoke his mind, a rabble-rouser without deep ties to the institutional radicalism expressed by the Progressive Era's trade-union movement. Baldwin, on the other hand, a longtime contributor to the *Oregon Labor Press*, provides some insight into how the Klan disrupted any kind of broad, interreligious solidarity within the labor movement.

Baldwin provides none of the expected clues to explain her embrace of the Klan and anti-Catholicism. For many progressives, racial equality was not a pressing issue; in fact, the Progressive Era was marked by the expansion of Jim Crow laws in the South and West and acquiescence in the North. For some, the Klan represented a change in emphasis, but not necessarily a new outlook. But an examination of the way that Baldwin

Tom Burns was active in socialist politics during Baldwin's time in Portland and like Baldwin would at least briefly support the Ku Klux Klan. Courtesy of the Oregon Historical Society, ORHI77727

discussed race and immigration suggests anything but a tendency toward bigotry; her writing exhibits a tolerance that was hardly universal among West Coast progressives and socialists. She frequently urged her readers to be sympathetic to immigrants domestically and to colonized people abroad. Before and during the war she espoused pacifist views, as many others within the socialist circle had. "The Woman's Point of View" provides an opportunity to inquire into the kind of questions that would later roil Portland and the labor movement in the postwar era. Simply put, Baldwin's columns portray a racially and culturally tolerant writer.

Defense of the Immigrant

During the "new" immigration that reached its peak in the years prior to World War I, immigrants came increasingly from non-Protestant lands in eastern and southern Europe that were experiencing state building and the spread of capitalist markets, as well as from the modernizing Asian nation of Japan. In most large industrial cities in the eastern and midwestern United States, most inhabitants were either immigrants or the children of immigrants, and although that was not true of Portland, concerns about immigration proliferated there as well as nationally. While nativist expressions could be made by those who feared competition in labor markets with immigrants, they also came from those who thought that the United States was to be overwhelmed, both culturally and genetically, by inferior races. That line of thinking may have reached its apex in Madison Grant's widely read *The Passing of the Great Race*, published for the first time in 1916, which borrowed from Mendelian genetics and applied it to human racial types. An officer of the New York Zoological Association, of the Immigration Restriction League, and of the American Eugenics Society, Grant constructed a highly developed, yet unstable Nordic race that was in danger of genetically reverting to "original" or more "primitive" types through intermarriage with these new immigrants, which he described as representatives of more stable and primitive peoples. Grant summed up the danger: "the children of mixed marriages between contrasted races belong to the lower type, the importance of transmitting in unimpaired purity the blood inheritance of ages will be appreciated at its full value." Between 1916 and when immigration was nearly completely cut off by Congress in 1924 on a mostly racial or ethnic basis, the book went through six editions. The early twentieth century witnessed the largest burst of immigration to the United States, and at the same time a highly anxiety-ridden response from many native-born Protestants.[8]

Yet not from Baldwin, though she had hardly been insulated from the fact of mass immigration. She had witnessed a demographic transformation of her native Naugatuck, which had been mostly native born and Protestant in her youth, only to become largely immigrant and Roman Catholic by the end of the century, but she and her brother Henry had dwelled less on cultural and religious change than they did industrial transformation. Baldwin did come into contact with readers of her column who opposed immigration, but she argued against intolerance. Viola Burr, a frequent correspondent to the *Oregon City Courier,* asked "why every foreigner who comes to this country wants to run our Government? If things are so much better in the old countries, why do they come and crowd us out of our wealth and our homes?" A few weeks later, Burr pressed Baldwin further, arguing that immigrants divide the available wealth, depriving locals from the bounty of their labor. They come to America, she claimed, "with absolutely nothing,"

and they bring nothing with them "to add to our wealth." She complained that immigrants impoverished native-born workers, imagining
that the economy was a zero-sum game, in which gains to some had to
be balanced by losses by others. She asserted that the original residents
of a town that had doubled in size because of immigration "would only
have one-half dollar each to do business with" for every dollar that they
previously had.[9] Burr asked questions that northwesterners, especially
those who had organized—sometimes violently—in response to Chinese and Japanese immigration, had been asking for years.

Baldwin responded with a defense of immigrants, beginning with
their motives for leaving for the United States. Russian Jews, she argued,
came "to get a chance to exist," while "Armenians came here in droves
a few years ago, when the unspeakable Turk was on the rampage." She
noted, "a good many German and Italian men (and so, of course, their
families or sweethearts) come to escape compulsory military service,"
while others immigrated to "escape punishment for being 'political
criminals.'" Consistent with her approach to discipline and punishment,
she made clear to her readers that she did not take the last category
literally, arguing that the "political criminal" was "very likely to be an
honest man that a corrupt government finds it necessary to shut up or
kill." She likewise challenged Burr's assertions regarding the economic
effect of immigration, asserting that her "political economy is almost as
funny as [that of] Malthus.'" She contradicted Burr's assessment that
the immigrant brings nothing but poverty, asserting, "the immigrant
himself is a commercial asset—so much added to the wealth of the Nation. Many of these immigrants have been the means of developing and
distributing vastly more wealth than they have ever consumed from the
common stock. Never forget," she told her readers, "the human being
himself, possessed of normal health and faculties, is himself wealth in
potency."

Yet she revealed some agreement with people like Burr when
she implicitly agreed that immigrants posed a threat to a high-wage
economy by blaming the steamship companies for the massive wave
of immigration. The owners of these companies registered what she
called the "Yankee love of money, the Yankee hustle, the Yankee habit of
referring to just plain malicious, wicked lies as 'business,'" and many
immigrants came under mistaken notions of life in America. At the same
time, Baldwin blamed the poverty of immigrant workers on industrial

"corporations who employ vast numbers of men at unskilled labor and who buy labor as they do their coal or iron, where it is the cheapest." To further put the onus on corporations, she extensively quoted from an article that described industrial employers as "veritable lords, whose employes are regarded and treated as mere slaves. The National glorification of the wonderful American industries is an empty patriotic boast; the real producers are to a very large extent immigrant proletarians." She explained that the capitalist welcomes immigrants because of their wealth-generating potential, and pays them such that the capitalist "retains his profit, which is what the laborer has produced over and above his wage." In this Baldwin expressed sympathy for the immigrant while reiterating aspects of her critique of capitalism.[10]

Her sympathies extended to immigrant communities in Portland, including those against which the Klan would organize in later years. In a column on the Council of Jewish Women and the Neighborhood House, Baldwin gave readers insight into the workings of the Jewish immigrant community. Founded in 1899 by prosperous German Jewish immigrants concerned about the poverty and customs of more recent Jewish immigrants from Russia who were settling on the South Side of Portland, the Neighborhood House started by offering sewing classes to the girls of south Portland, open to Jews and non-Jews alike, and within a few years had constructed a new building and opened a kindergarten. Baldwin noted that the institution provided a broad set of services, which included a gymnasium, classes in English, the "Hebrew Bible," Jewish history, and cooking. Baldwin assessed the value of the institution with demonstrated sympathy for the disorientation felt by immigrants:

> It is not only a place where the children are taught and
> trained and entertained, but one where the mothers and
> fathers are beginning to go for help, in this alien land where
> the language is unknown to them and everything is new and
> strange. . . . In innumerable ways the immigrant finds just
> what he needs. Just the heartening and help required to dull
> the pain of homesickness or else make him forget the horrors
> from which perhaps he felt.

Baldwin pointed out that the Neighborhood House and the Council had received honors in Paris and at the Jamestown Exposition of 1907 for their work in the immigrant community, which Baldwin said was "of interest to the whole city because the whole city shares in the honor."[11]

A visit to the kindergarten at Neighborhood House, attended by sixty-nine children, mostly Russian Jews and a few Italians, elicited from Baldwin some comments that went against the grain of nativist eugenics. Instead of registering concern about the impact of foreign gene pools as Madison Grant would, Baldwin did the opposite. For instance, she told her readers, "There is no use denying that the pure-blooded American is developing a facial sameness that but for the infusion of foreign blood would become wearisome, and so, fatal to beauty." To this more homogeneous native phenotype, Baldwin portrayed "these blessed little foreigners" as bringing a potential broadening of the American type with their "large, liquid, long-lashed eyes, mobile features and rich coloring." Similarly, she found their home environments to be, despite their poverty, culturally rich. On visiting the home of some ill children, Baldwin described the mother as "a true-hearted, warm-hearted woman."[12]

In her discussions of the Jewish immigrant community, Baldwin showed no signs of hostility, no sign that she would eventually make her way to the cultural orbit of the KKK. In an extended review of Madison C. Peters's *Justice to the Jew*, Baldwin suggested that the book would better inform "those who still retain a silly prejudice against the Jews."[13] When fellow New Thought writer Elizabeth Towne questioned the severity of Russian persecutions of Jews, Baldwin expressed disappointment that "so bright a woman as Mrs. Towne . . . may fail utterly to grasp a situation when she must evolve her knowledge of it from her inner consciousness, instead of having it burned into her soul by sight and sound and the actual dread experience." She went on to list some of the discriminating practices that put severe limitations on Jewish liberty in Russia, noting, "They are not allowed to live out in the open country, to own land and be farmers. They are tolerated only in the cities, and naturally they live in communities for self-preservation and society—and that explains their 'clannishness.'" Addressing the travails of a Jewish woman whom she visited in Portland, Baldwin related that her village had been attacked "by the Cossacks," who "invaded" her home and "dashed out her baby's brains," and while they did not "murder the mother—they did worse."[14]

Yet it was Asian immigrants who tended to bring forth the greatest amount of invective and anxiety from white people in Portland and elsewhere on the Pacific Coast. In the winter of 1886, the local Knights of Labor had attempted to forcibly remove all Chinese from the Portland area, a scenario that would be replayed nearly forty years later when union men forced out Japanese employees of a mill in the coastal town of Toledo. In a measure supported by the Ku Klux Klan, Oregonians in the 1920s voted to deprive Japanese and other Asian immigrants of the right to own land in the state, adopting a legal formula that California had pioneered in 1913. This so-called Alien Land Act prevented those foreign nationals who were "ineligible for citizenship" under the terms of the Naturalization Act of 1790, which had limited naturalization to "white persons," from owning land in the state.[15] Anti-Asian sentiment had been a mainstay of Oregon and Pacific Coast working-class politics since the late nineteenth century, long preceding the arrival of the Klan.

Among those who indulged in anti-Asian politics were Portland women associated with the political left, women a lot like Baldwin but who had embraced the racist movement to exclude first Chinese and then Japanese immigrants. Sue Ross Keenan, for instance, who had been active in the effort to force the Chinese out of Portland in 1886, ran as a Populist Party candidate for school superintendent in 1892. In the twentieth century, socialist orator and writer Nina Wood, whom Baldwin praised on numerous occasions, borrowed from this racist tradition. In her book *Crimes of the Profit Furnace*, Wood engaged the tropes of anti-Asian politics, condemning the enslavement of "white women" in "Chinese dens" where they "are required to adopt the dress, ornaments, oils and perfumes peculiar to Chinese women." She warned that procurers of young white women traveled through the small towns seeking recruits, "willing or unwilling, bond or free" to work in the "unspeakable madness of these unspeakable hells."[16]

Though she found much to admire in Wood's analysis of capitalism, Baldwin avoided anti-Asian rhetoric. Instead, she found much to praise among both the Chinese and the Japanese. In a column that publicized a contest for the best work produced by boys enrolled in the manual training schools, Baldwin used Chinese artistry to set the bar high for American craft workers, suggesting that it would be fabulous if "an American could even imitate with any degree of accuracy the delicate wood carving of the Chinese."[17] When writing of Chinese funerary rites, Baldwin suggested that readers who might disregard them as "heathenish" consider that "Our rites are just as heathenish to them as theirs are to you," adding that the Chinese "regard us as 'heathen devils,' too, and that 'by the same token,' we have now and then lived up to the reputation they give us."[18] The Japanese were similarly discussed as a civilized people who were not only unfairly dismissed as backward by many Americans, but who, like the Chinese wood carvers, were set up as paragons of high-minded living. In a discussion of poor deportment among some at the Rose Festival, Baldwin suggested that it would be better if American crowds "were as cultivated as the Japanese," for then they would take in parades quietly and respectfully.[19] She also noted that the Japanese displayed a more conservation-minded relationship with nature, so when she appealed to her readers to allow the dogwoods in surrounding woods "time to grow," she suggested that Americans might "learn the artistic restraint of the Japanese that finds ample satisfaction for beauty hunger in two or three perfect blossoms."[20] Baldwin also deployed the example of the Japanese when she attacked the whipping-post law, discussed in chapter 4. In that instance, she related a conversation with the sheriff's deputy, whose responsibility it was to administer the lash to the incarcerated wife beater. The deputy, she informed her reader, "smiled cynically when told that the Japanese officers apologize to a man before placing him under arrest."[21]

Baldwin's connections to the New Thought community may have rendered her more open to Asian influences. Other emerging metaphysical traditions, notably theosophy, drew her journalistic attention. The Theosophical Society was the creation of the meeting of the fertile spiritual imagination of Madame Helena Petrovna Blavatsky and the rationalist spiritualist inquiry of Henry Steel Olcott. The new tradition revitalized the belief in spiritual adepts who, informed by Eastern philosophy, would gain command of mind and matter, revealing mystical knowledge of ancient cultures. Blavatsky's views were first articulated in *Isis Unveiled*, published in 1877. More elitist than New Thought in its implications, reliant on a hierarchy of adepts, theosophy led its followers into the world of Hindu spirituality, especially when Blavatsky and Olcott moved to India in 1880. Theosophy was of interest to many who emerged from the spiritualist tradition, and it helped pave the way for Hindu religious leaders like Swami Vivekananda to find an American audience in the 1890s.[22]

"The Woman's Point of View" did not ignore this tendency, and in many ways it reflected and demonstrated Baldwin's heightened appreciation for Asian cultures. In a hostile review of a ministerial denunciation of female authority in the church, Baldwin pointed out that many women found better guidance from "Oriental teachers" whom they know "to be men of profound scholarship, broad culture, and a loftiness of spirituality and keenness of perception that shame nine-tenths of the clergymen in Christian pulpits."[23] When Annie Besant, the British woman who would come to head the Theosophist Society, received hostile press for an ascribed belief in the transmigration of souls, Baldwin defended her "superb intellectual equipment," and challenged the reporters for their lack of knowledge of theosophy. Similarly, Baldwin chastised reporters for blemishing the reputation of Point Loma theosophist Katherine Tingley by accusing her of taking orders from a dog to whose body a prior mentor's soul had allegedly migrated. She repeated that theosophists did not believe in the transmigration of souls, and suggested that the press would do better to focus on Tingley's efforts to establish "Raja Yoga" schools in Cuba. Baldwin also detailed the way in which woman's rights advocate Clara Colby had become "awakened to the immense field for thought in the Oriental religions by some theosophists in Spokane," and that she had subsequently hosted "those Oriental teachers who were prominent at the great Parliament of Religions" at the Columbian Exposition in Chicago, among them Swami Vivekananda.[24] The metaphysics of New Thought led Baldwin—and the same can be said of the other local female New Thought editors, Colby and Mallory—to display an appreciation for the Hindu religious tradition.

In this, Baldwin and her fellow New Thought believers reflected an aspect of a broader cultural response of Americans who grew to understand their own religious traditions to be cold and austere. Searching for something more vital in an increasingly mechanized world, many Americans, particularly among the educated bourgeoisie, were influenced by the Arts and Crafts movement, which celebrated handicraft and sometimes, especially in England, came with a critique of capitalism. Similarly, Americans turned to Asian religion and art, as well as the European medieval tradition, for cultural sources of vitality and spirit.

In some places, the collection of Asian art went hand in hand with an aesthetic embrace of primitivism—the raising of the medieval over the Renaissance, the fascination with Native American art—which was in some cases a means of signifying the superiority of the white race. In other places, the collection of goods from the Orient reflected a greater openness to the international and non-Western world.[25]

It is not surprising then that Baldwin would object to the racist outbreak that prevented a white woman, Helen Emery, from marrying Japanese immigrant Gunjiro Aoki in Corte Madera, California, just outside of San Francisco. Aoki, who was quickly labeled by antimiscegenationists as a sexually aggressive violator of racial boundaries, received threats that he would be tarred and feathered if he went through with the marriage. The Emery family was at first treated, as historian Peggy Pascoe puts it, like "a virtuous White family in peril." But as Emery and Aoki persisted in their efforts to marry, aided by her mother, pressure mounted on the family. Mrs. Emery was asked to leave her position as local president of the Episcopal Ladies Guild, and Helen's father was asked to resign from his position as an Episcopal archdeacon. Japanese organizations, anxious to calm white fears, tried to convince the couple to desist. But they would have none of it, as the two young people traveled with Helen's mother up the Pacific Coast to find a place where they could legally wed. They found just as hostile a reception in Portland, where the *Oregonian* warned that while the laws of the state might not prevent the marriage, "public sentiment in Oregon is revolted by it. And the spirit of the statutes, if not the letter, condemns it." The newspaper noted that the district attorney warned the couple that should they "appear arm in arms, as is the case of true sweethearts, that they will be arrested as common nuisances." After being hounded out of Portland, the couple finally married in Seattle, which lacked an antimiscegenation law that had given local officials the tenuous legal grounding to deny the right to marry in Oregon.[26]

For Baldwin, the movement to prevent the marriage of Aoki to Emery, as well as the resulting expansion of miscegenation laws in the western United States, was evidence of "madness," which while "discouragingly chronic" was not "incurable." She described Aoki as a "clear, honorable, bright young fellow" who had "wooed and won an American girl." She mocked the "good church women" in Corte Madera who were "thrown into fits because a girl kisses her Jap lover in public," and asked if they "are moving heaven and earth as they should be to prevent the white slave traffic in their own city of brazen corruption." Of the young men who threatened Aoki with violence, she asserted, "you might safely wager all your diamonds that these young men haven't an intelligent idea about municipal government, which is the personal business of every last one of us." Referring to the potential couple, Baldwin asserted that the choice to marry was "strictly their business," and that others should recognize it was "none of their affair," which they would normally understand "if they were not hopelessly insane on the race question."[27]

Then she took on miscegenation and the concerns of eugenicists in ways that reflect the arguments she had made fifteen years before in Naugatuck in response to the appeal for women to have more children to avert "race suicide." The opponents of the Aoki-Emery marriage argued that the resulting children "have a right to be well born," and that they cannot be in a mixed-race marriage. In these cases, it was concern over the continued dominance of the white race, and for some like Madison Grant that would mean white persons of northern European extraction. None of that mattered to Baldwin, who considered the lack of love in marriage as the thing that violates the "birthright" of the child. She objected to any kind of argument that reduced parents to "mere breeders of their kind," and pointed out that many married couples never had children, rendering this argument of "race fanatics . . . wholly gratuitous." What did matter was that the parents love each other:

> To be born of truly loving parents, who are ready to extend
> that love and transmute it into joyous welcome to any child
> born of it, is to be well born. Nobody is well born or shall
> we say best born, who comes into the world without that
> sanction and seal of legitimacy and welcome. It is time we
> stopped playing with humbug and falsehood and recognized
> this one divine truth. Should Aoki and his bride have
> children, the chances are, judging from their devotion to each
> other, that those children will be well born.[28]

Most significantly, Baldwin perceived in the effort to stop the Aoki-Emery marriage an atavistic impulse that prevented progress. Ever since "supposed rational human beings" appeared on the earth, Baldwin insisted they have allowed prejudice to lead them "into the same mud of race hatred." She spoke specifically of the Irish, who had once been "in much the same situation as the Japanese are today," but who now are "good Americans, ready to fan into flame the same old sheeplike antipathy of race and to lead their following over the bluff into the same old stupid race prejudice, forgetting their own fight against it." She pointed out that "First Chief Deputy District Attorney" bore the Irish last name of Fitzgerald, and accused him of forbidding the marriage because "he thinks the Japanese can be classed as Mongols." Similarly, the Irish-American county clerk had "issued positive orders to all his deputies . . . to decline the couple of marriage license in the event they appeared in the Courthouse." The problem, she concluded, was "the idiotic race prejudice of the unthinking mass of people."[29]

It was the mostly implicit conflation of the irrational mob with the Irish that caught the attention of J. Hennessy Murphy, a local lawyer who was closely connected with the Catholic Church, frequently defending its interests. When Murphy wrote to the editor of the *Telegram*, he began by questioning the value of a woman's column. He asserted that women are a "nuisance" on a newspaper, as "ninety per cent of them cannot rise above twaddle." The result he warned was that "a good pastry chef is lost for a silly scribe when these women are turned loose to give their 'point of view,' a view by the way, seldom with a point." He asserted that the editor of the *Telegram* had undoubtedly not read the column before it went to print, speaking to a propensity of male editors to ignore the woman's page that had given women journalists an opportunity to be, as Sarah A. Evans had put it, "the intellectuals, the revolutionists, the revolters" because they flew under the broader editorial radar of the paper. Murphy would make sure that the editor of the *Telegram*, John Carroll, now paid attention.

His chief objection was that Baldwin had engaged in what he called a "gratuitous and uncalled for insult to a whole race of people." Denying that ethnicity and race were critical categories that defined individuals, Murphy claimed it was the branding of the district attorney as Irish that was offensive, explaining that Fitzgerald carried an "Irish name, but . . . never to my knowledge interested himself in Irish affairs directly or indirectly." For Murphy, the identification of the officials as Irish cast an ethnic shadow on all those who opposed the interracial marriage as "sheep" who were motivated "by prejudice and race hatred." Similarly, he took offense at the assertion of the preconceived notion that Irish had controlled saloons and city governments, insisting that Irish Catholics "are among the most pronounced and successful advocates of teetotalism and temperance." Murphy claimed the Irish did not "as a race take any hand in the late 'convulsions'" regarding the "Aoki-Emery episode." In fact, he denied that race prejudice was much of a factor, asserting that whatever hostility demonstrated in this instance by Irish men was "economic" in motivation, as poor people fought to hold their turf rather than express hatred toward the people of a different race. Any blame for the concern over "race degeneracy" had been registered "mostly by old maids." He concluded by pointedly asserting that those Irish "connected with the press . . . have other assignments than 'points of view.'"[30]

Murphy therefore argued that there was something more essential about gender than there was about race and ethnicity, at least when it came to the Irish. Women were categorically better deployed in the kitchen than in the pressroom; women journalists wrote mere "twaddle"; women expressed mere "points of view"; and women agitated questions of race degeneracy, demonstrating small and intolerant minds. In this, gender was a natural category that fully defined female capabilities and their proper social roles within the family. Any statement about the Irish, on the other hand, was a mere demonstration of intolerance, a failure to recognize the urban and economic context in which the Irish immigrant had adapted to American life. There was nothing natural about any Irish propensities; they were fully individualized human beings. Murphy took any kind of implicit assertion by Baldwin that could be interpreted as a blanket statement about the Irish as a direct insult against an entire people. In this, the Aoki-Emery episode came to expose the precarious position held by women journalists who aspired to serious discussion of society and politics. And it had to rankle Baldwin, who had stressed the capability of women to transcend any gendered limitations.

Baldwin certainly understood what was at stake. She responded with her own assessment that Murphy, instead of attacking an individual, had assaulted "women journalists in general" and his use of "old maid" marked him as a "hopeless vulgarian." She accurately denied that she had labeled the Irish as a race as "sheep," and had used that term to "include any and all races who are bitten with the

race-prejudice microbe," though she had singled out the Irish for discussion. But on the subject of the Aoki-Emery wedding, she began to
backtrack, claiming she "was not defending what Mr. J. Hennessey
Murphy is pleased to call miscegenation" but rather the rights of two
people to act "without the interference of two states." Nonetheless, she
concluded with a forceful assessment that Murphy was incapable of
seeing that "race prejudice per se is the same, whether directed against
the Irish, the Jap, the Italian or Hebrew. It is despicable, the mark of
a narrow mind; one of the greatest obstacles today in the path of the
world's progress."[31]

Ten days later, Baldwin wrote her final column. There was no mention of Murphy, and it remains unclear whether the exchange with him
had led to her loss of employment. In fact, there was no explanation of
her departure, and at the end of the final column—it would disappear
from the *Telegram*—Baldwin assessed the importance of what she had
spent three years creating. She asserted that in the city and countryside
of the Northwest, there had been and remained a need for "light," and
that the women who sought it "could not be put off with silly chaff,
meant to deaden the mind, and not to stimulate it to life." The job remained unfinished, however. She left her readers with what she called
"a word of exhortation":

> The welfare work of the world was never as urgent as now; it
> never had the attention of so many thoughtful and splendidly
> equipped men and women as now. Indeed, it is safe to say
> that all men and women whose intellects place them above
> the level of human drift are keenly awake to these problems
> of mind and matter and industry and economics that daily
> grow more pressing.[32]

With that, "The Woman's Point of View" ceased to be written.
In an episode that began with her defense of a Japanese man from the
forces of intolerance, which she associated with Irish Catholics, Baldwin
ironically displayed some signs of anti-Irish prejudice that may have
been grounded in a New England Protestant's biases against the Catholic Church. If that were the case, it would await the rise of the Ku Klux
Klan a decade later for Baldwin to give it fuller expression.

Colonialism, Imperialism, and War

In her *Telegram* columns, Baldwin scoffed at pretensions to white supremacy, condemning police brutality toward African Americans who breached the racial separation that had been imposed by Jim Crow, and asking her readers to ponder the "tragedy of being born black in a country of white domination."[33] Her disdain for domestic racism was paralleled by her dismissal of any good intentions espoused for imperialism. When she provided her readers details from the writings of anthropologist Frederick Starr, who exposed the brutal exploitations of the Congolese by Belgians, she pointed out "the amazing similarity between United States rule in the Philippines and Leopold rule in the Congo State." Baldwin concluded that Starr's work about the Congo "has brought a charge against us of the white race that we cannot deny, for hundreds of common acts of everyday life confirm it." On another occasion, Baldwin suggested that white people would benefit from putting themselves "in the place of dark-skinned people and see—not how heathenish and wicked they look to us—but how brutal and covetous, sniveling and hypocritical we look to them." Discussing an Indian speaker, Baldwin pointed out that the "Hindoo missionary" who aimed to "lift a little of the heavy weight of the British yoke from his people" distinguished himself from his Western counterparts because "he never utters a word of violence or menace." Closer to home, Baldwin criticized a celebration of "Empire Day" in Portland that lacked any Indian presence, though "British India is larger than any other of the King's dependencies." The absence led her to recall sentimentally "the dark-faced men with their heads wrapped in yards of soft cloth, that had walked so silently through Portland streets, feeling the loneliness of an alien—a loneliness we cannot imagine because it is that of color and race." Baldwin rejected the vision of racial hierarchy and empire altogether, lecturing her readers, "We may wriggle and twist as we will, but just the same, the brown and the black and the yellow peoples are of our race."[34]

The rejection of the notion of Christian uplift as a legitimate reason for empire was part of an overall opposition to militarism of any kind, one infused with the language of female mission to overcome the interests of men. In the columns, Baldwin expressed this in a few different ways. While discussing the female capability to fly airplanes, she had pointed out that men quickly turned a wonderful technology into a killing machine.[35] In March 1908, Baldwin charged that "the world's great money lenders" and the manufacturers of armaments were fomenting war between the United States and Japan, and she called on women, organized in peace societies, to do all they could to resist "the men representing the interests."[36] Women had roles to play in moving the world away from warfare and imperialism. Mothers, she said, should provide lessons in altruism, providing role models like Johnny Appleseed rather than the soldier.[37] She called on women to pay the man in uniform less respect, which was a necessity if there would be any hope to end war.[38] In the summer of 1908, she did exactly that when confronted with members of the Second Idaho militia in a restaurant. When the young men sat down at her table, she mused, "It isn't often a woman comes face to face with such visible proof of the fact that the world is still ruled by force and bloodshed as that room full of men in khaki represented." She told them that she "didn't believe in war at all," and challenged them by asserting that if "all the world went as earnestly to work to make people healthy and happy as it does to sustain the foolish business of armies and navies and to perfect murdering machines of all sorts, there would be no need of war," to which she reportedly received agreement from the young men. She concluded by labeling war as "just plain murder by wholesale."[39]

For Decoration Day (now Memorial Day) in 1907, Baldwin provided her readers with the declaration of principles adopted by the American Peace Society, which reiterated the rights of all people to life, liberty, and the pursuit of happiness, while defining "helpful kindness to all creatures and civic intelligence" as the "basis of true citizenship." Inspired by the writings of Leo Tolstoy, Baldwin envisioned a day when "by a secret but universal compact among the common soldiers of every civilized land," they all refused, "en masse, to be ordered out by a few Generals to kill each other."[40] The outbreak of World War I in Europe in the summer of 1914 led Baldwin, now freed of her daily column responsibilities, to develop such ideas in the pursuit of peace. In 1915, she published a short story, "The White Zeppelin," in a collection published by the Christian Women's Peace Movement, an umbrella organization that included missionaries, the Young Women's Christian Association (YWCA), and the Parent-Teacher Association (PTA). The organization aimed to avoid politics and "confine our effort to a peace propaganda based on the teaching and spirit of Jesus." Other women, many of them feminists, were ultimately drawn to the Women's Peace Party, chaired by Jane Addams.[41]

In Baldwin's story, politics and blame for the war were avoided, as the Germans, French, and British were treated, with one exception, similarly. The appearance of the White Zeppelin, acting as a force upon the mind, defused any martial spirit held by the soldiers, leading them to refuse to fight. For the generals, however, "the peaceful dirigible had become a cause of unreasoning terror, bordering upon superstitious panic" because its appearance is "invariably followed by a waning zest for battle upon the part of their troops."[42] One British officer, the Irish-born Lieutenant Murphy, was awakened to the irrationality of war by the vision of "Mars recumbent" on the dirigible's wall:

Too long we've pampered his delicate appetite with dum dum bullets, shrapnel, bombs, floating mines, then mine sweepers to destroy the mines; then dreadnoughts, then torpedo boats that destroy the dreadnoughts; then submarines to blow up the whole outfit not to mention peaceful fishing craft and passenger boats; then air machines, then air guns to destroy the air machines—like the one yonder—and all the time Mars—the old divil [sic]—getting huskier and harder to handle. It's a game for lunatics and idiots, that's what it is.[43]

The White Zeppelin brought rational thought to the battlefield, and frustrated generals realized that no matter how "deadly efficient" their arms were, "it is after all, 'the spirit in man' which fights battles."[44] When it rained down white and mauve lilacs on the battlefield, men crushed them "fiercely to their lips in a spasm of homesick longing," and "borne on the sweetness of the lilacs, thoughts of peace penetrated the inmost souls of these men."[45] When it disappeared, sanity departed as well, and the killing resumed. When the dirigible returned for the final scene, when both sides were preparing for a climactic battle, a frustrated German general shot it down out of the sky, only to reveal that it had been staffed entirely by women of all nationalities. Their feminine sacrifice brought the men in uniform, including the generals, to sanity, and finally "the demon of armaments and bloodshed was exorcised." Taught by "the gentle crew of the White Zeppelin," humanity "had come into its own,--had found its oneness."[46]

Amid the tragedy of the war, Baldwin produced a hopeful and utopian short story that expressed her progressive vision infused with New Thought spirituality. The narrative spoke of deeply embedded but vague interests that obscured the true objectives of humanity and the direction of history. "The White Zeppelin," acting as a spiritual conduit of a higher purpose on the soldiers, cut through the patriotic nonsense that led men to kill each other and to regain their reason. If the story was silent about arms manufacturers and financiers to whom she had previously attributed the persistence of the martial spirit, it redirected blame for war on passionate generals who sought to obscure reason and keep the men in the trenches.

As Germany resumed unrestricted submarine warfare in early 1917 and the US Congress debated entry into the war, Baldwin made clearer the relationship between industry, finance, and the killing fields of Europe. In a letter to the *Oregon Labor Press,* she challenged national-ist patriotism and anti-German propaganda, arguing that the US steel industry had killed more civilian Americans in their factories than Ger-many had with its use of submarines. True patriotism, she reminded her trade-union readership, demanded "square dealing, individual health happiness and prosperity for EVERY man, woman and child under the flag," and warned that the war fever and preparedness had unleashed "a diseased, imbecile patriotism that can only feel itself 'patriotic' when the blood of our best is being spilled."[47]

Radicalism and Anti-Catholicism in 1920s Oregon

The war heightened class tensions in factories, shipyards, and log-ging camps, and concern about the impact of work stoppages on war-related production motivated the Wilson administration to develop an unprecedented level of regulation. For instance, the War Labor Board (WLB), with its blend of labor and business representatives, sought to prevent productivity breakdowns due to labor conflict, and under the leadership of Frank Walsh the WLB did so by providing protections for union organizing and the negotiation of better conditions. By imposing gains for labor that were justified as necessary to avoid long shutdowns resulting from industrial disputes, the WLB created conditions that stimulated union organization of workers who lacked a craft tradition and a traditional trade union. As industry increasingly became reliant on "semiskilled" workers, industrial unionization would be the wave of the future, a future enabled by the Wagner Act and the New Deal, but the way was paved by the WLB. For these reasons, conservatives grew to hate the WLB and to blame the Wilson administration for inciting class conflict.[48]

Once the war was over, corporate leaders could afford to ignore rulings from the WLB, stalling the growth of unionization. At the same time, conservatives mounted a counterattack, most notably in the use of federal authority under Attorney General A. Mitchell Palmer to harass and imprison those on the left. Socialists who had flocked to the communist banner in the wake of the Russian Revolution found themselves under federal surveillance, as their offices were raided, papers seized, and officers arrested. Those who had too strenuously objected to the war had already found themselves imprisoned, and it was in this context that longtime Socialist Party leader Eugene Debs ran for president from a prison cell.[49]

In the context of heightened repression of the radical left, Baldwin's own writings became increasingly argumentative and bombastic. Once the war ended, Baldwin's writings focused on what she perceived to be the two institutional breaks on freedom and equality: bankers and the Catholic Church. With regard to the former, Baldwin continued to lecture the trade-unionist readership of the *Oregon Labor Press* about the nature of money. She denounced one correspondent's criticisms of her New Thought treatise on money as a "verbal jungle" accompanied by a "smoke screen and awful gas barrage, only to find myself confronted with the golden calf—dear to all usurers and parasites of whatever race or clime." She promised that she would respond to his arguments if he ever would "emerge from his jungle fastness of apologetic economics— devised as a defense for the indefensible," and that she would "be only too happy" to engage him in the newspaper. Instead, she lambasted an economic civilization that had accumulated billions of dollars' worth of gold only to use it to impose massive debt "upon the back of labor while it fought to 'make the world safe for democracy.'"[50] A week later, Baldwin condemned mainstream political economists, whom she charged used "words, rather than force," to enable the "parasite class . . . to keep intact the old order." A favorite tactic, she wrote, was to "scare the timid and law-abiding with the terrible word BOLSHEVIST!"[51] Baldwin condemned the Red Scare. She denounced the raiding of offices of "reputable labor unions" by the local police and the newly created FBI, whom she termed "protectors of parasites." Moreover, she charged that the raids demonstrated that the "war was in reality fought to make the world safe for hypocrisy." The boys who "turned their backs upon life to go down into the hells of modern warfare in European infernos" as well as the women "who toiled, and prayed for them with aching hearts at home," found what Baldwin considered the awful truth: "Somebody lied. It has proved a war to perpetuate war."[52]

While she continued to denounce financiers and bankers, Baldwin soon became involved in a movement that identified a threat to republican institutions from the Catholic Church, which increasingly animated Portland and Oregon politics in the early 1920s. A year before she would distinguish between "religion" and "ecclesiasticism," which had allowed her to portray the Bolsheviks in Russia as tolerant of religion, Baldwin entered the religious fray during the school board election in June 1920. On the basis of a conversation in which a Catholic candidate had condemned her opponents for "injecting religion" into the schools, Baldwin urged "all lovers of a true public schools not to support her." Baldwin rejected any notion that Protestants like herself had done any such thing, and in so doing began to articulate what she meant by "religion." She pointed out that in New England in an earlier era, "the Bible was the one non-sectarian book of conduct and morals," read daily by teachers and students. But she mourned that the "Bible has vanished from our public schools, spirited away by the same sinister clerical hand which still burns Bibles wherever it can be done safely." This removal of the King James Bible from the classroom, a demand of growing Catholic communities in the nineteenth century, was the moment when Baldwin insisted that the "'religious question' was 'injected' for the first time into the school problem."[53]

Baldwin then proceeded to articulate Protestant grievances against the Papacy that went as far back as the Reformation. She asked her readers, "What sect is it that hates the Bible? What sect burned at the stake men who translated it into the tongues of the multitude for the multitude to read? What sect is it which burned Bibles in free America; which still destroys them in Ireland; and since the Spanish War has fed them to the flames by the hundred in the Philippines?"[54] Then she took on the local sins of the Catholic Church, condemning it for establishing schools "to fit sectarian-trained teachers for our non-sectarian public schools." She censured school directors who hired nuns to teach in the public schools of Marion and Washington Counties, "forcing parents of other faiths to endure the humiliation and the danger of seeing their children papal-trained." Baldwin attempted to demonstrate that the Catholic Church had historically sought control over education, and the most important result she argued was the ignorance of the people in lands where the Catholic Church dominated. The school board election, as far as Baldwin was concerned, was about keeping Catholic influence out of the schools and maintaining the United States as a progressive society. She concluded by stating, "No American boy or girl is fitted for citizenship unless fortified with an intelligent knowledge of the past and present activities of the Roman hierarchy, the controlling power in the Catholic Church—and trained to cope with the trickery and fraud constantly practiced by its right hand—the Jesuit order, in its effort to gain power and money."[55] As many during the immediate postwar years had done with the Bolsheviks, Baldwin did with the Catholic Church, identifying it as the great threat to the American Republic. Any threat to this Protestant vision of citizenship was tantamount to "injecting religion" into politics.

These were astounding claims, ones that could not help but set Catholic against Protestant union brethren, but the interesting thing about them is that they pose a naturalness to Protestantism that is compatible with New Thought and spiritualism in that they pose natural progress and human improvement as the result of the focused mind. Imposition of the King James Bible on all children in the public schools was not understood by Baldwin as "injecting religion," whereas the Catholic resistance to it was, especially since it was guided by a priestly hierarchy interested in containing minds of parishioners. In many regards, Baldwin's anti-Catholic discourse reflects the kind of blend of secular and spiritual modes of knowing that John Lardas Modern has stressed as emergent in the mid-nineteenth century, naturalizing religious practices and beliefs.[56] In these ways, Baldwin insinuated herself in the rising ethnic and religious tensions that would threaten the unity of the Portland Central Labor Council and the Oregon State Federation of Labor.

It did not take long for Catholic trade unionists to respond. A response written by A. J. Dooney, the president of the Portland City Fire Fighters' Union No. 43, who apparently did not know her personally, charged Baldwin with fomenting "discord in our ranks," and he accused

her of "ignorance and bigotry." Dooney denied that the Catholic hierarchy had imposed the ban of the Bible in the schools, and denied that
Catholics were opposed to the Bible but rather to "its children having
a faulty, garbled translation crammed down their throats." As to the
charge that the Catholic Church was opposed to education, Dooney
replied with caustic logic: "It is an enemy of schools because it builds
schools! Just so, Mr. Baldwin is an enemy of labor, because he belongs
to a labor union! The state is an enemy of order because it makes laws."
Dooney summed up the Baldwin position:

> Of course, we should pay taxes for the schools, and allow the
> enlightened Mr. Baldwin to run them. We have nothing to
> say. No Catholics should be allowed to teach. All anti-Catholic
> lies should be taught as facts. The Protestant translation of
> the Bible should be read. And the Jew, Catholic and others
> should sit with folded hands while their children are led
> away from the religion of their fathers—thanking God they
> were still allowed to live in this land of the free.[57]

The school board election witnessed the victory of the anti-Catholic slate by a two-to-one margin, despite the opposition of local daily
newspapers. It was a bellwether for the more serious breach occasioned
by the appearance of the Ku Klux Klan shortly thereafter that would
severely weaken the local labor movement and roil Oregon politics. The
Klan's rise to prominence was felt most dramatically in the 1922 election, in which its support helped Democratic candidate Walter Pierce
overcome incumbent Ben Olcott, and during which the voters of Oregon
passed the initiative closing all private, mostly Catholic, schools. In
1922, the legislature passed the Alien Land Act, which intended to end
Japanese landholding within the state. In that year, Oregon nativism
and electoral racism reached a high-water mark.

Yet the impulses that drove it were contradictory. The Klan-
supported effort to close down the Catholic school system sought to
force Catholic children into the public schools, where they would be
protected from priestly influence; it was an attempt to force a Protestant
Americanization on both native-born and immigrant Catholics. In the
aftermath of the Red Scare, when the full force of the federal government was arrayed against radical organizations like the Communist and

Socialist Parties as well as the Industrial Workers of the World (IWW), public school education seemed to many a necessary inoculation against radicalism in the youth of the immigrant community. Recognizing the reactionary politics of this effort, the *Oregon Labor Press*, edited by Clarence Rynerson, came out strongly against the Klan. Rynerson warned that the Klan was an agent of employers, and presciently he added that wherever it went it sewed discord between workers. Nonetheless, Rynerson would find that the Klan had insinuated itself throughout the Portland labor community, and in 1922 the deeply divided Portland Central Labor Council (CLC) would fail to endorse a slate of candidates or take a stand on the private school bill, an unprecedented move for the usually politically active CLC. Rynerson and the *Oregon Labor Press* would grow silent about the KKK. Signs of Klan strength were evident in neighborhood newspapers like the *Sunnyside Gazette*, which had long espoused support for the radical single tax, but which now printed the pro-Klan sentiments of Reverend T. H. Gallagher of the Sunnyside Methodist Church. Gallagher had been vice president of the Portland Ministerial Association just a year earlier, and had served as a well-received delegate to the CLC in 1921. There was no simple division between the house of labor and its middle-class progressive supporters on the one hand and the Klan on the other. In some cases, like that of Eleanor Baldwin, they were one and the same. Baldwin was hardly anomalous.[58]

The linkages between the rise of Protestant militancy and progressivism are there to be found, and there is no better example than longtime progressive leader William U'Ren, the mastermind of the turn-of-the-century movement to overcome legislative objections to direct democracy—including the initiative, referendum, recall, and direct election of US senators. A product of an artisanal home in the Midwest, U'Ren discovered the writings of Henry George while traveling in the West, and became a confirmed supporter of the single tax. When he located to Clackamas County, just south of Portland, he fell in with a group of populists who shared his interest in both George and in spiritualism, and who would help elect him to the legislature. In the legislature, U'Ren would adopt a do-anything strategy to pass measures promoting direct democracy, and these efforts in particular earned him national fame and the moniker of Oregon's "lawgiver." Yet that was merely the means to achieve a Georgite end; once the initiative had been established into electoral law, U'Ren led a number of campaigns for the implementation of the single tax through the initiative process, which aimed to practically socialize land. But he was active in other ways that furthered his credentials as a progressive radical. As a lawyer, he served as a counsel for unions, and during the First World War he worked with the nascent American Civil Liberties Union defending communists from governmental prosecution. In many ways, U'Ren stands as the embodiment of the kind of middle-class radicalism about which Robert Johnston has written.[59]

But signs of cultural complexity run through U'Ren's political and legal career, as they do Baldwin's journalistic one. While running as a candidate for governor, he came out strongly in favor of both women's rights and Prohibition, and it would be Democratic gubernatorial candidate Walter Pierce's support for temperance that led the Republican U'Ren to endorse the Democrat for governor in 1918 over the incumbent Republican governor, James Withycombe. Earlier, U'Ren had advocated a minimum wage so that young women would not be forced into prostitution, declaring in a 1912 article in the *California Outlook*, "Our mothers and wives and the mothers that are to be are rebelling against growing girls for the white slave traffic and for mistresses for men whose wages do not permit them to marry a wife and raise a family of good children and decent citizens."[60] While U'Ren supported reforms that grew out of a Protestant sense of social morality, he, like Baldwin, did not identify with anti-Catholic politics in the prewar era.

In 1922, however, with the rise of the KKK, U'Ren became party to a Klan-supported challenge to the outcome of a Republican primary election that centered on the role of the Catholic hierarchy in politics. It was charged that numerous Catholic Democrats had changed their party affiliations at the direction of their priests so that they could vote in the primary for Republican Governor Ben Olcott, an avowed opponent of the Klan. As attorney for the Olcott opponents, U'Ren explained the basis of the challenge: "We have the names of a very large number of Catholic democrats who entered the polls and changed their party registrations who we believe would tell that story if we had the right to question them along that line." When the court rejected his plea to interrogate Catholic voters regarding priestly influence, U'Ren said he would go to the legislature to seek amendments to the primary law that would prevent such "exercise of influence on the voters by the church or other organizations." The battle lines of the case were further exposed when Olcott attorney Jay Bowerman offered "to announce my readiness to join with Mr. U'Ren in his determination to strengthen the primary law . . . providing he will agree to include also a provision which will prevent kleagles, wizards, and goblins from coming into a community and attempting to dictate to the electors."[61] By 1922, the father of Oregon's direct democracy had become embroiled in a controversy as to what constituted a threat to local democracy. At least temporarily, U'Ren sided with the Klan.

Though Baldwin's crusade against the Catholic Church began with the public school controversies, her anti-Catholic politics may have reached its conspiratorial zenith in an article that she wrote for the *Western American*, the weekly newspaper of the Oregon Klan. Written after the school and gubernatorial election of 1922, when Klan influence was at its peak, Baldwin addressed the so-called Corfu Incident. The precipitating event was an international crisis generated by a border dispute between Albania and Greece and exacerbated by the murder of an Italian negotiating team, headed by General Enrico Tellini, by unknown assailants. Mussolini blamed the Greeks for the murders and denied that the League of Nations had any legitimate interest in resolving the matter; instead, the Italians used the incident as a pretext to invade and occupy the island of Corfu. Baldwin rejected *Il Duce's* interpretation of events, asserting that it was Italy, not Greece, who stood to benefit from the murders. But Mussolini did not act alone, she warned. "It is an open secret," Baldwin told her Klan-supporting readers, "that the Vatican has been scheming before and ever since the world war to absorb the Greek Catholic church with all its wealth of church property for herself." Alleging that the incident would further the Vatican's ambitions, Baldwin charged that "the Scarlet Woman on the seven hills feeds best on the blood diet and gets it whenever she can with safety to herself." With the cooperation of the press, over which the Vatican has "sufficient control," the world ignored the Catholic Church's grasp for power. Baldwin called on the Klan to join the "Masons, and other anti-clericals in general, to do the world a good turn" by remaining wide awake against worldwide papal conspiracies.[62]

It is unclear whether Baldwin's association with the Klan accompanied a broader intolerance. By and large, the Klan, in its efforts to preserve a white Protestant culture from what it considered the mongrelizing effects of immigration and race mixing, took up the mantle of white supremacy. What this relationship meant for radicals like William U'Ren or Eleanor Baldwin, who were concerned with what they perceived to be the corrupting power of the Catholic Church, is unclear, and there is not a lot of literary evidence regarding either of these otherwise progressive Klan supporters. That the two were on the political left cannot be seen as an anomaly, as so many on the Pacific Coast had long simultaneously held socialist and racist beliefs; the Irish-born iron molder Frank Roney in Gilded Age San Francisco was one such example, and Nina Wood of course was a latter-day one.[63] Baldwin's lionizing of the antisemitic Henry Ford suggests the possibility that her intolerance extended beyond the Catholic Church, which if so would have amounted to a reversal of an explicit tolerance that she articulated in "The Woman's Point of View." But the extent to which she embraced Ford is unclear.

Many on the left, including the *Oregon Labor Press*, celebrated Henry Ford for his demonstration that high wages were compatible with a successful manufacturing enterprise and for what they must have thought was his penchant to speak producerist truth to finance capital power. Raised in rural Michigan, and delighted to escape the loneliness and tedium of the farm, Ford would carry his rural background with him in ways that became increasingly clear with time. Though he celebrated consumerism and understood high wages as fostering broader consumption, he consistently interpreted conflicts and lawsuits in a dualistic manner that was compatible with a populist worldview, identifying himself as a noble producer who sought to be freed of corporate and nonproductive stockholders—he often called them "parasites"—who sought to rake in high dividends and prevent the expansion of productive capacity.[64] The *Oregon Labor Press* praised Ford for demonstrating that the pessimism of neo-Malthusians about wage rates was wrong, that industrial progress did not inevitably lead to wage stagnation. Further, in the early 1920s, the trade-union paper supported his effort to gain the rights to develop the hydropower potential of the Muscle Shoals site on the Tennessee River, which would eventually come under the control of the Tennessee Valley Authority a decade later. The paper condemned Oregon Senator Charles McNary, who had supported Senator George Norris's vision of public development of the river, for opposing the Ford proposal, which Ford would withdraw in 1924.[65]

Baldwin too was enamored with the "Flivver King." In an un-published manuscript that she wrote as a follow-up treatise to *Money Talks*, Baldwin quoted Ford's suggestion that an economic system that imposed unemployment and poverty on the masses "has neither the right to exist nor the soundness with which to endure."[66] But Ford did more than give expression to Baldwin's sense that capitalism was im-moral; he also engaged the question of money and finance on a regular basis, blaming business downturns on the machinations of financiers. Approvingly, she quoted from an article that he wrote, titled "Farmers Are Serfs of the Money Lenders," and Baldwin added, "All industries are equally slaves to the money-lenders."[67] For Baldwin, celebration of Ford went hand in hand with her anticapitalist message.

There may have been other reasons for Baldwin to embrace Ford. In 1915, Ford undertook the organization of a "Peace Ship" that was meant to convey to the populations of Europe the folly of war, a venture that Baldwin must have thought had striking parallels to the White Zeppelin of her imagination. The highly publicized effort proved to be a disaster, as Ford announced the participation of numerous leading peace advocates, most of whom ultimately decided not to set sail with him. Those that did engaged in constant argument, as passage on the Peace Ship proved to be anything but pacific. Perhaps most disturbing to Ford was the evidence that populations had knowingly cast their lot with the generals and the politicians. Still, Ford continued to interpret the war as having been caused by bankers and arms producers. While these were positions unlikely to bother Baldwin or much of the socialist left, it did engender hostility from much of the rest of society. Respond-ing to negative press associated with his antiwar efforts, Ford claimed in 1921, "The capitalistic newspapers began a campaign against me. They misquoted me, distorted what I said, told lies about me."[68]

By that time, Ford's *Dearborn Independent* was already indulging in an antisemitic campaign, having launched its infamous "The Interna-tional Jew" series in the spring of 1920. The series, ninety installments in all, recapitulated the arguments of the tsarist forgery, *Protocols of the Elders of Zion*. All the destructive qualities that Ford had associated with bankers and speculators were now categorically attributed to Jews, and in this too Ford and his associates revealed their debt to farmer populism of the 1890s. Populist intolerance has been a source of histori-cal controversy over the years. In the wake of McCarthyism, Richard

Hofstadter characterized populists as having been driven by irrational intolerance, and he particularly noted their rhetorical excesses against Jews. Walter Nugent, on the other hand, delved deep into heartland archival material to examine populism in Kansas and found that while there were occasional diatribes against the Rothschild banking house, populists there exhibited little hostility toward Jews and immigrants in general, and that their rhetorical excesses were not unique in American society. There is no such disagreement about Ford's antisemitism: it was consistent until he was forced in an out-of-court settlement to apologize in 1927.[69]

There is no mention of Ford's antisemitism in Baldwin's treatise. Instead, in her efforts to show how finance capitalists had used debt to enslave the masses across the globe, she used firms that did not have Jewish-sounding names, like Brown Brothers, whom she identified as "debt-dealers of New York City" and whom she charged with entangling Nicaragua in so much debt that it was in danger of losing its independence to American marines. In discussing the burden of debt under which the city of Portland labored, she referenced Blyth, Witter & Company. Though she sometimes used heightened language that racists often deployed, as when she denounced "our great financiers" who traffic in "interest-bearing debt" as "sub-human," Baldwin never identified a Jewish firm as such.[70] In this she did not follow earlier Greenback writers with whom she was undoubtedly familiar, men like Ignatius Donnelly and William "Coin" Harvey, who had drawn a link between financial elites and Jews, nor did she follow in the path of populist, temperance advocate, and suffragist Mary Elizabeth Lease, who called Grover Cleveland "the agent of Jewish bankers and British gold."[71]

And yet when Baldwin laid out a political path to oppose finance capitalists, she demonstrated how complicated the politics of left and right could be. She urged readers of her treatise to reelect two men, Senators Thomas E. Watson of Georgia and Robert La Follette of Wisconsin, both of whom she identified as "militant fighters against the debt-clans."[72] Baldwin placed herself within the broad range of the left, much of which would come together to support a La Follette presidential run in 1924, but Watson is a reminder of how culturally complex anticapitalism could be. Watson, we might remember, had positively reviewed the original treatise, *Money Talks*, expressing a latter-day populist understanding of banking and finance. But he had also been among those who praised the rise of the second Ku Klux Klan, and he had celebrated the manhood of those who broke into the jail in Atlanta to lynch Leo Frank, the Jewish superintendent in a textile factory, convicted of raping and murdering a female white employee but pardoned by the Georgia governor.[73] Baldwin apparently saw nothing troubling about Watson's engagement with the Klan, which was more overtly based on racial domination than her own anti-Catholicism.

And yet these Klan-based affiliations raise questions about the meaning that Klan involvement held for radicals like Baldwin. A 1927 letter that Eleanor received from E. M. Baldwin sheds some light on the nature of her affiliations, but it hardly answers the questions that they raise. E. M. Baldwin, who had lived in the Northwest but had in old age moved to San Diego, understood himself to be engaged in an effort to "forward fundamental Americanism . . . doing nothing else but spreading this kind of gospel over the country," which included the preparation of "patriotic matter" for newspapers. What he meant by fundamental Americanism was in line with Klan understandings, as he complained to Eleanor that the Los Angeles Public Library did not have a copy of the King James Bible. He recounted that in a couple of suburban towns he had the same experience, and was told by a librarian in one of them that if he wanted it so badly he "might buy a copy." He asked Eleanor if Portland's public library had a copy. Posing a war against Protestant Christianity, he suggested that a movement was afoot to "throw this book out of all Public Libraries as well as out of the schools." The letter, though opaque about many things, is thematically oriented around issues that might, if they were clear enough, help us understand Eleanor's participation with the Klan. The correspondent responded to an inquiry Eleanor had made regarding the Dreyfus case, asserting that, aside from some comments regarding Zola's relationship with his wife, he did "not for a moment doubt it was as you say." He also recommended that Eleanor read an editorial in the *Dearborn Independent* "on the attack Jews have made upon Mr. Ford's assertions regarding their control of the Federal banking system," and asked for her opinion of it. He referred to Eleanor's "suggestion concerning Mr. Ford's surroundings and the influences which may be directing affairs for him unknown to himself," and assured her "that this information will be handled carefully, if at all." He continued by stating, "I am bumping into all sorts of situations which are, to say the least, puzzling."[74]

There is no record of Eleanor Baldwin's side of the correspondence, just these few mentions in the response that she received. And that leaves us with the task of making an assessment without a complete record. In that way, it is like the second Ku Klux Klan itself, as historians have found the organization difficult to pin down. Some historians, particularly those who have examined the Klan in the West, have portrayed the Klan as a grassroots organization dedicated to challenging local elites and ensuring the application of law to those who violated community values. As Shawn Lay summarizes this scholarship, "the great bulk of Klansmen were not aberrationally racist, religiously bigoted, or socially alienated, although they were more likely to openly express and act upon their views."[75] Other scholars have found a darker, more regressive Klan in the historical record. For Nancy MacLean, the Klan represented a "reactionary populism" that posed a strong resemblance to the rise of fascism in Europe, and that its success was dependent on the weakness of the labor movement in the early 1920s. Contrary to the qualified depictions by Lay and others, MacLean argues there was little progressive about the Klan. Concerned about growing assertiveness among both African Americans and women, the Klan sought to impose a traditional order on a rapidly changing culture. For MacLean, violence and lynchings were central to their purpose. In his assessment of the Oregon Klan, Robert Johnston portrays a Klan that diluted the radical content of produceristic language. He asserts, "if the Portland Klan had any connection to populism, it came through hijacking the grand tradition of Portland's direct democrats rather than serving as a vehicle for combat with elites." The Klan's leadership worked actively, Johnston writes, to "disconnect those in the middle from anti-elitist politics of any kind, whether reactionary or radical."[76]

And yet some committed progressives found their way to the Klan. In her history of women and the KKK, Kathleen Blee recounts the personal history of Indianan Lillian Rouse, a strong progressive and women's rights advocate who described herself as a socialist who supported a guaranteed living wage and governmental aid for the elderly. Blee concludes that Rouse "saw no contradiction between those positions and the Klan."[77] In Portland, there are signs that the emergence of Baldwin's anti-Catholic political writings did little to damage her reputation or limit the circles in which she moved. In 1920, she was elected corresponding secretary of the Woman's Press Club, a position to which she was named again in 1925. Her condemnations of the Catholic Church certainly did not make her an outcast.[78]

But we don't know what Eleanor Baldwin felt about the Ku Klux Klan. She contributed to the Klan newspaper and supported the anti-Catholic politics out of which the Klan would grow in Oregon, but we know too little about what she thought about that organization to make any firm conclusions regarding the meaning of her experience. It was an astounding leap for the daughter of an abolitionist who maintained the integrity of that position well into her adult professional life. She understood the history of the original Klan, the way in which it was deployed to terrorize recently freed African Americans, and that its Progressive Era revival was in many regards grounded in an increasing rapprochement between whites in the North with those of the South. This growing racial solidarity of white people may have been furthered by the romance of the old South and the Lost Cause, bringing with it an appreciation for the anti-industrial and premodern elements of Southern culture, much as those concerns had stimulated an aesthetic and philosophical interest in things Asian and in the Arts and Crafts movement. Much of the cultural response to industrialism was compatible with the Klan's emphasis on honor and the protection of women. Yet there is nothing in Baldwin's prior writings to suggest that she could absorb the full ethos of the revived KKK.

But we can draw a few conclusions: there is no evidence that Klan involvement mitigated her own radicalism; her defense of the Bolshevik Revolution in the nascent Soviet Union and her heightened anti-banker language suggest that certain Klan measures, especially if oriented toward limiting the influence of the Catholic Church, were understood to be populist radical measures. For Baldwin, the Catholic hierarchy appeared as an encrusted reactionary organization devoted to hindering the liberation of all working people from oppression, and she relied on old Protestant adages about the Catholic Church to make her arguments. That says more about Baldwin and the idiosyncratic way in which she responded to postwar society and politics than it does about the Klan itself. There were others like W. S. U'Ren, otherwise a strong civil libertarian who was concerned about the Catholic hierarchy's interest in curbing the spread of democratic values. Defending Communists and challenging Catholic votes in a primary may not have been understood by U'Ren as contradictions. In a sense, the KKK may have provided many Americans with a Rorschach test: attracting a variety of prejudices and concerns, the Klan provided many with the hope that it could reinvigorate a progressive worldview. The Klan, in the minds of those who flocked to its banner in the early 1920s, could be many different and contradictory things. The abrupt collapse of the Klan in the middle of the 1920s may have been a reflection of the ideological incoherence of that organization.

Baldwin's anti-Catholic activism sheds some light on how some Oregon radicals, ranging from Tom Burns to William U'Ren, could find in the Ku Klux Klan, if only for a moment, a progressive social movement. There is little evidence that any of these folks shared the racial antagonisms that so many Klansmen and Klanswomen possessed and often expressed. While living in an environment in which leftist politics and racist anti-Asian politics had long been strange bedfellows, Baldwin resisted the temptation to stoke those fires, and early in her Portland career, she defended Asian immigrants as talented newcomers who would make good citizens. Similarly, she made plain her high regard for Jewish immigrants in Portland, and objected to statements that they had not suffered from antisemitism in the Russian Empire. She may have lost her column in the *Telegram* in 1909 because her defense of a white woman and Japanese man's right to marry led her into an unforeseen conflict over Irishness and civility. There may have been unacknowledged anti-Catholic prejudices that led her to make the assertion about the Irish that so offended J. Hennessey Murphy; this was a line of thinking not particularly unexpected, as so many New England Protestants shared an antipathy toward the Irish and Catholicism. But prior to the postwar era, there is little evidence of even that intolerant streak. Her expressions of support for recent immigrants, including Jews from eastern Europe, suggest that her intolerance was finely honed toward the Catholic hierarchy. For there are few signs, other than her associations in an era in which intolerance was on the rise, that anything had changed.

Yet the political climate had changed around her, and she articulated a response in two apparently contradictory ways: in her support for the Bolsheviks and her anti-Catholic writings. In the first instance, Baldwin responded to unexpected developments in eastern Europe that had been unleashed by the war, and she, like so many others on the political left, welcomed the communist revolution as a bellwether of a better, more egalitarian world, one in which individuals would no longer be crushed by poverty and the opprobrium of the wealthy. A new social world, one that she had assumed would eventually be brought into being by the spread of New Thought principles, and one in which the liberty of all to live decent and meaningful lives would be finally established. She did not see the Catholic Church in that way; in the aftermath of war, Baldwin concluded that the Catholic hierarchy sought to stop any such new social world from appearing, and she, like William U'Ren, sought to protect the schools and the ballot box from the influence of the Papacy.

Epilogue

After three years of illness, Eleanor Baldwin died on December 26, 1928, having been attended to during her long decline by friends. She was remembered in local obituaries in ways that were consistent with the manner in which she had written about herself. Local newspapers noted that her father had been a minister and "active abolitionist," and the *Oregonian* explained that she had "acquired her father's love for freedom and devoted a considerable [part] of her life to writing for the advancement of 'wage slaves.'"

The Oregon *Journal* similarly described her as possessing "a delicate, sensitive and sympathetic nature," and that "she felt keenly the oppression and injustice of the world's financial system." Three of the local dailies mentioned her work as the writer of "The Woman's Point of View" and *Money Talks*.[1] Though she lived long enough to praise the Bolsheviks and to work with the second Ku Klux Klan, there was no mention of these moments of more extreme politics. Instead, her obituaries depict her as representative of the development of a kind of liberalism that began with the insistence that individuals must be free, as manifest by abolition, and came to understand that freedom could be impinged upon by social and economic forces other than slavery.

Her death came a little more than four years before Franklin Delano Roosevelt would take office and intensify the process of inscribing statist interventions as a significant element of the twentieth-century liberal imagination. As the New Deal moved increasingly toward the interests of working people and the poor in 1935 with the passage of measures like the Social Security Act and the National Industrial Relations Act, the linkage between the House of Labor and the Democratic Party became a more permanent fixture of American politics. We do not know how Baldwin would have responded to this transforming moment in American politics, but some other Oregonians of her era provide examples of radicals who rejected the statist implications of the New Deal. Marie Equi, the Industrial Workers of the World–supporting radical physician who articulated anticapitalist positions similar to Baldwin's, never warmed to FDR even though he granted her a full pardon for her conviction under the wartime Sedition Act. She found him to be "slippery as an eel," and she believed that his talk of peace in the 1930s masked preparation for war. Her recent biographer presumes that she voted Republican upon regaining her citizenship.[2]

Perhaps more telling is the personal political trajectory of William S. U'Ren, who remained politically active into the 1920s and 1930s. After moving to Portland from Oregon City, he defended striking workers and communists in court against employers and the government, and he would become a leading advocate of civil liberties. Though he dismissed the Bolshevist ideal of the dictatorship of the proletariat as "the rankest nonsense," he stated, "there is much commendable in the communist state the communist party seeks to install in America." Yet the radical U'Ren, so strongly influenced by Henry George and the labor theory of value, could not make the transition to the Democratic Party, instead condemning the New Deal's paternalism. Despite his sustained belief that everyone had a right to a job, he opposed the New Deal and its panoply of work-relief agencies. U'Ren embraced the vision of an economically independent citizenry, which was ultimately incompatible with what he considered the "dole." As Oregon journalist Richard Neuberger put it, U'Ren came to believe "that political authority has become too concentrated in Washington D.C." Neuberger added that U'Ren worried about the "'growing influence of the military' in government." By his death at midcentury, Oregon's lawgiver had concluded that the New Deal state did not fulfill the objectives of progressive radicalism.[3] And we might remember that U'Ren, like Baldwin, had been imbued not only with an economically radical politics, but also with a Protestant sense of morality that may have led both into some kind of temporary alliance with the KKK. The political trajectories of U'Ren and Equi remind us that the development of the modern left in the United States was not preordained or linear. Some radicals turned to the Republican Party after the Great Depression and in reaction against the New Deal.

For Baldwin, who did not live long enough to grapple with the statist liberalism of the New Deal, the best clues we have are the concerns that she registered in the manuscript that she was working on in the 1920s, one that would never find its way into print. The new political tract seemed to move further from the liberal's notion of individualism than its predecessor, *Money Talks*, as Baldwin increasingly stressed the organic nature of society. Children, she declared, must be taught that their sense of "separateness" is "mistaken," and instead must come to realize that, like the cells that compose our bodies,

> our physical bodies are vitally and closely related—each to
> all the others—so in the great social body of which we are
> parts, the relationship is just as vital, whether we wish it or
> not—between us and all the millions of other human units,
> which are, with us the structural cells of the social body,
> "Our Country," the United States of America. It is because
> of this fact that enlightened selfishness must promptly, in
> defense begin to realize and act upon the scientific truth that
> "an injury to one is an injury to all."[4]

The problem with socialists, she claimed, was not that they criticized individualism, it was that they did not see that it was the money-lenders who destroyed the organic unity of the social organism.

But the manuscript, with all its internal contradictions, was not aimed at getting socialists to pay more attention to money and finance. Instead, it was Baldwin's attempt to move New Thought philosophy away from the celebration of the self, a direction in which it was inexorably moving. "To be content to have substance provided for us, knowing ourselves to be a part of this ailing social body," she posed, "without doing our best to heal it of its malady, cannot be the highest type of New Thought." She pleaded with the "great body of New Thought readers of the Elizabeth Towne Publishing Company's literature and philosophy" to recognize that their "consciousness of Infinite Substance . . . demands all the same freedom from economic slavery and starvation that you claim individually."[5] She wrote to "urge the souls of New Thoughters" to recognize the cause of "the millions in torment," even those "whom we call the criminals, because as an alternative to any one of the other phases of poverty banditry suits their temperament better, since more honorable if less dangerous employment is denied them" by the manipulation of the economy by bankers.

She called on the metaphysical community to recognize the humanity of "the wretchedly weak—also products of our sick social body—who drift into bread lines, shelter, alms houses, prisons, jails and many who at last die, penniless suicides on the dissecting table."[6] Baldwin sought to take the themes of prosperity that often ran through New Thought discourse and orient them toward social justice rather than mere personal success by stressing the interconnectedness of minds and bodies, asserting:

> As surely as God has decreed health, wealth, happiness and brotherhood as the rewards of obedience of the laws of the social body, disobedience of these laws persisted in a little longer will certainly slay this living organism in which you and I are structural cells and twentieth century civilization plunge downward to death over the same path traversed by the nations of old, from Babylon to Rome.[7]

The analysis still offered the same historical trajectory of progress and liberation that had accompanied much of her writing. She denounced capital as "the last refuge of those who would enslave to themselves the rest of the human race." Indebtedness imposed on the masses of humanity "all the hardships, humiliations, and degradation of slavery." This was a form of slavery that was not as obvious as chattel slavery; the belief held by debtors they are "citizens in a 'free country' . . . is what has kept them in bond-age." And overcoming it would bring ultimate liberation; she termed "interest-bearing debt" as "the last shackle that will hold in slavery the millions to a few of their kind. There is nothing to follow its removal but—Freedom!"[8] In the 1920s, Baldwin attempted to reinvigorate the socialistic strain in New Thought that was manifest by others like J. Wilson Stitt and Henry Victor Morgan. But she was tilting at consumerist windmills.

Some liberals like Rex Tugwell, who would reorient New Deal policy toward embracing mass consumerism, had been influenced by University of Pennsylvania economist Simon Patten, whom historian William Leach has called "America's most influential economist of capitalist abundance and consumption." Patten was among those economists who moved the question of how to assess value from the position that labor was the source, a view held by earlier political economists like Adam Smith as well as generations of labor radicals, to the notion of marginal utility, in which consumer preferences ultimately determine the value of a commodity. Many liberals would come to understand mass consumption as the means of overcoming older patterns of boom and bust that were grounded in industrial overproduction. For his emphasis on mass consumption, Patten has been termed by Leach as a "mind-cure" economist. While Patten took New Thought–type thinking in the direction of mass consumption, he also signaled the changing theoretical approach to the relationship between corporations, banking, and the state that would characterize liberal political economy in the middle of the twentieth century. Instead of condemning bankers as nonproducers, Patten celebrated their role in moving money through the national economy. He termed "banker morality" as "the highest morality because it lacks the limits that national, local, or creed morality possesses." Modern liberalism embraced the logic of consumerism and attempted to use the state to spread its benefits more broadly.[9]

Progressive Era radicalism was a different moral universe in Baldwin's hands. In "The Woman's Point of View," Baldwin had squared up against the consumerist logic of the woman's page on many occasions, questioning degrading practices by employers and calling on women to resist the lure of fashion, especially when it came at the cost of animal life. Her journalistic career was organized at one of the critical spots in the development of mass consumer society, where female consumers patronized the new marketplaces in city centers. But Baldwin was poised between new and old social ethics, and she always had been. On the one hand, she had rejected the self-denial that was such a hallmark of Victorian womanhood, seeing it as conflicting with her aspirations for a future full of independent women who lived their own lives rather than subordinating them entirely for the benefit of husbands and children. Many female New Thought writers had taken a similar position, suggesting that women, like all human beings, needed to strive for self-fulfillment.[10] Yet Baldwin, like some who leaned toward socialism in the New Thought community, still condemned economic selfishness, seeing it as a sign of atavistic thinking that prevented true progress and evolution from occurring. Baldwin's thinking is reminiscent of that of Charlotte Perkins Gilman, who similarly saw in female subordination a destructive self-denial and argued that female independence would not only benefit women, but ultimately would lead men to act better. Gilman had argued that a man, engaged in the evolutionary competition for women, would no longer find it necessary to subordinate the social good to earn enough money to attract a wife and potential mother, since the woman herself was economically independent and no longer dependent on a man for sustenance. Instead of being concerned about being economically supported, the woman would choose the man who would make the best father. Less female self-denial meant that men would become less selfish and that society would be put on the evolutionary path toward progress.[11]

As much as female activists sought to break free of Victorian conventions that placed women at the center of the home, opting instead to move them to the center of society, there was still much in the Victorian mind-set that underlay their activism. Many continued to embrace the Victorian code of self-denial, understanding it as a set of social prescriptions that prevented men from abusing women and capitalists from abusing workers. Though many sexologists and psychologists had for decades been publishing work that challenged the vision of the passionless woman, the flowering of a more sexualized consumer culture in the 1920s would shift the ground on which many women lived their lives and engaged in advocacy. Women like Jane Addams and Charlotte Perkins Gilman would reject the hyperheterosexual culture in which young, independent women engaged during that era, the former complaining of their "astounding emphasis on sex," and the latter in a similar vein writing, "It is sickening to see so many of the newly freed abusing that freedom in a mere imitation of masculine weakness and vice."[12]

Baldwin would live out her last years, the last three of them mired in illness, during this period; we have no sense of how she responded to the Jazz Age. But her earlier writings indicate that she occupied much of the ground that many women held at the turn of the twentieth century. Women like Jane Addams and Florence Kelley in Chicago not only worked for social justice through politics and outreach at Hull House, the settlement house that they founded to work with impoverished immigrant working-class communities, but they also operated the house as a source of female community in which independent single women could maintain themselves. For many women reformers, economic reform and challenges to the dictates of capitalists went

hand in hand with an expansion of women's rights and growing opportunities for women to maintain an independent existence outside
of marriage. That Baldwin lived such a life and was concerned that
housing be provided for others like her put her squarely within this
emerging and expanding realm of female public activity. What makes
her particularly interesting is that she articulated this understanding
on a daily basis in a woman's column.

The meaning of her dalliance with the Klan complicates our understanding of her life, such as how the embrace of Victorian standards
of sexual restraint might complicate our grasp of other women like
Gilman and Addams. But we have no shortage of examples of people
getting caught unexpectedly by the forces of change. The capture of
the Republican Party by a billionaire real estate developer and reality
show host who appealed to white working-class people by raising fears
of violence by Muslims, Mexican immigrants, and African Americans
and by decrying elites who benefit from global trade provides us with
a reflection of how the political ground on which we rest is capable of
being shaken to the core. Many conservative populists, the kind who
have used Oregon's initiative process to try to criminalize abortion
and limit the rights of gay citizens, rallied to Donald Trump's message
even though his commitment to their position on those issues was at
best unclear and potentially hostile. But so have many Republican
Party stalwart politicians who recognize that Trump does not align
himself with all the positions that Republicans expect their party to
take, including on matters of foreign policy. And many of the supporters of socialist Bernie Sanders who declared "Never Hillary" and who
seemed unfazed by a potential Trump presidency further remind us
that events move quickly, and that unexpected alliances may form that
with hindsight may seem inexplicable.[13] In such uncertain moments,
when political structures appear to be in disarray and new threats
seemingly emerge, individuals must make relatively quick decisions
as to where the threats to the good society lie. In the aftermath of
World War I, the identification of the Catholic hierarchy as a threat to
a progressive future seemed credible to U'Ren and Baldwin; that it led
them to work with the Klan and its forces of reaction confounds us. In
hindsight, the Klan seems like it was the much greater threat to personal liberty and progress. But to them, the Catholic Church seemed to
endanger processes that promised further progressive development.

And so Eleanor Baldwin reminds us that the past is as difficult to navigate as the present, filled with all the complications that make up individual human beings, and all the more true with complex modern societies. In many ways, she is the beginning of a conversation that I first imagined when researching microfilm at the Oregon Historical Society, precipitated by a moment mentioned in the preface. It was then that I heard the young woman next to me exclaim that the labor movement's opposition to Prohibition was a natural position, exactly what she had expected to find. As a history professor who has taught undergraduates for nearly three decades, I have sufficient opportunities to respond to students who want an easily understood and rational past, "it's more complicated than that." I did not feel a need to make that instance in the microfilm room a teaching moment.

But this book provides a more nuanced approach to the past, one that historians often desire our students to adopt. It is probably clear that I find Eleanor Baldwin to have had many admirable traits, that she was a woman who used her education to become a public intellectual of sorts, espousing the values of human liberation. Her insistence that women not only have political rights but also should be included in all aspects of social life as independent citizens speaks to the continuing global fight that equate women's independence with social improvement. Her hatred of the levels of economic inequality that had emerged during the Gilded Age speaks to the widening cleavages in our own society between financiers and corporate executives, the threatened middle class, and an increasingly marginalized working class. In the wake of the Occupy Wall Street movement of 2011, and the surprising enthusiasm with which socialist Bernie Sanders challenged the more moderate Hillary Clinton for the Democratic Party presidential nomination, class themes have new resonance in contemporary political life. For those who might find Thomas Piketty's magnum opus long and tedious, Baldwin's columns still clearly and simply speak truth to power. Much of this clarity was rooted in two contradictory religious traditions: the moral reform of her Wesleyan Methodist father, who understood the battle against slavery as a confrontation with evil, and the emerging New Thought tradition, which provided the philosophical certainty that the world was moving steadily and naturally toward true progress. This is most likely at the heart of her support for the

Klan and its anti-Catholic politics, which may seem to readers like a contradiction—as would her lifelong embrace of abolitionism—but it more likely made it an imperative.

Notes

PREFACE

1 *Western American*, September 7, 1923.
2 Lawrence Levine, *Defender of the Faith: William Jennings Bryan, the Last Decade 1915-1925* (Cambridge, MA: Harvard University Press, 1987); C. Vann Woodward, *Tom Watson: Agrarian Rebel* (New York: Oxford University Press, 1963); Peter Sleeth, "Read You Mutt! The Life and Times of Tom Burns, the Most Arrested Man in Portland," *Oregon Historical Quarterly* 112 (Spring 2011): 58-81.
3 Oregon *Daily Journal*, January 1, 1929; *Oregonian*, December 30, 1928

INTRODUCTION

1 On literacy and knowledge in women's clubs, see Sandra Haarsager, *Organized Womanhood: Cultural Politics in the Pacific Northwest, 1840-1920* (Norman: University of Oklahoma Press, 1997), 13-14.
2 Alice Fahs, *Out on Assignment: Newspaper Women and the Making of Modern Public Space* (Chapel Hill: University of North Carolina Press, 2011), 13; Elizabeth Faue, *Writing the Wrongs: Eva Valesh and the Rise of Labor Journalism* (Ithaca, NY: Cornell University Press, 2002).
3 *Oregonian*, May 5, 1912.
4 *Oregonian*, May 5, 1912.
5 *Oregonian*, March 6, 1913.
6 Membership List, 1904-1925, Folder 2, Box 6, Portland Women's Club, mss. 1084, Oregon Historical Society (OHS) Library; *Oregonian*, January 6 and 23, 1910; March 6, 1910. On women's clubs, see Haarsager, *Organized Womanhood*; and Martha Killian Barefoot, "Between 'True Women' and 'New Women': Oregon Women's Clubs, 1890-1916 (MA thesis, University of Oregon, 1994), Folder 49, Box 10, Portland Woman's Club Records, mss 1084, OHS Library.
7 For instances in which Baldwin gave talks or led a Woman's Press Club meeting, see *Oregonian*, December 2, 1908; January 7, 1909; February 27, 1910; January 28, 1912; January 11, 1914; February 3, 1915; March 14, 1917; January 5, 1918; December 4, 1918; January 6, 1920; February 8, 1920; January 9, 1921; October 5, 1924. Baldwin was elected corresponding secretary of the Woman's Press Club more than once. *Oregonian*, May 9, 1920; May 8, 1921.
8 *Oregonian*, February 7, 1915.
9 *Oregonian*, January 17 and 18, 1908; November 6, 1908.
10 *Oregonian*, November 19, 1918.
11 Ruth Barnes Moynihan, *Rebel for Rights: Abigail Scott Duniway* (New Haven, CT: Yale University Press, 1983); Kimberly Jensen, "'Neither Head Nor Tail to the Campaign': Esther Pohl Lovejoy and the Oregon Woman Suffrage Victory of 1912," *Oregon Historical Quarterly* 108 (Fall 2007): 350-83; and idem,

Oregon's Doctor to the World: Esther Pohl Lovejoy and a Life in Activism (Seattle: University of Washington Press, 2012); Janice Dilg, "'For Working Women in Oregon': Caroline Gleason/Sister Miriam Theresa and Oregon's Minimum Wage Law, *Oregon Historical Quarterly* 110 (Spring 2009): 96-129; Michael Helquist, *Marie Equi: Radical Politics and Outlaw Passions* (Corvallis: Oregon State University Press, 2015); and Kimberly Mangun, *A Force for Change: Beatrice Morrow Cannady and the Struggle for Civil Rights in Oregon, 1912-1936* (Corvallis: Oregon State University Press, 2010).

12 Maureen A. Flanagan, *Seeing with Their Hearts: Chicago Women and the Vision of the Good City, 1871-1933* (Princeton, NJ: Princeton University Press, 2002), 8.

13 Maureen A. Flanagan, *America Reformed: Progressives and Progressivisms, 1890s-1920s* (New York: Oxford University Press, 2007).

14 Valentine Prichard, "Origin and Development of Settlement Work in Portland Including Free Medical Work," typescript, 1942, OHS Library.

15 Millie R. Trumbull, *The Child Who Works* (Portland: Oregon State Congress of Mothers, OHS Library, n.d.). On Trumbull's public denunciation of racism in the 1920s, see Mangun, *Force for Change*, 166-67.

16 *Woman's Tribune*, August 11, 1906, as quoted in Robert D. Johnston, *The Radical Middle Class: Populist Democracy and the Question of Capitalism in Progressive Era Portland, Oregon* (Princeton, NJ: Princeton University Press, 2003), 22. Alice Kessler-Harris, *In Pursuit of Equity: Women, Men, and the Quest for Economic Citizenship in 20th-Century America* (New York: Oxford University Press, 2001), 19-63; Nancy Cott, *The Grounding of Modern Feminism* (New Haven, CT: Yale University Press, 1989).

17 Molly Ladd-Taylor, *Mother-Work: Women, Child-Welfare, and the State, 1890-1930* (Urbana: University of Illinois Press, 1994), 7. Ladd-Taylor argues that maternalists and feminists helped shape the nature of the social welfare state, the former by failing to move beyond the vision of the domestic mother, the latter by neglecting to offer a different model of the welfare state. For an argument that stresses female professional identity as structuring the shape of reform, see Robyn Muncy, *Creating a Female Dominion in American Reform, 1890-1935* (New York: Oxford University Press, 1991). See also Seth Koven and Sonya Michel, "Womanly Duties: Maternalist Politics and the Origins of Welfare States in France, Germany, and the United States, 1880-1920," *American Historical Review* 95 (October 1990): 1076-108, quotation on 1077.

18 Eleanor Baldwin, *Money Talks* (Holyoke, MA: Elizabeth Towne, c. 1915), 2.

19 Nearly forty years ago, Herbert Gutman demonstrated the limits of capitalist cultural authority in the Gilded Age in *Work, Culture and Society in Industrializing America* (New York: Vintage Books, 1977), which has inspired numerous works produced by a range of talented scholars. For an interesting variant of this analysis, which argues that in the 1890s capitalists turned to the federal courts and the use of the injunction to evade the hostility of local jury trials in industrial disputes, see William E. Forbath, *Law and the Shaping of the American Labor Movement* (Cambridge, MA: Harvard University Press, 1991).

20 Her petty bourgeois origins distinguish Baldwin from other female journalists who wrote to support labor politics, women like the much wealthier radical Mary Heaton Vorse and the working-class Eva Valesh, who wrote primarily for labor and populist newspapers. Dee Garrison, *Mary Heaton Vorse: Life of an American Insurgent* (Philadelphia, PA: Temple University Press, 1989); and Faue, *Writing the Wrongs*.

21 Johnston, *Radical Middle Class*.

22 G. Thomas Edwards, *Sowing Good Seeds: The Northwest Suffrage Campaigns of Susan B. Anthony* (Portland: Oregon Historical Society Press, 1990), 230; Ida Husted Harper, ed., *The History of Woman Suffrage* (New York: J. J. Little and Ives, 1922), 5:147.

23 Rebecca Mead, *How the Vote Was Won: Woman Suffrage in the Western United States, 1868-1914* (New York: New York University Press, 2004); Jensen, "'Neither Head Nor Tail to the Campaign.'" On the growing conservatism of the national suffrage leadership, see Aileen Kraditor, *The Ideas of the Woman Suffrage Movement, 1890-1920* (New York: Columbia University Press, 1965). Duniway had long made class resentment a part of her appeal to rural women, and she supported much of what appeared on the platforms of the Knights of Labor and the People's (Populist) Party. Her failed 1910 initiative to grant the vote to women "taxpayers" was a break with this pattern. As Oregon writer and activist Sarah Evans wrote, "Both men and women, many of them the staunchest suffragists, openly opposed it and it was bitterly fought by labor and the fraternal organizations," and "there was general satisfaction when it was defeated." Harper, *History of Woman Suffrage*, 6:544.

24 Charles Postel, *The Populist Vision* (New York: Oxford University Press, 2007), 76. In this, the populist movement as a whole was more supportive of woman suffrage and equal rights than the Socialist Party, which on the national level reacted with some aloofness to what many perceived as a bourgeois-dominated movement. Mari Jo Buhle, *Women and American Socialism, 1870-1920* (Urbana: University of Illinois Press, 1981).

25 Harry Stein, "Printers and Press Operators: The *Oregonian* Remembered," *Oregon Historical Quarterly* 115 (Summer 2014): 208-23; George S. Turnbull, *History of Oregon Newspapers* (Portland, OR: Binfords & Mort, 1939), 178-80. Marshall N. Dana, longtime editor of the *Journal*, would remember Carroll (who had edited the *Journal* before moving on to the *Telegram*) as the kind of editor who "delighted in a crusade." *The First 50 Years of the Oregon Journal: A Newspaper Story* (Portland, OR: Binford & Morts, 1951), 73. On the existence of a Portland establishment, see E. Kimbark MacColl, *Merchants, Money and Power: The Portland, 1843-1913* (Portland, OR: Georgian Press, 1988).

26 For the women who worked at Hull House in Chicago, see Kathryn Kish Sklar, *Florence Kelley and the Nation's Work* (New Haven, CT: Yale University Press, 1995). The efforts of Lillian Wald, who founded the Henry Street Settlement in New York City, to bridge the gap between rich and poor, are covered in David Huyssen's *Progressive Inequality: Rich and Poor in New York, 1890-1920* (Cambridge, MA: Harvard University Press, 2014), chaps. 6-8. On Pohl Lovejoy, see Jensen, *Oregon's Doctor to the World*, chap. 5.

27 Her sister, Celia, criticized Henry George for putting land reform ahead of currency and banking reform as the proper radical remedy for poverty. Another sister, Maria Jerusha Small, had a son, J. T. Small, who ran for office on labor tickets in Provincetown, Massachusetts, where he ran a bakery and advertised radical currency tracts. See Celia Baldwin Whitehead, "Henry George and Nehemiah," *The Arena* 15 (1896): 196-201, and on J. T. Small, see Barnstable *Patriot*, September 27 and November 8, 1887.

28 Tension between labor activists and former abolitionists is nicely developed in David Montgomery, *Beyond Equality: Labor and the Radical Republicans* (Urbana: University of Illinois Press, 1981). For relations between abolitionists and the antebellum labor movement, see Eric Foner, "Abolitionism and the Labor Movement in Antebellum America," in *Anti-Slavery, Religion, and Reform:*

Essays in Memory of Roger Anstey, ed. Christine Bolt and Seymour Drescher (Folkestone, UK: Wm Dawson & Son, 1980), 254-71.

29 William James, *The Varieties of Religious Experience: A Study in Human Nature* (New York: Longman, Green, 1917), 105-6.

30 William Leach provides a good example. Speaking of New Thought and other "mind-cure" traditions, Leach argued that they reflected "in the most committed way the American conviction that people could shape their own destinies and find total happiness." For Leach, New Thought was the paradigmatic consumer-ist religion, one whose influence transcended its small number of full adherents as Americans adopted the ethos of the department store and mass consumption. *Land of Desire: Merchants, Power, and the Rise of a New American Culture* (New York: Vintage Books, 1993), 226-30, quotation on 237. A similar characterization of New Thought is provided by Gail Thain Parker, *Mind Cure in New England: From the Civil War to World War I* (Hanover, NH: University Press of New England, 1973). More recently, Kate Bowler has posed New Thought as the source of the modern "prosperity gospel" movement in American Protestantism. *Blessed: A History of the American Prosperity Gospel* (New York: Oxford University Press, 2013), esp. chap. 1.

31 Catharine L. Albanese, "Introduction: Awash in a Sea of Metaphysics," *Journal of the American Academy of Religion* 75 (September 2007): 582-88. Albanese's magisterial *A Republic of Mind and Spirit: A Cultural History of American Metaphysical Religion* (New Haven, CT: Yale University Press, 2008) is the best introduction to the subject. On Peale, see Richard Weiss, *The American Myth of Success: From Horatio Alger to Norman Vincent Peale* (Urbana: University of Illinois Press, 1988), 223-34. For Jackson Lears, the metaphysical traditions reflected a broader cultural rejection of the cold certainties of Calvinist religion and an adoption of a "therapeutic ethos" that helped smooth the path toward a mass consumer society. *No Place of Grace: Antimodernism and the Transformation of American Culture, 1880-1920* (New York: Pantheon, 1981).

32 Beryl Satter, *Each Mind a Kingdom: American Women, Sexual Purity, and the New Thought Movement, 1875-1920* (Berkeley: University of California Press, 2001). On women's rights and the earlier spiritualist movement, see Anne Braude, *Radical Spirits: Spiritualism and Women's Rights in Nineteenth-Century America* (Boston, MA: Beacon Press, 1989).

33 Weiss, *American Myth of Success*, 162. Weiss's recognition of contradictory ele-ments in New Thought attitudes about consumerism is consistent with the work of historians examining the origins of consumerism among nineteenth-century labor advocates. See Lawrence Glickman, *A Living Wage: American Workers and the Making of Consumer Society* (Ithaca, NY: Cornell University Press, 1999).

34 Wallace D. Wattles, *Financial Success through Creative Thought, or The Science of Getting Rich* (Holyoke, MA: Elizabeth Towne, 1915, reprinted by Health Research Books, 1998), 49, emphasis in original.

35 Ann Braude says that Duniway was not a spiritualist, and that she appreciated them only because they invited her to speak. *Radical Spirits*, 96. Stacey M. Robertson characterizes her as both a spiritualist and free religionist. *Parker Pillsbury, Radical Abolitionist, Male Feminist* (Ithaca, NY: Cornell University Press, 2000), 166. Ruth Barnes Moynihan portrays Duniway's interest in spiritu-alism as an outgrowth of her religious rationalism. *Rebel for Rights*, 133. Carole Glauber notes that independent photographer Lily White was connected to the New Thought community. "Eyes of the Earth: Lily White, Sarah Ladd, and the Oregon Camera Club," *Oregon Historical Quarterly* 108 (Spring 2007): 34-67.

36 See Michael Saler, "Modernity and Enchantment: A Historiographic Review," *American Historical Review* 111 (June 2006): 692-716. For a discussion of secular thought, enchantment, and religious sensibilities that stresses the hold of common sense philosophy over evangelicals and spiritualists alike, see John Lardas Modern, *Secularism in Antebellum America, with Reference to Ghosts, Protestant Subcultures, Machines, and Their Metaphors* (Chicago, IL: University of Chicago Press, 2011).

37 Ann Taves, *Fits, Trances, and Visions: Experiencing Religious and Explaining Experience from Wesley to James* (Princeton, NJ: Princeton University Press, 1999), 172-73.

38 The seminal work that has complicated our understanding of progressive "movements," is Samuel P. Hays, *Conservation and the Gospel of Efficiency: The Progressive Conservation Movement, 1890-1920* (Cambridge, MA: Harvard University Press, 1959). Hays's work has generated a great deal of scholarship, particularly its insights that conservation was rooted less in a rising of democratic forces against the "interests" and more in expertise and bureaucratic forms that often were supported by those very corporate forces. In many ways, Hays opened the door for others to subject progressivism to more critical inquiry. See James Weinstein, *The Corporate Ideal in the Liberal State, 1900-1918* (Boston: Beacon Press, 1968); and Gabriel Kolko, *The Triumph of Conservatism: A Reinterpretation of American History, 1900-1916* (New York: Free Press, 1963).

39 Recent works that have emphasized democratic progressive reform include Alan Dawley, *Struggles for Justice: Social Responsibility and the Liberal State* (Cambridge, MA: Belknap Press of Harvard University Press, 1991); idem, *Changing the World: American Progressives in War and Revolution* (Princeton, NJ: Princeton University Press, 2003); and Jackson Lears, *Rebirth of a Nation: The Making of Modern America, 1877-1920* (New York: HarperCollins, 2009). A survey of the Gilded Age that emphasizes continuity rather than disjuncture with the Progressive Era can be found in Rebecca Edwards, *New Spirits: Americans in the Gilded Age, 1865-1905* (New York: Oxford University Press, 2006).

40 The linkage between Progressive Era radicalism and abolition was manifest in the Cridge family. A prominent Portland single-taxer, Alfred Cridge (the younger), a member of the Typographical Union, wrote proudly that his father had been an abolitionist and by the 1880s was advocating the adoption of the initiative and referendum, governmental ownership of public utilities, and a proportional representation scheme that would increase the influence of working people. *American Federationist: Official Magazine of the American Federation of Labor* 19 (July 1912): 929.

41 Thomas Piketty, *Capital in the Twenty-First Century* (Cambridge, MA: Harvard University Press, 2014). Piketty correlates growing inequality with lower growth rates. Robert J. Gordon argues that the high rates of growth, which fueled higher wages, experienced for a century between 1870 and 1970 were a result of a unique concatenation of significant, life-altering inventions. *The Rise and Fall of American Growth: The U.S. Standard of Living Since the Civil War* (Princeton, NJ: Princeton University Press, 2016).

42 See the forum on "Populists and Progressives, Capitalism and Democracy," *Journal of the Gilded Age and Progressive Era* 13 (July 2014): 377-433.

43 Lawrence M. Lipin, *Workers and the Wild: Conservation, Consumerism, and Labor in Oregon, 1910-30* (Urbana: University of Illinois Press, 2007).

CHAPTER 1: THE SPREADING OF ABOLITIONIST ROOTS

1   Alfred Kazin, "Introduction," in Harriet Beecher Stowe, Uncle Tom's Cabin (NY: Bantam Books, 1981), vii.

2   There is a long literature on the causes of the Civil War; the interested reader might start with Michael F. Holt, *The Fate of Their Country: Politicians, Slavery Extension, and the Coming of the Civil War* (New York: Hill and Wang, 2004).

3   *The Nation*, August 2, 1877.

4   *Sunday Oregonian*, February 3, 1907, p. 7.

5   Harriet Beecher Stowe, *Uncle Tom's Cabin* (Toronto: Bantam Books, 1981), 442, emphasis in original.

6   Emphasis mine.

7   Eleanor F. Baldwin, "The Woman's Point of View," *Telegram*, February 5, 1907.

8   Pennsylvania, Church and Town Records, 1708-1985; Berlin Vital Records, vol. 1, p. 31, Connecticut State Library.

9   Henry Baldwin, "Personal Recollections of Naugatuck about 70 Years Ago," No. 1, reprinted in Naugatuck *Daily News*, July 30, 1927, photocopies held in File H 103, Naugatuck Historical Society Museum. The apple incident can be found in "Personal Recollections," No. 9. The 1860 Census lists Lucius as owning two thousand dollars in real estate and three hundred dollars in personal property. The town of Waterbury, from which Naugatuck seceded in 1844, records a purchase by Lucius of some of the family land as early as 1834. Town of Waterbury, Waterbury Land Records, vol. 44 (1834), p. 78.

10 "Personal Recollections," No. 29.

11 "Personal Recollections," Nos. 22 and 26.

12 See the 1870 Census: Massachusetts, County of Essex, Lynn, Ward 6; Connecticut Headstone Inscriptions, Hale Collection, vol. 78, Naugatuck, pp. 1-325, Connecticut State Library; Town of Naugatuck, Births, Marriages, Deaths, vol. 1, 1863-1884, p. 10, Naugatuck City Clerk Office.

13 "Personal Recollections," No. 7.

14 Constance McLaughlin Green, *History of Naugatuck, Connecticut* (New Haven, CT: Yale University Press, 1948), 51.

15 Green, 123.

16 Eric Baldwin, "'The Devil Begins to Roar': Opposition to Early Methodists in New England," *Church History* 75 (March 2006): 94-119; Nathan O. Hatch, "The Puzzle of American Methodism," *Church History* 63 (June 1994): 175-89. On the historical relationship between Methodism and challenges to orthodoxy, see Ann Taves, *Fits, Trances, and Visions: Experiencing Religion and Explaining Experience from Wesley to James* (Princeton, NJ: Princeton University Press, 1999).

17 Marlene Taylor, *A History of the Naugatuck Methodist Church in Connecticut* (Naugatuck, CT: Naugatuck United Methodist Church, 1988), 2-3. Taylor relies on material from the Naugatuck *Agitator*, a labor-friendly newspaper that was at times edited by Henry C. Baldwin.

18 "Personal Recollections," No. 13.

19 "Personal Recollections," Nos. 10, 14, and 45. On temperance within the New England Methodist Church, see Douglas J. Williamson, "The Rise of the New England Methodist Temperance Movement, 1823-1836," *Methodist History* 21 (1982): 3-28.

20 "Personal Recollections," No. 14; Douglas M. Strong, "Partners in Political Abolitionism: The Liberty Party and the Wesleyan Methodist Connection," *Methodist History* 23 (January 1985): 99-115; Chris Padget, "Hearing the

Antislavery Rank-and-File: The Wesleyan Methodist Schism of 1843," *Journal of the Early Republic* 12 (Spring 1992): 63-84.

21 *The True Wesleyan* (Boston), April 29, 1843.

22 "Personal Recollections," No. 48.

23 "Personal Recollections," No. 38.

24 Sheldon B. Thorpe, *The History of the Fifteenth Connecticut Volunteers in the War for the Defense of the Union, 1861-1865* (New Haven, CT: Price, Lee & Adkins, 1893), 156-57, 168, and 239-49.

25 Henry C. Baldwin to Charles D. Lewis, February 1, 1863, Soldier Studies: Civil War Voices, accessed February 10, 2017, http://www.soldierstudies.org/index.php?action=view_letter&Letter=299.

26 "Personal Recollections," No. 1.

27 Celia Baldwin Whitehead, "Pessimism," *North American Review* 108 (November 1918): 799-800.

28 See the 1870 Census, Naugatuck.

29 H. F. Donlan, *The Citizen Souvenir* (Waterbury, CT: A. C. Northrup, 1895), 30; Roger W. Tuttle, ed., *Biographies of Graduates of the Yale Law School, 1824-1899* (New Haven, CT: Tuttle, Morehouse, and Taylor, n.d.), 275; *Commemorative Biographical Record of New Haven County, Connecticut* (Chicago, IL: J. H. Beers, 1902), 1026-27.

30 See the 1880 Census, Naugatuck.

31 Naugatuck *Enterprise*, September 10, 1880; *New York Times*, September 16, 1884; *John Swinton's Paper*, September 14, 1884; Philadelphia *Inquirer*, July 6, 1880; New Haven *Register*, July 26, 1880.

32 *New York Times*, June 14, 1892; July 5, 1894; July 19, 1896; Tuttle, *Biographies of Graduates*, 275; *Obituary Record of Graduates of Yale University Deceased during the Academical Year Ending in June 1897*, no. 7 of the fourth printed series (June 1897), 489. On currency battles of the post–Civil War era, see Gretchen Ritter, *Goldbugs and Greenbacks: The Antimonopoly Tradition and the Politics of Finance in America* (Cambridge: Cambridge University Press, 1997); Milton Friedman and Anna Jacobson Schwartz, *A Monetary History of the United States, 1867-1960* (Princeton, NJ: Princeton University Press, 1963). On populism in the 1890s and its impact on early twentieth-century reform, see James Livingston, *Origins of the Federal Reserve System: Money, Class and Corporate Capitalism, 1890-1913* (Ithaca, NY: Cornell University Press, 1986).

33 Steven Minh, *A Nation of Counterfeiters: Capitalists, Con Men, and the Making of the United States* (Cambridge, MA: Harvard University Press, 2009). Still valuable is Bray Hammond, *Banks and Politics in America from the Revolution to the Civil War* (Princeton, NJ: Princeton University Press, 1957); and Robert V. Remini, *Andrew Jackson and the Bank War* (New York: W. W. Norton, 1967).

34 Irwin Unger, *The Greenback Era: A Social and Political History of American Finance, 1865-1879* (Princeton, NJ: Princeton University Press, 1964), 106.

34 Gretchen Ritter, *Goldbugs and Greenback*, 73.

36 "Personal Recollections," No. 40.

37 *John Swinton's Paper*, January 13, 1884.

38 *John Swinton's Paper*, October 18, 1885.

39 New Haven *Register*, October 7, 1882; Naugatuck *Weekly Review*, April 13, 1883.

40 *New York Times*, July 19, 1896.

41 *John Swinton's Paper*, November 29, 1885. In another letter, Baldwin surmised that Grant's "days of usefulness to the cause of freedom and justice ended when he ceased to be a soldier and took up the scepter of civilian rule." Ibid.,

September 15, 1885. The handling of the debt was a long-term concern of
Baldwin's. As chair of the Connecticut Greenback Convention in 1880, Baldwin
claimed "the country would be richer to-day had the national debt of two
billions been wiped out in two years after the war; then the country would not
be mortgaged for forty years." New Haven *Register*, March 19, 1880.

42 Eric Foner, *Free Soil, Free Labor, Free Men: The Ideology of the Republican Party
    before the Civil War* (New York: Oxford University Press, 1970).

43 *John Swinton's Paper*, June 15, 1884.

44 *John Swinton's Paper*, September 27, 1885. Italics in original.

45 *John Swinton's Paper*, March 7, 1886.

46 Naugatuck *Agitator*, November 19, 1887, Naugatuck Historical Society Museum.
    The New Haven *Register* of October 11, 1887, provides an account of a speech
    defending the convicted anarchists. On the Haymarket Affair, see James Green,
    *Death in the Haymarket: A Story of Chicago, the First Labor Movement and the
    Bombing That Divided Gilded Age America* (New York: Pantheon Books, 2006).

47 On the Knights' electoral activity in select cities, see Leon Fink, *Workingmen's
    Democracy: The Knights of Labor and American Politics* (Urbana: University of
    Illinois Press, 1985). For a discussion of the George campaign, see Robert Weir,
    "A Fragile Alliance: Henry George and the Knights of Labor," *American Journal
    of Economics and Sociology* 56 (October 1997): 421-39; David Scobey, "Boycotting
    the Politics Factory: Labor Radicals and the New York City Mayoral Election of
    1886," *Radical History Review* (1984): 280-325; and Lawrence M. Lipin, "Nature,
    the City, and the Family Circle: Domesticity and the Urban Home in Henry
    George's Thought," *Journal of the Gilded Age and Progressive Era* 13 (July 2014):
    305-35.

48 *John Swinton's Paper*, October 10, 1886, and November 21, 1886.

49 New Haven *Register,* October 21, 1890, and November 3, 1890.

50 On populism and the rise of the People's Party, see Lawrence Goodwyn,
    Democratic Promise: The Populist Movement in America (New York: Oxford
    University Press, 1976); Robert C. McMath Jr., *American Populism: A Social
    History 1877-1898* (New York: Hill and Wang, 1993); Charles Postel, *The Populist
    Vision* (New York: Oxford University Press, 2009).

51 The industrial themes of populism are discussed in Norman Pollack, *The Populist
    Response to Industrial America: Midwestern Populist Thought* (Cambridge, MA:
    Harvard University Press, 1976). On the use of the courts in labor struggles,
    see William Forbath, *Law and the Shaping of the American Labor Movement*
    (Cambridge, MA: Harvard University Press, 1991).

52 *New York Times*, May 13, 1894.

53 New Haven *Register*, August 2, 1894. The editor termed Baldwin "the socialist
    orator."

54 Hartford *Courant*, August 8, 1895.

55 Photocopies of Henry Baldwin's "Personal Recollections of Naugatuck about 70
    Years Ago," as they were printed in the Naugatuck *News*, beginning July 30,
    1927, are located in File H 103, Naugatuck Historical Society Museum,.

56 "Personal Recollections," No. 1. In a speech at a Labor Day celebration in New
    Haven, Baldwin condemned both the monopolies of money and of land as
    sources of working-class poverty. New Haven *Register*, September 3, 1894.

57 "Personal Recollections," No. 8.

58 "Personal Recollections," No. 9.

59 "Personal Recollections," No. 34.

60 "Personal Recollections," Nos. 14 and 49.

61 "Personal Recollections," No. 10.

62 "Personal Recollections," No. 49.

63 "Personal Recollections," No. 10.

64 "Personal Recollections," No. 49.

65 Among other family members engaged in Greenback-Labor politics, there is Eleanor's brother-in-law, Seth D. Bingham, who had married Frances Adelaide Baldwin, the sibling born just before Henry. Bingham was named to the state committee for the independent labor campaign of 1890, which had named Henry as the candidate for governor. New Haven *Register*, October 21, 1890. It is unclear how or whether the family's Methodism might explain the anticapitalist ethics of many of Eleanor's siblings. On the Methodist tradition's ambiguous relationship with capitalist ethics, see William R. Sutton, *Journeymen for Jesus: Evangelical Artisans Confront Capitalism in Jacksonian Baltimore* (University Park: Pennsylvania State University Press, 1998), esp. chaps. 2 and 3.

66 Connecticut Headstone Inscriptions, Hale Collection, vol. 78: Naugatuck, 145; Church and Town Records, Pennsylvania, 1708-1985, entry 372; Manuscript Census records for 1870, 1880 and 1900, courtesy of ancestry.com.

67 Records of the Alumni Association, Connecticut Normal School, Central Connecticut State University, Burritt Library Archives, p. 69. On Catharine Beecher's efforts on the behalf of female teachers, see Kathryn Kish Sklar, *Catharine Beecher: A Study in American Domesticity* (New York: W. W. Norton, 1976).

68 Henry E. Fowler, *A Century of Teacher Education in Connecticut: The Story of the New Britain State Normal School and the Teachers College of Connecticut, 1849-1949* (New Britain: Teachers College of Connecticut, 1949).

69 *Catalogue and Circular of the Connecticut State Normal School at New Britain Year Ending June 25, 1880* (New Britain, CT: Adkins Brothers, 1880), 10-12.

70 New Haven *Evening Register*, January 24, 1880; Hartford *Courant*, January 24, 1880.

71 Records of the Alumni Association, p. 71.

72 One such alumna was Adelaide R. Pender, the daughter of a machinist, who matriculated half a decade after Baldwin graduated. Pender supported herself for decades through employment as a writer and proofreader with the Meriden *Daily Journal*, as an associate editor by the Kellogg Publishing Company of New York, and as a clerical worker in the Connecticut governmental bureaucracy. Adelaide R. Pender, "At the New Britain Normal School 1886-1888," typescript, Central Connecticut State University, Burritt Library Archives, title page and p. 2.

73 Eleanor Baldwin, *Money Talks* (Holyoke, MA: Elizabeth Towne, 1915), 2.

74 Celia Baldwin Whitehead, "Henry George and Nehemiah," *The Arena* 15 (1896): 196-201.

75 *John Swinton's Paper*, September 26, 1886. The local county history mentions the Puritan Shirt Factory, owned by E. A. Buffinton of Leominster, having been destroyed by a fire in January 1886, about three-quarters of a year before Baldwin wrote this correspondence. Perhaps the factory was rebuilt in the interim, which would explain her declaration that it was new. Simeon L. Deyo, ed., *History of Barnstable County, Massachusetts* (New York: H. W. Blake, 1890), 973, http://capecodhistory.us/Deyo/Provincetown-Deyo.htm. On Joshua T. Small's proprietorship of the bakery, see ibid., 1007. Small followed the same path as his Uncle Henry, running on the local labor party ticket in 1887 for secretary of state. Barnstable *Patriot*, November 8, 1887. Fifteen years later, he

penned a call for revolution in an anarchist periodical, *Free Society* [Chicago], July 13, 1902, p. 3.

76 *John Swinton's Paper*, November 7, 1886.

77 Boston *Daily Globe*, July 11, 1894.

78 Kansas *Agitator*, January 1, 1897.

79 Gail Bederman, *Manliness and Civilization: A Cultural History of Gender and Race in the United States, 1880-1917* (Chicago, IL: University of Chicago Press, 1996), 170-216.

80 Naugatuck *Citizen*, January 30, 1892.

81 When women are no longer subject to the financial dependency that was the basis of what she termed the "sexuo-economic relation," Gilman asserted, "Men who are not equal to good fatherhood under such conditions will have no chance to become fathers, and will die with general pity instead of living with general condemnation." *Women and Economics: The Economic Factor between Men and Women as a Factor in Social Evolution* (New York: Harper and Row, 1966; originally published 1898), 186. Gilman relied heavily on the reform Darwinism of Lester Ward. See Mary A. Hill, *Charlotte Perkins Gilman: The Making of a Radical Feminist, 1860-1896* (Philadelphia, PA: Temple University Press, 1980), esp. 264-72.

82 On Celia's relationship to the suffrage movement, see "Celia Baldwin Whitehead, Denver 1932," pp. 5-9, Carle Whitehead Papers, WH390, Western History Collection, Denver Public Library; Ida Husted Harper, ed., *History of Woman Suffrage*, vol. 6 (New York: J. J. Little and Ives, 1922), 61.

CHAPTER 2: A VISION OF PROGRESSIVE WOMANHOOD

Epigraph. Henry Victor Morgan, "The Song of the Singer," in *Songs of Victory* (Chicago, IL: Library Shelf, 1911), p. 15, Box 1, Victor Henry Morgan Papers, Accession Number 0167-002, University of Washington Libraries.

1 On the newspaper publisher's interest in convincing advertisers that they had a considerable female readership, see Julia A. Golia, "Courting Women, Courting Advertisers: The Woman's Page and the Transformation of the American Newspaper, 1895-1935," *Journal of American History* 103 (December 2016): 606-28. On the cultural power of advertising, see William Leach, *Land of Desire: Merchants, Power, and the Rise of a New American Culture* (New York: Vintage Books, 1993), 20; Stuart Ewen, *Captains of Consciousness: Advertising and the Social Roots of the Consumer Culture* (New York: McGraw Hill, 1976); Daniel Horowitz, *The Morality of Spending: Attitudes toward the Consumer Society in America, 1875-1940* (Chicago, IL: Ivan R. Dee, 1985).

2 *Evening Telegram*, January 16, 1909; Deborah M. Olsen, "Fair Connections: Women's Separatism and the Lewis and Clark Exposition of 1905," *Oregon Historical Quarterly* 109 (Summer 2008): 174-203, esp. 3-4.

3 There is a considerable literature on the relationship between progressivism and female activism: Maureen A. Flanagan, *American Reformed: Progressives and Progressivisms, 1890s-1920s* (Oxford: Oxford University Press, 2007); Kathryn Kish Sklar, *Florence Kelley and the Nation's Work* (New Haven, CT: Yale University Press, 1995); Seth Koven and Sonya Michel, "Womanly Duties: Maternalist Politics and the Origins of Welfare States in France, Germany, and the United States, 1880-1920," *American Historical Review* 95 (October 1990): 1076-108.

4 Alice Fahs, *Out on Assignment: Newspaper Women and the Making of Modern Public Space* (Chapel Hill: University of North Carolina Press, 2011), 7.

5 Ibid., 59.

6 Marshal N. Dana, *Newspaper Story: Fifty Years of the Oregon Journal, 1902-1952* (Portland, OR: Binfords & Mort, 1951), 75-76.

7 Daniel Walker Howe, ed., *American Victorianism* (Philadelphia, PA: University of Pennsylvania Press, 1976); idem., *What Hath God Wrought: The Transformation of America, 1815-1848* (New York: Oxford University Press, 2009).

8 George Rogers Taylor, *The Transportation Revolution, 1815-1860* (New York: M. E. Sharpe, 1977); Charles Sellers, *The Market Revolution: Jacksonian America, 1815-1846* (New York: Oxford University Press, 1994); John Lauritz Larson, *The Market Revolution in America: Liberty, Ambition, and the Eclipse of the Common Good* (Cambridge: Cambridge University Press, 2009). See also William Cronon, *Nature's Metropolis: Chicago and the Great West* (New York: W. W. Norton, 1991), esp. chap. 2.

9 W. J. Rohrbaugh, *The Alcoholic Republic* (New York: Oxford University Press, 1981); Stephen Thernstrom, *Poverty and Progress: Social Mobility in a Nineteenth Century City* (Cambridge, MA: Harvard University Press, 1964).

10 Stephen Mihm, *A Nation of Counterfeiters: Capitalists, Con Men, and the Making of the United States* (Cambridge, MA: Harvard University Press, 2009).

11 Stephen Nissenbaum, *Sex, Diet and Debility in Jacksonian America: Sylvester Graham and Health Reform* (Westport, CT: Greenwood Press, 1980). Catherine McNeur's brief discussion of adulterated milk in antebellum New York City will provide the reader with a sense of the problems that Graham and his followers perceived. *Taming Manhattan: Environmental Battles in the Antebellum City* (Cambridge, MA: Harvard University Press, 2014).

12 Carroll Smith Rosenberg, "Beauty, the Beast and the Militant Woman: A Case Study in Sex Roles and Social Stress in Jacksonian America," *Disorderly Conduct: Visions of Gender in Victorian America* (New York: Oxford University Press, 1986), 90-108.

13 Elizabeth Cady Stanton, "Address Delivered at Seneca Falls," in *Elizabeth Cady Stanton, Susan B. Anthony: Correspondence, Writings, Speeches*, ed. Ellen Carol DuBois (New York: Schocken Books, 1987), 32; Susan B. Anthony as quoted in Nancy Woloch, *Women and the American Experience* (New York: Knopf, 1984), 340. See also Sue Davis, *The Political Thought of Elizabeth Cady Stanton: Women's Rights and the American Political Traditions* (New York: New York University Press, 2008). Abigail Scott Duniway, herself a pioneer and farm wife, rejected the linkage between the vote and temperance and urged the Oregon suffrage movement to steer clear of the latter. So would Baldwin.

14 Barbara Leslie Epstein, *The Politics of Domesticity: Women, Evangelism, and Temperance in Nineteenth-Century America* (Middletown, CT: Wesleyan, 1981); Ruth Bordin, *Women and Temperance: The Quest for Power and Liberty, 1873-1900* (Philadelphia, PA: Temple University Press, 1981); Jack S. Blocker Jr., *"Give to the Wind Thy Fears": The Women's Temperance Crusade, 1873-1874* (Westport, CT: Praeger, 1985).

15 Many activists like Stanton rejected the notion that there were clear biological causes of the differences between men and women. These were cultural differences; society had made greater efforts to inscribe morality into the character of women than it had for men. For many such women, the objective was not to make women less moral, but rather to make men more so.

16 Paula Baker, "The Domestication of Politics: Women and American Political
    Society, 1780-1920," *American Historical Review* 89 (June 1984): 620-47, quota-
    tion on 633. Baker points to changes in government and the political culture of
    separate spheres, and suggests that an era was coming to an end by the time that
    women got the vote.

17 On the Portland exposition, see Lisa Blee, "Conflating Lewis and Clark's
    Westward March: Exhibiting a History of Empire at the 1905 World's
    Fair," *Oregon Historical Quarterly* 106 (Summer 2005): 232-53; Olsen, "Fair
    Connections"; Carl Abbott, *The Great Extravaganza: Portland and the Exposition*
    (Portland: Oregon Historical Society, 1981); and Robert W. Rydell, *All the
    World's a Fair: Visions of Empire at American International Expositions, 1876-
    1916* (Chicago, IL: University of Chicago, 1984), 184-207. On the literary and
    political effort to honor Sacagawea, see Sheri Bartlett Browne, *Eva Emery Dye:
    Romance with the West* (Corvallis: Oregon State University Press, 2004), 72-115.

18 Fahs, *Out on Assignment*, 65.

19 David Paul Nord, *Communities of Journalism: A History of American Newspapers
    and Their Readers* (Urbana: University of Illinois Press, 2001), 247, 269.

20 *Telegram*, July 30, 1907.

21 *Telegram*, July 30, 1907.

22 *Telegram*, January 19, 1907.

23 For instance, see the excerpt of T. S. Arthur's *Sweethearts and Wives*, originally
    serialized in *Godey's Lady's Book* in 1841, and reprinted in Nancy F. Cott, ed.,
    Root of Bitterness: Documents of the Social History of American Women (Lebanon,
    NH: Northeastern University Press, 1996), 138-47.

24 *Telegram*, June 27, 1906.

25 *Telegram*, September 14, 1906.

26 *Telegram*, May 7, 1908.

27 Mrs. R. H. Tate, as quoted in "The Woman's Point of View," *Telegram*, September
    22, 1906. On the relationship of the HTA to the State Congress of Mothers, see
    Baldwin's column of July 28, 1906. On the activities of the Mothers' Congress,
    see National Congress of Mothers, *Report of the National Congress of Mothers,
    Held in the City of Washington, D. C., March 10-17, 1905* (Washington, DC:
    National Congress of Mothers, 1905). See also Mrs. Frederic Schoff, "The
    National Congress of Mothers and Parent-Teacher Associations," *Annals of the
    American Academy of Political and Social Science* 67 (September 1916): 139-47.

28 *Telegram*, March 9, 1908.

29 *Telegram*, January 3, 1907.

30 *Telegram*, September 28, 1906; Program for the Year 1907-1908, Branch Circle
    No. 5, Associations, Institutions, etc., mss 1511, Box 16, Folder 7, Home Training
    Association, OHS Library.

31 *Telegram*, October 14, 1907.

32 *Telegram*, October 28, 1907.

33 *Telegram*, October 22, 1908.

34 *Telegram*, May 19, 1908.

35 *Telegram*, February 1, 1907. Yet Baldwin could be critical of this kind of elite
    attention to the poor. In a different column, she critically described the "elite"
    belief that they are "divinely appointed to play the missionary." *Telegram*,
    December 16, 1907.

36 *Telegram*, May 4, 1908. Trumbull's concerns for the poor was not racially
    limited; she was a subscriber to the local black newspaper, *The Advocate*, to
    which she wrote in the wake of racially charged violence in the era of the Ku

Klux Klan: "It is not an easy thing to preach tolerance in this 'land of the free and the home of the brave,' our black men and women are sacrificed to the hate and cruelty of the white race; it is not easy to preach love and kindliness under the weary pettinesses of social ostracism which we white people do not hesitate to practice against our black neighbors." Quoted in Kimberly Mangun, *A Force for Change: Beatrice Morrow Cannady and the Struggle for Civil Rights in Oregon, 1912-1936* (Corvallis: Oregon State University Press, 2010), 166-67.

37 Christine Stansell, *City of Women: Sex and Class in New York, 1789-1860* (New York: Alfred A. Knopf, 1982); Mary P. Ryan, *Cradle of the Middle Class: The Family in Oneida County, New York, 1790-1865* (Cambridge: Cambridge University Press, 1981); and Joan Waugh, *Sentimental Reformer: The Life of Josephine Shaw Lowell* (Cambridge, MA: Harvard University Press, 1998).

38 *Telegram*, October 17, 1906.

39 *Telegram*, February 1, 1909. Some settlement house workers came to appreciate the culture of poor immigrants, overcoming the nativism and class bias that afflicted many other philanthropic ventures. For the women who worked at Hull House in Chicago, see Kathryn Kish Sklar, *Florence Kelley and the Nation's Work* (New Haven, CT: Yale University Press, 1995). The efforts of Lillian Wald, who founded the Henry Street Settlement in New York City, to bridge the gap between rich and poor, is covered in David Huyssen's *Progressive Inequality: Rich and Poor in New York, 1890-1920* (Cambridge, MA: Harvard University Press, 2014), chaps. 6-8.

40 *Telegram*, February 20, 1909.

41 *Telegram*, November 5, 1908. Peter Boag, *Same-Sex Affairs: Constructing and Controlling Homosexuality in the Pacific Northwest* (Berkeley: University of California Press, 2003), 188-93.

42 *Telegram*, July 24, 1906. On the national organization, see the reports of Elizabeth Barstow in "Report of Travelers' Aid Committee," *Girls' Friendly Society in America* 8 (January 1905): 34-36. On the local efforts, see Gloria E. Myers, *A Municipal Mother: Portland's Lola Greene Baldwin, America's First Policewoman* (Corvallis: Oregon State University Press, 1995).

43 Katharine G. Aiken, *Harnessing the Power of Motherhood: The National Florence Crittenton Mission* (Knoxville: University of Tennessee Press, 1998).

44 *Telegram*, July 24, 1906.

45 *Telegram*, November 30, 1907, and June 30, 1906. Three years later, Baldwin sounded the alarm that interests tied to the saloon and the brothel were pressuring the city to end the relationship between Lola Baldwin and the police department. She credited her with shutting down illegitimate businesses, and giving "thought and sympathy and individual friendliness and help to the individual girl," nearly five hundred in number. *Telegram*, January 12, 1909.

46 Paper written by Dr. E. J. Welty, Read in the Congregational Church, May 1910, Memorabilia Folder, Box 1, Portland Women's Union, Mss. 1443, OHS Library; Sandra Haarsager, *Organized Womanhood: Cultural Politics in the Pacific Northwest, 1840-1920* (Norman: University of Oklahoma Press, 1997), 190.

47 Lori Ginzburg, *Women and the Work of Benevolence: Morality, Politics, and Class in the Nineteenth-Century United States* (New Haven, CT: Yale University Press, 1992).

48 Abigail Scott Duniway to Clara Colby, March 22, 1905, Box 1, Folder 3, Abigail Scott Duniway Papers, Series I: Suffrage Records, Subseries A, correspondence, Collection 232 B, Special Collections, Knight Library, University of Oregon; *Telegram*, June 4, 1908; Abigail Scott Duniway, *Path Breaking: An*

Autobiographical History of the Equal Suffrage Movement in Pacific Coast States (Portland, OR: James, Kerns & Abbott, 1914), 229 and 259; Rebecca Mead, *How the Vote Was Won: Woman Suffrage in the Western States, 1868-1914* (New York: New York University Press, 2004), 102-5; Ruth Barnes Moynihan, *Rebel for Rights: Abigail Scott Duniway* (New Haven, CT: Yale University Press, 1983), 210-12.

49 *Telegram*, November 23, 1908.

50 *Telegram*, March 19, 1909.

51 *Telegram*, November 11, 1907.

52 *Telegram*, June 19, 1907.

53 *Telegram*, January 8, 1907, and March 2, 1907. See also Kate Rousmaniere, *Citizen Teacher: The Life and Leadership of Margaret Haley* (Albany: State University of New York Press, 2005), 59-91; Maureen A. Flanagan, *Chicago Women and the Vision of the Good City, 1871-1933* (Princeton, NJ: Princeton University Press, 2002), 65-70.

54 *Telegram*, June 19, 1907. As quoted in Janet Calligani Casey, "Marie Corelli and Fin de Siecle Feminism," *English Literature in Transition, 1880-1920* 35, no. 2 (1992): 162-78, quotation on 168. Casey notes that Corelli sold as many as 100,000 copies of her works in a single year; that her work had been translated into other European languages; and that it outsold the works of H. G. Wells, Rudyard Kipling, and Arthur Conan Doyle combined. She attributes her popularity to her ability to "give her readers precisely what they wanted: the illusion of a feminist spirit couched in a fundamentally conventional Victorian ideology."

55 *Telegram*, November 11, 1907.

56 *Telegram*, December 18, 1908.

57 *Telegram*, December 25, 1906.

58 *Telegram*, November 24, 1908.

59 *Telegram*, June 4, 1906.

60 *Telegram*, October 29, 1907.

61 *Telegram*, March 27, 1908.

62 *Telegram*, May 31, 1907.

63 *Telegram*, April 20, 1907.

64 *Telegram*, August 28, 1906.

65 *Telegram*, December 3, 1908.

66 Gordon Wood reminds us that American wage laborers during the Revolutionary War refused to call their employers "master" because it connoted a degraded status for the employee; instead, they chose the Dutch word "boss," which meant "master" but lacked the same connotation in the new nation. *The Radicalism of the American Revolution* (New York: Alfred Knopf, 1991), 184.

67 *Telegram*, April 16, 1909. See Susan Porter Benson, *Counter Cultures: Saleswomen, Managers, and Customers in American Department Stores, 1890-1940* (Urbana: University of Illinois Press, 1988).

68 *Telegram*, February 2, 1907.

69 *Telegram*, May 16, 1906, and July 19, 1906.

70 *Telegram*, February 15, 1907.

71 *Telegram*, July 9, 1907.

72 *Telegram*, October 19, 1908; see also *Oregonian*, October 18, 1908.

73 *Telegram*, February 17, 1909.

74 *Telegram*, March 13, 1909.

75 *Telegram*, August 3, 1906.

76 *Telegram*, May 25, 1906.

77 *Telegram*, August 20, 1906.

78 *Telegram*, August 20, 1906, and December 1, 1906. On the relationship between constraining dress and female submissiveness, see Helene E. Roberts, "The Exquisite Slave: The Role of Clothes in the Making of the Victorian Woman," *Signs* 2 (spring 1977): 554-59.

79 *Telegram*, January 3, 1908.

80 *Telegram*, October 5, 1908.

81 *Telegram*, January 3, 1908.

82 *Telegram*, March 26, 1909, and July 20, 1907.

83 Alice B. Stockham, *Tokology: A Book for Every Woman* (New York: R. F. Fenno, 1893), 139.

84 On the relationship between dress reform and women's rights in the mid-nineteenth century, see Amy Kesselman, "The 'Freedom Suit': Feminism and Dress Reform in the United States, 1848-1875," *Gender and Society* 5 (December 1991): 495-510.

85 Jennifer Price, *Flight Maps: Adventures with Nature in Modern America* (New York: Basic Books, 1999), 59.

86 *Telegram*, January 4, 1908.

87 Price, *Flight Maps,* 72.

88 *Telegram*, April 15, 1909; *Oregonian*, February 9, 1910; and Worth Mathewson, *William L. Finley: Pioneer Wildlife Photographer* (Corvallis: Oregon State University Press, 1986).

89 *Telegram*, October 5, 1907.

90 *Telegram*, July 31, 1907.

91 *Telegram*, May 4, 1907.

92 The examples listed here were all drawn from *Telegram*, November 5, 1908.

93 *Telegram*, January 4, 1908.

CHAPTER 3: THE RADICAL ASSAULT ON CAPITALISM

Epigraph. Henry Victor Morgan, "Pioneers," in *Songs of Victory* (Chicago, IL: Library Shelf, 1911), p. 18, Box 1, Victor Henry Morgan Papers, Accession Number 0167-002, University of Washington Libraries.

1 Mari Jo Buhle, *Women and American Socialism, 1870-1920* (Urbana: University of Illinois Press, 1981), 49-51. Charles Postel provides a chapter on women's activists within the populist movement in *The Populist Vision* (New York: Oxford University Press, 2007), 69-101.

2 Robert D. Johnston, *The Radical Middle Class: Populist Democracy and the Question of Capitalism in Progressive Era Portland, Oregon* (Princeton, NJ: Princeton University Press, 2003); Lawrence M. Lipin, *Workers and the Wild: Conservation, Consumerism, and Labor in Oregon, 1910-30* (Urbana: University of Illinois Press, 2007).

3 *Telegram*, January 12, 1909.

4 *Telegram*, May 5, 1908.

5 *Telegram*, December 14, 1908.

6 *Telegram*, July 12, 1906.

7 *Telegram*, April 26, 1907.

8 John Fabian Witt, *The Accidental Republic: Crippled Workingmen, Destitute Widows, and the Remaking of American Law* (Cambridge, MA: Harvard University Press, 2004), 2-3.

9 Karen Orren emphasizes feudal-style hierarchies as leading to judicial decisions that granted employers superiority in claims from their employees; a highly skilled worker, earning a considerable wage, it was often argued, understood the risks involved in their employments, allowing the employer to claim a lack of responsibility. *Belated Feudalism: Labor, the Law, and Liberal Development in the United States* (Cambridge: Cambridge University Press, 1991), 91-111. Peter Karsten, *Heart versus Head: Judge-Made Law in Nineteenth-Century America* (Chapel Hill: University of North Carolina Press, 1997), 114-22, also emphasizes continuities in explaining the development of American jurisprudence, including the fellow-servant doctrine, which he asserts was not imposed by American judges on a body of common law that previously held masters responsible. For a different perspective that emphasizes changes in law that paralleled changes in industry, see Morton Horwitz, *The Transformation of American Law, 1870-1960* (Oxford: Oxford University Press, 1992), 51-63.

10 *Telegram,* May 23, 1907.

11 *Telegram,* April 27, 1907.

12 *Telegram,* May 23, 1907.

13 *Telegram,* May 23, 1907, and February 25, 1908.

14 *Telegram,* January 10, 1908; *Bridgemen's Magazine,* March 8, 1908, 119-20.

15 *Telegram,* January 10, 1908.

16 *Telegram,* August 31, 1907.

17 *Telegram,* September 8, 1908. Margaret Haley is mentioned in chap. 2 of this volume.

18 *Telegram,* July 18, 1906.

19 *Telegram,* July 5, 1907, and January 5, 1909.

20 *Telegram,* December 20, 1906.

21 *Telegram,* December 20, 1906.

22 *Telegram,* February 15, 1909.

23 *Telegram,* March 25, 1909.

24 *Telegram,* February 13, 1908.

25 *Telegram,* December 10, 1907. For a recent discussion of the problem of tenement housing in New York City, one that posits the reformers as possessing imperial designs to remake the poor in their own image, see David Huyssen, *Progressive Inequality: Rich and Poor in New York, 1890-1920* (Cambridge, MA: Harvard University Press, 2014).

26 *Telegram,* April 25, 1907.

27 *Telegram,* July 3, 1907.

28 *Telegram,* January 2, 1907.

29 *Telegram,* June 24, 1907.

30 *Telegram,* July 27, 1908.

31 *Telegram,* September 16, 1907.

32 *Telegram,* February 22, 1909.

33 *Telegram,* September 29, 1906. In a state that held out opportunities of pretty proprietorship for families of modest means, the scandal smacked of land monopoly, and it would help sustain much of the radical efforts to pass the single tax in the following decade. See John Messing, "Public Lands, Politics,

and Progressives: The Oregon Land Fraud Trials, 1903-1910," *Pacific Historical Review* 35 (February 1966): 35-66.

34 *Telegram,* November 19, 1907.

35 *Telegram,* May 12, 1908.

36 *Telegram,* January 14, 1909, and November 14, 1908.

37 *Telegram,* January 14, 1909.

38 *Telegram,* May 21, 1908.

39 *Telegram,* October 3, 1906.

40 *Telegram,* November 8, 1906.

41 *Telegram,* April 25, 1908.

42 *Telegram,* November 11, 1914. I am grateful to Kim Jensen for providing me with this reference. In her column of March 4, 1909, Baldwin described the speech, with some sympathy, of Frances McHenry, state lecturer and organizer for the National Grand Lodge of Good Templars, who spoke of the saloon as the kind of "poor man's club" that beat them into "staying poor in the interest of politicians and other predatory classes."

43 *Telegram,* October 11, 1907.

44 *Telegram,* May 17, 1907.

45 *Telegram,* November 4, 1907.

46 Eileen Boris, *Art and Labor: Ruskin, Morris, and the Craftsman Ideal in America* (Philadelphia, PA: Temple University Press, 1986; Jackson Lears, *No Place of Grace: Antimodernism and the Transformation of American Culture, 1880-1920* (New York: Pantheon Books, 1981), 60-96. See also David Shi's depiction of the Arts and Crafts movement as poised between republican simplicity and conspicuous consumption. *The Simple Life: Plain Living and High Thinking in American Culture* (New York: Oxford University Press, 1985).

47 *Telegram,* April 14, 1909.

48 *Telegram,* March 20, 1909.

49 *Telegram,* April 14, 1909, and July 17, 1907.

50 *Oregonian,* January 9, 1910.

51 *Telegram,* July 17, 1907. See also "The Woman's Point of View" column for June 10, 1907.

52 *The Craftsman* 28 (April 1915): 114-16.

53 *Telegram,* December 23, 1907. Richard S. Christen describes the Portland society as uninterested in social and economic change and asserts that its leaders were content to teach "privileged individuals how to construct a personal and emotional sphere that would offset the harshness of industrialization and its workplaces." Nonetheless, the society, founded in the fall of 1907, would sponsor activities that were "accessible to a wide audience." "Julia Hoffman and the Arts and Crafts Society of Portland: An Aesthetic Response to Industrialization," *Oregon Historical Quarterly* 109 (Winter 2008): 510-35, quotations on 512-13 and 526; Boris, *Art and Labor,* 34-45.

54 *Telegram,* January 21, 1908.

55 *Telegram,* February 8, 1908.

56 *Telegram,* August 4, 1906.

57 *Telegram,* October 29, 1907.

58 *Telegram,* March 3, 1909.

59 *Telegram,* February 7, 1908.

60 *Telegram,* February 6, 1908. Baldwin's sentiments on these matters paralleled those of the women like Florence Kelley, who established the National

Consumers' League at the end of the nineteenth century. See Kathryn Kish Sklar, *Florence Kelley and the Nation's Work: The Rise of Women's Political Culture, 1830-1900* (New Haven, CT: Yale University Press, 1995).

61 *Telegram,* August 20, 1907. Many states had passed homestead exemption legislation to protect the homesteads and productive property of farmers.

62 *Telegram,* November 2, 1907.

63 *Telegram,* November 28, 1908. Susan Porter Benson discusses the complicated relationships between department store managers, saleswomen, and the customers who could at times sympathize with them against their employers. *Counter Cultures: Saleswomen, Managers, and Customers in American Department Stores, 1890-1940* (Urbana: University of Illinois Press, 1986).

64 *Telegram,* March 22, 1909.

65 *Telegram,* March 23, 1907.

66 *Telegram,* September 9, 1907.

67 *Telegram,* September 15, 1906.

68 *Telegram,* November 10, 1906.

69 E. P. Thomson's *The Making of the English Working Class* (New York: Vintage, 1966) is magisterial in its coverage of the rise of this tradition in England. For the United States, see Sean Wilentz, *Chants Democratic: New York City and the Rise of the American Working Class* (New York: Oxford University Press, 1984); and Bruce Laurie, *Working People of Philadelphia, 1800-1850* (Philadelphia, PA: Temple University Press, 1980).

70 *Telegram,* September 8, 1906.

71 *Telegram,* August 21, 1907.

72 *Telegram,* January 4, 1908.

73 *Telegram,* January 21, 1907. Though she does not identify as a socialist in the columns, there is evidence, mostly from the *Oregonian,* of a closer tie than she otherwise let on. In January 1910, she gave brief talk on William Morris; a few months later she wrote a defense of socialism for a Tacoma newspaper that drew the attention of an editorial in the *Oregonian*; and she lectured on "State Capitalism or Socialism: Which?" *Oregonian,* January 9, 1910; June 10, 1910; and October 10, 1913. On the other hand, she applauded the "dispassionate, calm, temperate and philosophic" tone of the *Single Tax Review,* comparing it favorably to socialist and anarchist periodicals, which she thought were "aggressive" and "caustic." *Telegram,* September 9, 1908. While renewing her subscription to socialist Ida Crouch Hazelett's *Montana News,* published in Helena, Baldwin denied that she was a socialist. See the issue of July 9, 1908.

74 *Telegram,* March 19, 1907.

75 *Telegram,* March 6, 1907.

76 Nina E. Wood, *Crimes of the Profit Furnace* (Portland, OR: Mann & Beach, 1906), 5-6, 50, and 55-56.

77 *Telegram,* March 18, 1907.

78 *Telegram,* April 17, 1909.

79 *Oregonian,* May 5, 1912; September 12, 1912; and December 19, 1917.

80 *Telegram,* April 25, 1907.

CHAPTER 4: THE CERTAINTY OF PROGRESS

Epigraph. *Telegram,* April 16, 1908.

1 On Elizabeth Towne and her position on desire and corporate capitalism, see Beryl Sattler, *Each Mind a Kingdom: American Women, Sexual Purity, and the New Thought Movement* (Berkeley: University of California Press, 1999), 234-38.

2 *Telegram*, August 6, 1907.

3 *Telegram*, January 4, 1907.

4 *Telegram*, May 30, 1907.

5 *Telegram*, April 13, 1908.

6 Dan McKanan, "The Implicit Religion of Radicalism: Socialist Party Theology, 1900-1934," *Journal of the Academy of Religion* 78 (September 2010): 750-89. For a discussion of Wilson's embrace of women's rights, see Stephen E. Barton, "'This Social Mother in Whose Household We All Live': Berkeley Mayor J. Stitt Wilson's Early Twentieth-Century Socialist Feminism," *Journal of the Gilded Age and Progressive Era* 13 (October 2014): 532-63. Henry Victor Morgan's son told a potential biographer of his father that "Dad was a life-long socialist—and pacifist." Victor H. Morgan to Mr. Margolis, February 4, 1976, Correspondence, Box 1, Henry Victor Morgan Papers, Accession Number 0167-002, University of Washington Libraries.

7 *Nautilus* 12 (November 1909): 12.

8 *Oregonian*, September 4, 1920, p. 9, Vertical File, Lucy A. Rose Mallory, Oregon Historical Society Library; Marsha Silberman, "Leo Tolstoy's Use of Lucy Mallory's Moralistic Writing in the Circle of Reading," *Tolstoy Studies Journal* 23 (2011): 84. For an example of the broad labor and farmer reform posture adopted by the early Mallory, see the October 1891 issue. Though Mallory technically published two magazines as one—the *World's Advance-Thought* and *The Universal Republic*—both will be referred to as the *World's Advance-Thought*.

9 *Telegram*, January 1, 1908.

10 For Trumbull, see *Telegram*, November 7, 1908. For Duniway, see the same and the issue of June 29, 1908, in which Baldwin quotes extensively from Duniway's speech, during which she was said to have "charmed her audience" when she spoke of her being consoled by the spirit of her only daughter, who after death provided signs that "she still lived and loved her." At a Spiritualist camp meeting outside of Oregon City, Duniway spoke about Abigail Adams's efforts to have her husband and the others at the constitutional convention write gender equality into the Constitution. *Evening Telegram*, September 12, 1908. See also Ruth Barnes Moynihan, *Rebel for Rights: Abigail Scott Duniway* (New Haven, CT: Yale University Press, 1983), 133.

11 *World's Advance Thought and Universal Republic* 20 (June 1906): 186.

12 U'Ren held séances at the home of Seth and Alfred Lewelling. Robert C. Woodward, "William S. U'Ren: A Progressive Era Personality," in *Experiences in a Promised Land: Essays in Pacific Northwest History*, ed. G. Thomas Edwards and Carlos Schwantes (Seattle: University of Washington Press, 1986), 196.

13 Alan Dawley, *Changing the World: American Progressives in War and Revolution* (Princeton, NJ: Princeton University Press, 2003), 43.

14 *Telegram*, February 12, 1908; *World's Advance-Thought* (April-May 1906): 162. Emphasis in original.

15 *Practical Christian* 1, no. 9 (December 1910), Box 1, Henry Victor Morgan Papers, Accession Number 0167-001, University of Washington Libraries.

16 *Telegram*, August 7, 1907. Compare Baldwin's use of science and technology with that of mid-nineteenth-century spiritualist John Murray Spear's: "Between the Grand Central Mind and all inferior minds there subsists a connection, a telegraphic communication, by means of what may be termed an Electric chain,

composed of a greater or lesser number of intermediate links." As quoted in John
Lardas Modern, *Secularism in Antebellum America, with Reference to Ghosts,
Protestant Subcultures, Machines and Their Metaphors* (Chicago, IL: University
of Chicago Press, 2011), 40. Also see R. Laurence Moore, *In Search of White
Crows: Spiritualism, Parapsychology, and American Culture* (New York: Oxford
University Press, 1977).

17 *World's Advance-Thought* 21 (December 1907): 179.

18 Elizabeth E. McAdams and Raymond Bayless, *Life after Death: Parapsychologists
Look at the Evidence* (Chicago, IL: Nelson-Hall, 1981), 127-28.

19 *Telegram*, January 1, 1908.

20 *World's Advance-Thought* 20 (April-May 1906): 163.

21 Edgar Lucien Larkin, "Electricity the Base of Nature," *World's Advance-Thought*
22 (March 1908): 23-24; Lucien, "Digging around the Base of Nature," *World's
Advance-Thought*, 22 (May 1908): 38-39.

22 *Telegram*, April 10, 1909.

23 *Telegram*, September 27, 1906.

24 *Telegram*, August 27, 1906. Baldwin often wrote columns about Mallory on the
twenty-seventh of the month, when the world-soul communion was to occur.

25 *Telegram*, May 24, 1906.

26 *Telegram*, February 4, 1908.

27 *Telegram*, June 20, 1906.

28 *Telegram*, August 16, 1906.

29 *Telegram*, June 20, 1906.

30 *Telegram*, January 29, 1907.

31 *Telegram*, December 15, 1908.

32 *Telegram*, January 18, 1908.

33 *Telegram*, March 5, 1907.

34 *Telegram*, January 8, 1908.

35 *World's Advance-Thought* 21 (January 1907): 85.

36 Mallory wrote, "every piece of flesh food is the product of murder," but she also
emphasized that it infected consumers with "cancer, consumption, smallpox,
and other diseases, and sending countless numbers of early graves." Perhaps
worse was that it hardened the "budding sympathetic nature of the youth
of the land, leading to cruelty in various forms; and also marks the gestating
offspring of unnumbered mothers with a blood-thirstiness and cruelty." The sins
multiplied, as flesh eating creates a "thirst for liquors," increases combativeness,
and "sustains war." Vegetarians, on the other hand, "lose all desire for liquor and
there are not drunkards among them." *World's Advance-Thought* 20 (April-May
1906): 169-70.

37 *Telegram*, March 5, 1907.

38 Robert D. Johnston, *The Radical Middle Class: Populist Democracy and the
Question of Capitalism in Progressive Era Portland, Oregon* (Princeton, NJ:
Princeton University Press, 2003), 191-206. See also Nadav Davidovitch,
"Homeopathy and Anti-Vaccinationism at the Turn of the Twentieth Century,"
in *The Politics of Healing: Histories of Alternative Medicine in Twentieth-Century
North America*, ed. Robert D. Johnston (New York: Routledge, 2004), 9-26.

39 B. O. Flower, *Progressive Men, Women, and Movements of the Past Twenty-Five
Years*, as quoted in Johnston, *Radical Middle Class*, 179. On Flower's embrace of
the New Thought mental healing movement, see Sattler, *Each Mind a Kingdom*,
188-92.

40 *World's Advance-Thought* 23 (January 1910): 75; ibid., 26 (November 1913): 78.
41 *Telegram*, March 5, 1907.
42 *Telegram*, November 23, 1908.
43 *World's Advance-Thought* 25 (February 1912): 30.
44 *World's Advance-Thought* 25 (January 1913): 127.
45 Lora C. Little, "Health in the Suburbs," *Mt. Scott Herald*, January 21, 1915, and February 4, 1915.
46 Lora C. Little, "Health in the Suburbs," *Mt. Scott Herald*, January 21, 1915.
47 *Telegram*, November 28, 1906.
48 *Telegram*, May 18, 1907.
49 *Telegram*, June 5, 1907.
50 *Telegram*, June 5, 1907. Thomas Jefferson had argued that the environment was important in the character formation of the child when he stated that in a slave society "the parent storms, the child looks on, catches the lineaments of wrath, puts on the same airs in the circle of smaller slaves, give a loose to his worst of passions, and thus nursed, educated, and daily exercised in tyranny, cannot but be stamped by it with odious peculiarities. The man must be a prodigy who can retain his manners and morals undepraved by such circumstances." *Notes on the State of Virginia*, ed. William Peden (Chapel Hill: University of North Carolina Press, 1982), 162.
51 *Telegram*, May 28, 1906.
52 *Telegram*, August 17, 1907.
53 *Telegram*, August 24, 1907.
54 David Peterson Del Mar, "'His Face Is Weak and Sensual': Portland and the Whipping Post Law," in *Women in Pacific Northwest History*, rev. ed., ed. Karen Blair (Seattle: University of Washington Press, 2001): 59-89.
55 *Telegram*, May 28, 1906.
56 *Telegram*, August 24, 1906.
57 *Telegram*, April 19, 1907.
58 *Telegram*, February 4, 1907.
59 *Telegram*, April 19, 1907.
60 *Telegram*, August 15, 1907.
61 *Telegram*, February 4, 1907.
62 *Telegram*, May 13, 1907.
63 *Telegram*, February 4, 1907.
64 *Telegram*, July 27, 1906.
65 *Telegram*, August 15, 1907.
66 *Telegram*, January 31, 1908.
67 *Telegram*, August 21, 1907.
68 *Telegram*, January 30, 1908.
69 *Telegram*, February 18, 1909.
70 *Telegram*, April 19, 1907.
71 *Telegram*, August 15, 1907.
72 *Telegram*, December 5, 1906.
73 Eleanor Baldwin, *Money Talks* (Holyoke, MA: Elizabeth Towne, c. 1915), 2.
74 Ibid., 3.
75 Ibid., 20.
76 Ibid., 39.
77 Ibid., 21.
78 Ibid., 4.

79 Ibid., 6

80 Adrian Johns, *Piracy: The Intellectual Property Wars from Gutenberg to Gates* (Chicago, IL: University of Chicago Press, 2009), 314-15; Jeff Sklansky, *The Soul's Economy: Market Society and Selfhood in American Thought, 1820-1920* (Chapel Hill: University of North Carolina Press, 2002), 77-93.

81 *Money Talks*, 11.

82 Ibid., 13-14.

83 Ibid., 39.

84 Ibid., 15.

85 Ibid., 38.

86 Ibid., 26.

87 Ibid., 29.

88 Ibid., 26.

89 Ibid., 30 and 48.

90 Ibid., 45-46.

91 Ibid., 33-34.

92 Ibid., 35.

93 Ibid., 45-47. Cummings is one of only two authorities whom Baldwin acknowledges in the text. Ibid., 2. She would also reference him in a column written for the *Oregon Labor Press* on May 26, 1917.

94 *Journal of Education* 82 (November 11, 1915): 469, http://www.jstor.org/stable/42824789?seq=1#page_scan_tab_contents.

95 *American Education* 6 (April 1916): 502, https://books.google.com/books?id=HjI_AQAAMAAJ&pg=PA502&lpg=PA502&dq=eleanor+baldwin+money+talks&source=bl&ots=5l8kyW1ehs&sig=w9_zb2n7J3MDRVhfTPf_NUShZAw&hl=en&sa=X&ei=sIw6VZCdOtfcoASB7YDoCw&ved=0CDAQ6AEwBg#v=onepage&q=eleanor%20baldwin%20money%20talks&f=false.

96 *American Poultry Advocate*, 23 (June 1915): 607, https://books.google.com/books?id=cS5JAAAAYAAJ&pg=PA607&lpg=PA607&dq=eleanor+baldwin+money+talks&source=bl&ots=Lqb5jl6tJP&sig=8JM3AAzdeQpbjquWOklVXXoL5vQ&hl=en&sa=X&ei=sIw6VZCdOtfcoASB7YDoCw&ved=0CCUQ6AEwAg#v=onepage&q=eleanor%20baldwin%20money%20talks&f=false.

97 *Tom Watson's Magazine* 22 (February 1916): 224-25, https://books.google.com/books?id=CJhFAQAAMAAJ&pg=PA224&lpg=PA224&dq=eleanor+baldwin+money+talks&source=bl&ots=o-DP9lg1h2&sig=eMY2_GEKbWawZeQT1OVqkL1N__A&hl=en&sa=X&ei=sIw6VZCdOtfcoASB7YDoCw&ved=0CCkQ6AEwBA#v=onepage&q=eleanor%20baldwin%20money%20talks&f=false.

98 *Efficiency Magazine and Sales Manager* 6 (October 1915): 14, https://books.google.com/books?id=XOU-AQAAMAAJ&pg=PA18-IA174&lpg=PA18-IA174&dq=eleanor+baldwin+money+talks&source=bl&ots=Yxfg_zVuo_&sig=r9BoknHVmMNOq_c9fpCl3-zmvLU&hl=en&sa=X&ei=sIw6VZCdOtfcoASB7YDoCw&ved=0CDgQ6AEwCA#v=onepage&q=eleanor%20baldwin%20money%20talks&f=false.

99 *Oregon Labor Press*, May 26, 1917.

100 Joseph A. McCartin, *Labor's Great War: The Struggle for Industrial Democracy and the Origins of Modern American Labor Relations, 1912-1921* (Chapel Hill: University of North Carolina Press, 1998).

101 *Oregon Labor Press*, February 14, 1920.

102 Nancy Cohen, *The Reconstruction of American Liberalism, 1865-1914* (Chapel Hill: University of North Carolina Press, 2002); Kathleen Donohue, *Freedom from Want: American Liberalism and the Idea of the Consumer* (Baltimore: Johns

Hopkins University Press, 2003); Rosanne Currarino, *The Labor Question in America: Economic Democracy in the Gilded Age* (Urbana: University of Illinois Press, 2011).

CHAPTER 5: THE WORLD OF WAR, BOLSHEVIKS, AND THE KLAN

Epigraph. Elizabeth Towne, "The Point of View," *The Nautilus*, December 1905.
1 Henry F. May, *The End of American Innocence: The First Years of Our Own Time, 1912-1917* (New York: Oxford University Press, 1959), 393.
2 On these events, see Adam Hodges, *World War I and Urban Order: The Local Class Politics of National Mobilization* (New York: Palgrave Macmillan, 2016), 128-48.
3 *Oregon Labor Press*, June 10, 1921.
4 *Oregon Labor Press*, February 25, 1921, and April 22, 1921.
5 *Oregon Labor Press*, April 22, 1921.
6 See Paula Abrams, *Cross Purposes: Pierce v. Society of Sisters and the Struggle over Compulsory Public Education* (Ann Arbor: University of Michigan Press, 2009). The classic work on American nativism is John Higham's *Strangers in the Land: Patterns of American Nativism* (New Brunswick, NJ: Rutgers University Press, 1955).
7 I. D. Ransley, Henry Schoen, and Tom Burns, "On the Job in Oregon," *International Socialist Review* (September 1913): 163-66. Robert Johnston has described O'Hara as a "social justice Catholic priest" who "ended up accepting the basic economic order," calling for regulation of excesses rather than a wholesale restructuring of society. *The Radical Middle Class: Populist Democracy and the Question of Capitalism in Progressive Era Portland, Oregon* (Princeton, NJ: Princeton University Press, 2003), 25.
8 Higham, *Strangers in the Land*, 155; Leonard Dinnerstein, *Antisemitism in America* (New York: Oxford University Press, 1994), 66-67. See also Jonathan Peter Spiro, *Defending the Master Race: Conservation, Eugenics, and the Legacy of Madison Grant* (Burlington: University of Vermont Press, 2009);
9 *Telegram*, September 26, 1907, and October 10, 1907. Burr wrote Baldwin on other subjects; for instance, more than a year earlier she had questioned the practice of sending Christian missionaries to China. See the column for June 25, 1906.
10 *Telegram*, September 26, 1907, and October 10, 1907. Others within the woman's rights community saw things differently; for instance, physician and city health official Eliza Pohl Lovejoy called for the restriction of immigration, especially that of "unassimilable races." Kimberly Jensen, *Oregon's Doctor to the World: Esther Pohl Lovejoy and a Life in Activism* (Seattle: University of Washington Press, 2012), 154.
11 *Telegram*, January 6, 1908. Emily Zeien-Stuckman, "Creating New Citizens: The National Council of Jewish Women's Work at Neighborhood House in Portland, 1896-1912," *Oregon Historical Quarterly* 113 (Fall 1912): 312-33. The Neighborhood House was mentioned as the only other settlement house in the city in Valentine Pritchard's "Report of People's Institute," reprinted on the women's page of the *Evening Telegram Magazine*, February 20, 1909.
12 *Telegram*, February 9, 1907.
13 *Telegram*, April 15, 1908.
14 *Telegram*, October 15, 1906.

15 Roger Daniels, *The Politics of Prejudice: The Anti-Japanese Movement in California and the Struggle for Japanese Exclusion*, 2nd ed. (Berkeley: University of California Press, 1978); Daniel P. Johnson, "Anti-Japanese Legislation in Oregon, 1917-1923," *Oregon Historical Quarterly* 97 (Summer 1996): 176-210; Stefan Tanaka, "The Toledo Incident: The Deportation of the Nikkei from an Oregon Mill Town," *Pacific Northwest Quarterly* 69 (September 1978): 116-26; Eiichiro Azuma, "A History of Oregon's 'Issei,' 1880-1952," *Oregon Historical Quarterly* 94 (Winter 1993): 315-67.

16 Wood, *Crimes of the Profit Furnace* (Portland, OR: Mann and Beach, 1906), 32 and 38, http://babel.hathitrust.org/cgi/pt?id=coo.31924031895497;view=1u p;seq=5. Emphasis in original. For an earlier instance in which a movement opposing the dictates of capital expressed a vitriolic anti-Chinese racism, see Margaret K. Holden, "Gender and Protest Ideology: Sue Ross Keenan and the Oregon Anti-Chinese Movement," *Western Legal History* 7 (Summer/Fall 1994): 223-43. The classic account of this tendency in California remains Alexander Saxton's *Indispensable Enemy: Labor and the Anti-Chinese Movement in California* (Berkeley: University of California Press, 1975).

17 *Telegram*, April 14, 1908.

18 *Telegram*, August 10, 1906.

19 *Telegram*, June 11, 1908.

20 *Telegram*, April 12, 1909.

21 *Telegram*, August 17, 1907. A broader appreciation of Japanese and Chinese culture, with its aesthetic dimensions, was expressed by many upper-middle-class women in the embrace of Japanese and Chinese cultural products in the growing commercial marketplace. See Kristin Hoganson, *Consumers' Imperium: The Global Production of American Domesticity, 1865-1920* (Chapel Hill: University of North Carolina Press, 2007).

22 Catherine L. Albanese, *A Republic of Mind and Spirit: A Cultural History of American Metaphysical Religion* (New Haven, CT: Yale University Press, 2008), 270-83 and 354-57.

23 *Telegram*, June 23, 1908.

24 *Telegram*, October 30, 1906; September 18, 1907; and June 4, 1908.

25 Jackson Lears classifies the turn to Asian art as similar to the embrace of medieval art and stories. *No Place of Grace: Antimodernism and the Transformation of American Culture, 1880-1920* (New York: Pantheon Books, 1981), 184-215. On the Arts and Crafts movement, see Eileen Boris, *Art and Labor: Ruskin, Morris, and the Craftsman Ideal in America* (Philadelphia, PA: Temple University Press, 1986); also Lears, *No Place of Grace*, 60-96. For a discussion of the meanings that American housewives ascribed to the material production of non-Western peoples that they bought and placed in their homes, see Hoganson, *Consumers' Imperium*.

26 Peggy Pascoe, *What Comes Naturally: Miscegenation Law and the Making of Race in America* (New York: Oxford University Press, 2009), 87-89; *Oregonian*, March 26, 1909, The Oregon History Project, News Editorial, A Disgusting Spectacle, https://oregonhistoryproject.org/articles/historical-records/news-editorial-a-disgusting-spectacle/#.WKrybxiZPq0, accessed February 20, 2017; http://chroniclingamerica.loc.gov/lccn/sn85042462/1909-03-26/ed-1/seq-3.pdf. Katrine Barber and William Robbins note that Washington was the only state in the West without miscegenation laws. *Nature's Northwest: The North Pacific Slope in the Twentieth Century* (Tucson: University of Arizona Press, 2011), 32.

27 *Telegram*, March 18, 1909.

28 *Telegram*, March 30, 1909.

29 *Telegram*, March 29, 1909.

30 *Telegram*, April 5, 1909.

31 *Telegram*, April 7, 1909.

32 *Telegram,* April 17, 1909.

33 *Telegram*, March 5, 1908.

34 *Telegram*, May 29, 1908; July 31, 1907; and December 4, 1906.

35 *Telegram*, December 3, 1908.

36 *Telegram*, March 7, 1908.

37 *Telegram*, July 10, 1906.

38 *Telegram*, November 20, 1908.

39 *Telegram*, August 21, 1908.

40 *Telegram*, May 25, 1907.

41 "Editorial Notes," *Home Mission Monthly* 29 (June 1915): 202-3; Eleanor
    Baldwin, "The White Zeppelin," in *Called to the Colors and Other Stories* (West
    Medford, MA: Christian Women's Peace Movement, 1915): 53-69. The roster of
    women involved in the New York City antiwar parade of August 1914 includes
    Carrie Chapman Catt, Harriet Stanton Blatch, Lillian Wald, Rose Schneiderman,
    and Charlotte Perkins Gilman. Also prominent in the World War I–era peace
    movement were Jane Addams and Crystal Eastman, who would provide the New
    York branch of the Women's Peace Party a great deal of energy. An organizational
    history of the women's peace movement can be found in Harriet Hyman Alonso,
    *Peace as a Woman's Issue: A History of the U.S. Movement for World Peace and
    Women's Rights* (Syracuse, NY: Syracuse University Press, 1993), 56-84; and in C.
    Roland Marchand, *The American Peace Movement and Social Reform, 1898-1918*
    (Princeton, NJ: Princeton University Press, 1972), 182-222.

42 "The White Zeppelin," 54.

43 Ibid., 57-58.

44 Ibid., 54.

45 Ibid., 62.

46 Ibid., 66-69.

47 *Oregon Labor Press*, March 17, 1917. Baldwin's close friend Henry Victor
    Morgan, the New Thought preacher who now ministered to the Park Universalist
    Church in Tacoma, likewise spoke out against war and for socialism, arguing that
    Jesus challenged the power of Rome by "taking a few men" and "implanting in
    their minds the seeds of the great spiritual idea" that "nothing was impossible to
    love and faith." *Tacoma Times*, June 12, 1916. On the resistance to war by Pacific
    Northwest socialists, see Jeffrey A. Johnson, *"They Are All Red Out Here":
    Socialist Politics in the Pacific Northwest* (Norman: University of Oklahoma Press,
    2008), 143-59.

48 Joseph A. McCartin, *Labor's Great War: The Struggle for Industrial Democracy
    and the Origins of Modern American Labor Relations, 1912-1921* (Chapel Hill:
    University of North Carolina Press, 1998).

49 Robert K. Murray, *Red Scare: A Study in National Hysteria, 1919-1920*
    (Minneapolis: University of Minnesota Press, 1955).

50 *Oregon Labor Press*, March 6, 1920.

51 *Oregon Labor Press*, March 13, 1920.

52 *Oregon Labor Press*, May 15, 1920.

53 *Oregon Labor Press*, June 19, 1920. John Higham notes that during Baldwin's
    youth, the Catholic Church began (around 1869) to agitate for the end of the use

of the Protestant King James Bible, a demand that in the Philadelphia suburb of Kensington over a generation earlier had led to anti-Catholic riots. *Strangers in the Land*, 28; David Montgomery, "The Shuttle and the Cross: Weavers and Artisans in the Kensington Riots of 1844," *Journal of Social History* 5 (Summer 1972): 411-46.

54 *Oregon Labor Press*, June 19, 1920. Baldwin objected to the assertion of Mrs. D. A. Norton, who wrote in the *Daily Journal* that the candidate to whom Baldwin objected promised "teachers and contractors will stand or fall on their merit alone, and not because of their private religious beliefs." See *Daily Journal*, June 14, 1920.

55 *Oregon Labor Press*, June 19, 1920.

56 John Lardas Modern, *Secularism in Antebellum America, with Reference to Ghosts, Protestant Subcultures, Machines and Their Metaphors* (Chicago, IL: University of Chicago Press, 2011.

57 *Oregon Labor Press*, August 7, 1920.

58 Lawrence M. Lipin, *Workers and the Wild: Conservation, Consumerism, and Labor in Oregon, 1910-1930* (Urbana: University of Illinois Press, 2007), 123-32.

59 Johnston, *Radical Middle Class.*

60 Lawrence M. Lipin and William Lunch, "Moralistic Direct Democracy: Political Insurgents, Religion, and the State in Twentieth-Century Oregon," *Oregon Historical Quarterly* 110 (Winter 2009): 514-43, quotation on 522.

61 *Capital Journal* (Salem), August 15, 1922.

62 *Western American*, September 7, 1923.

63 On Frank Roney, see Saxton, *Indispensable Enemy*, 121–7.

64 Steven Watts, *The People's Tycoon: Henry Ford and the American Century* (New York: Knopf, 2005).

65 *Oregon Labor Press*, January 27, 1922, and July 21, 1922; Watts, *People's Tycoon*, 347.

66 Eleanor Baldwin, "Money Talks, Seven Years After," July 29, 1922, ms with revisions, p. 24, Folder One, Box One, Eleanor Baldwin Collection, Ax 223, Division of Special Collections and University Archives, University of Oregon.

67 Ibid., 31.

68 As quoted in Victoria Saker Woeste, *Henry Ford's War on Jews and the Legal Battle against Hate Speech* (Stanford, CA: Stanford University Press, 2012), 19. See also Watts, *People's Tycoon*, 228-35; and Dinnerstein, *Antisemitism in America*, 80-83.

69 Richard Hofstadter, *Age of Reform* (New York: Vintage Books, 1960; originally published in 1955); Walter T. K. Nugent, *Tolerant Populists: Kansas Populism and Nativism* (Chicago, IL: University of Chicago, 1963). On Ford's antisemitism, see Watts, *People's Tycoon*, 376-97, and Woeste, *Henry Ford's War on Jews*, esp. 19-52. For Woeste, Ford's antisemitism helped widen the growing chasm "between rural and urban America that has never ceased to characterize the nation's landscape and its enduring social and political divide." *Henry Ford's War on Jews*, 11.

70 Woeste, *Henry Ford's War on Jews*, 42 and 48.

71 Gretchen Ritter, *Goldbugs and Greenbacks: The Antimonopoly Tradition and the Politics of Finance in America* (Cambridge: Cambridge University Press, 1997), 191.

72 Ibid., 52.

73 Nancy MacLean, "The Leo Frank Case Reconsidered: Gender and Sexual Politics in the Making of Reactionary Populism," *Journal of American History* 78 (December 1991): 917-48.

74 E. M. Baldwin to Eleanor Baldwin, January 11, 1927. Letters, Writings, 1909-1927, Eleanor Florence Baldwin file, mss 2106, Oregon Historical Society.

75 Shawn Lay, ed., *The Invisible Empire in the West: Toward a New Historical Appraisal of the Ku Klux Klan of the 1920s* (Urbana: University of Illinois Press, 1992), 220. Other works that stress a populist reading of the Klan include Kenneth T. Jackson, *The Klan in the City, 1915-1930* (New York: Oxford University Press); and Leonard J. Moore, *Citizen Klansmen: The Ku Klux Klan in Indiana, 1921-1928* (Chapel Hill: University of North Carolina Press, 1991). A similar portrait of the Klan in Oregon is provided by Eckard V. Toy, "The Ku Klux Klan in Oregon," in *Experiences in a Promised Land: Essays in Pacific Northwest History*, ed. G. Thomas Edwards and Carlos A. Schwantes (Seattle: University of Washington Press, 1986), 269-86. For an emphasis on the Klan's fight to defend Victorian certainties, see Stanley Coben, *Rebellion against Victorianism: The Impetus for Cultural Change in 1920s America* (New York: Oxford University Press, 1991), 136-58. John Higham's discussion of the Klan builds on his larger analysis of long-standing antiradical, anti-Catholic themes among American nativists; he points out that during the peak of the Progressive Era, anti-Catholic publications stressed the threat that the Vatican posed to progressive efforts to control big business. *Strangers in the Land*, 178-82 and 286-99.

76 Nancy MacLean, *Behind the Mask of Chivalry: The Making of the Second Ku Klux Klan* (New York: Oxford University Press, 1994), xiii, 124-73, and 177-88; Johnston, *Radical Middle Class*, 235 and 238.

77 Kathleen M. Blee, *Women of the Klan: Racism and Gender in the 1920s* (Berkeley: University of California Press, 1991), 116-17.

78 *Oregonian*, May 9, 1920, and May 12, 1925.

EPILOGUE

Epigraph. Bob Dylan, "It's All Right Ma (I'm Only Bleeding)," *Bringing It All Back Home*, Columbia Records, 331/3 rpm, 1965.

1 *Oregonian*, December 30, 1928; *Telegram*, December 21, 1928; and Oregon *Journal*, January 1, 1929.

2 Michael Helquist, *Marie Equi: Radical Politics and Outlaw Passions* (Corvallis: Oregon State University Press, 2015), 229 and 236.

3 Robert D. Johnston, *The Radical Middle Class: Populist Democracy and the Question of Capitalism in Progressive Era Portland, Oregon* (Princeton, NJ: Princeton University Press, 2003), 133-35.

4 Eleanor Baldwin, "Money Talks, Seven Years After," July 29, 1922, ms with revisions, p. 4, Folder One, Box One, Eleanor Baldwin Collection, Ax 223, Division of Special Collections and University Archives, University of Oregon.

5 Ibid., 7.

6 Ibid., 8.

7 Ibid., 9.

8 Ibid., 49.

9 William Leach, *Land of Desire: Merchants, Power, and the Rise of a New American Culture* (New York: Vintage Books, 1993), 233 and 237. A different perspective on Patten, one that finds him more ambivalent toward mass culture, emerges in Daniel Horwitz, *The Morality of Spending: Attitudes toward the Consumer Society*

in America, 1875-1940 (Chicago, IL: Ivan Dee, 1985). On the early development of a modern liberal political economy, see Kathleen Donohue, *Freedom from Want: American Liberalism and the Idea of the Consumer* (Baltimore: Johns Hopkins University Press, 2003).

10 Beryl Sattler, *Each Mind a Kingdom: American Women, Sexual Purity, and the New Thought Movement* (Berkeley: University of California Press, 1999).

11 Charlotte Perkins Gilman, *Women and Economics: The Economic Factor between Men and Women as a Factor in Social Evolution* (New York: Harper and Row, 1966; originally published 1898); Mary A. Hill, *Charlotte Perkins Gilman: The Making of a Radical Feminist, 1860-1896* (Philadelphia, PA: Temple University Press, 1980).

12 Quoted in Nancy Woloch, *Women and the American Experience* (New York: Alfred A. Knopf, 1984), 399. For a discussion of Gilman that interrogates her thinking about progress and race, see Gail Bederman, *Manliness and Civilization: A Cultural History of Gender and Race in the United States* (Chicago, IL: University of Chicago Press, 1995), 121-69. On sexologists, see Carroll Smith-Rosenberg, *Disorderly Conduct: Visions of Gender in Victorian America* (New York: Alfred A. Knopf, 1985), 266-80.

13 A recent issue of *Foreign Affairs* was devoted to the international "Power of Populism." See in particular Michael Kazin's contribution, "Trump and American Populism: Old White, New Bottles," 95 *Foreign Affairs* (November/December 2016): 17-24.

Bibliography

Primary Sources

NEWSPAPERS AND MAGAZINES

American Federationist
Barnstable *Patriot*
Boston *Daily Globe*
Capital Journal [Salem]
Free Society [Chicago]
Hartford *Courant*
John Swinton's Paper
Kansas *Agitator*
Mt. Scott *Herald*
Naugatuck *Agitator*
Naugatuck *Citizen*
Naugatuck *Enterprise*
Naugatuck *Weekly Review*

Nautilus
New Haven *Register*
New York *Times*
Oregon *Daily Journal*
Oregon *Labor Press*
Oregonian
Philadelphia *Inquirer*
Portland *Evening Telegram*
Tacoma *Times*
The True Wesleyan [Boston]
Western American [Portland]
Woman's Tribune [Portland]
World's Advance Thought [Portland]

ARCHIVAL COLLECTIONS

Associations, Institutions, etc. Mss 1511. Oregon Historical Society Library.

Baldwin, Eleanor F. Letters. Ax223. University of Oregon Special Collections.

Baldwin, Eleanor F. Papers, 1909–1927. Mss 2106. Oregon Historical Society Library.

Connecticut Headstone inscriptions. Hale Collection. Connecticut State Library.

Duniway, Abigail Scott. Papers, Series I: Suffrage Records, Subseries A, correspondence. Collection 232 B. Special Collections, Knight Library, University of Oregon.

Morgan, Henry Victor. Papers. Accession Number 0167-002. University of Washington Libraries.

Pender, Adelaide R. "At the New Britain Normal School 1886–1888." Typescript. Central Connecticut State University, Burritt Library Archives.

Portland Woman's Club. Papers. Mss. 1084. Oregon Historical Society Library.

Prichard, Valentine. "Origin and Development of Settlement Work in Portland Including Free Medical Work." Typescript. 1942. OHS Library.

Welty, Dr. E. J. Paper read in the Congregational Church, May 1910. Memorabilia Folder, Box 1, Portland Women's Union. Mss. 1443. Oregon Historical Society.

Whitehead, Carle Papers. WH390. Western History Collection, Denver Public Library.

GOVERNMENT DOCUMENTS

Berlin Vital Records, vol. 1. Connecticut State Library.

Town of Naugatuck. Births, Marriages, Deaths, vol. 1, 1863 1884. Naugatuck City Clerk Office.

Town of Waterbury. Waterbury Land Records, vol. 44 (1834).

United States. Bureau of Census, 1870, 1880, 1900. Census manuscripts for Massachusetts and Connecticut, courtesy of ancestry.com.

PUBLISHED DOCUMENTS

Baldwin, Eleanor. "The White Zeppelin." In *Called to the Colors and Other Stories*. West Medford, MA: Christian Women's Peace Movement, 1915: 53–69.

Baldwin, Eleanor. *Money Talks*. Holyoke, MA: Elizabeth Towne, c. 1915.

Baldwin, Henry. "Personal Recollections of Naugatuck about 70 Years Ago." Reprinted in Naugatuck Daily News in 1927. Photocopies held in File H 103, Naugatuck Historical Society Museum.

Barstow, Elizabeth. "Report of Travelers' Aid Committee," *Girls' Friendly Society in America* 8 (January 1905): 34–36.

Catalogue and Circular of the Connecticut State Normal School at New Britain Year Ending June 25, 1880. New Britain, CT: Adkins Brothers, 1880.

Commemorative Biographical Record of New Haven County, Connecticut. Chicago, IL: J. H. Beers, 1902.

Deyo, Simeon L., ed. *History of Barnstable County, Massachusetts*. New York: H. W. Blake, 1890.

Donlan, H. F. *The Citizen Souvenir*. Waterbury, CT: A. C. Northrup, 1895

Duniway, Abigail Scott. *Path Breaking: An Autobiographical History of the Equal Suffrage Movement in Pacific Coast States*. Portland, OR: James, Kerns & Abbott, 1914.

Elizabeth Cady Stanton, Susan B. Anthony: Correspondence, Writings, Speeches. Edited by Ellen Carol DuBois. New York: Schocken Books, 1987.

Gilman, Charlotte Perkins. *Women and Economics: The Economic Factor between Men and Women as a Factor in Social Evolution*. New York: Harper and Row, 1966.

James, William. *The Varieties of Religious Experience: A Study in Human Nature*. New York: Longman, Green, 1917.

Morgan, Henry Victor. *Songs of Victory*. Chicago, IL: Library Shelf, 1911.

National Congress of Mothers, *Report of the National Congress of Mothers, Held in the City of Washington, D. C., March 10–17, 1905*. Washington, DC: National Congress of Mothers, 1905.

Obituary Record of Graduates of Yale University Deceased during the Academical Year Ending in June 1897, no. 7 of the fourth printed series. June 1897.

Ransley, I. D., Henry Schoen, and Tom Burns. "On the Job in Oregon," *International Socialist Review* (September 1913): 163–66.

Records of the Alumni Association. Connecticut Normal School. Housed in Burritt Library Archives, Central Connecticut State University.

Schoff, Mrs. Frederic. "The National Congress of Mothers and Parent-Teacher Associations." *Annals of the American Academy of Political and Social Science* 67 (September 1916): 139–47.

Stockham, Alice B. *Tokology: A Book for Every Woman*. New York: R. F. Fenno, 1893.

Thorpe, Sheldon B. *The History of the Fifteenth Connecticut Volunteers in the War for the Defense of the Union, 1861–1865*. New Haven, CT: Price, Lee & Adkins, 1893.

Trumbull, Millie R. *The Child Who Works*. Portland, OR: Oregon State Congress of Mothers. OHS Library, n.d.

Tuttle, Roger W., ed., *Biographies of Graduates of the Yale Law School, 1824–1899*. New Haven, CT: Tuttle, Morehouse, and Taylor, n.d.

Wattles, Wallace D. *Financial Success through Creative Thought, or The Science of Getting Rich*. Holyoke, MA: Elizabeth Towne, 1915, reprinted by Health Research Books, 1998.

Whitehead, Celia Baldwin. "Henry George and Nehemiah." *The Arena* 15 (1896): 196–201.

Whitehead, Celia Baldwin. "Pessimism." *North American Review* 108 (November 1918): 799–800.

Wood, Nina E. *Crimes of the Profit Furnace*. Portland, OR: Mann & Beach, 1906.

WEB-BASED PRIMARY DOCUMENTS

Henry C. Baldwin to Charles D. Lewis, February 1, 1863, Soldier Studies: Civil War Voices, accessed February 10, 2017, http://www.soldierstudies.org/index.php?action=view_letter&Letter=299.

Pennsylvania, Church and Town Records, 1708–1985, http://search.ancestry.com/Places/US/Pennsylvania/?cj=1&sid=102&netid=cj&o_xid=0000252276&o_lid=0000252276&o_sch=Affiliate+External.

Secondary Sources

ARTICLES AND CHAPTERS

Albanese, Catharine L. "Introduction: Awash in a Sea of Metaphysics." *Journal of the American Academy of Religion* 75 (September 2007): 582–88.

Azuma, Eiichiro. "A History of Oregon's 'Issei,' 1880–1952." *Oregon Historical Quarterly* 94 (Winter 1993): 315–67.

Baker, Paula. "The Domestication of Politics: Women and American Political Society, 1780–1920." *American Historical Review* 89 (June 1984): 620–47.

Baldwin, Eric. "'The Devil Begins to Roar': Opposition to Early Methodists in New England." *Church History* 75 (March 2006): 94–119.

Barton, Stephen E. "'This Social Mother in Whose Household We All Live': Berkeley Mayor J. Stitt Wilson's Early Twentieth-Century Socialist Feminism." *Journal of the Gilded Age and Progressive Era* 13 (October 2014): 532–63.

Blee, Lisa. "Conflating Lewis and Clark's Westward March: Exhibiting a History of Empire at the 1905 World's Fair." *Oregon Historical Quarterly* 106 (Summer 2005): 232–53.

Casey, Janet Calligani. "Marie Corelli and Fin de Siecle Feminism." *English Literature in Transition, 1880–1920* 35, no. 2 (1992): 162–78.

Christen, Robert H. "Julia Hoffman and the Arts and Crafts Society of Portland: An Aesthetic Response to Industrialization." *Oregon Historical Quarterly* 109 (Winter 2008): 510–35.

Davidovitch, Nadav. "Homeopathy and Anti-Vaccinationism at the Turn of the Twentieth Century." In Robert D. Johnston, ed. *The Politics of Healing: Histories of Alternative Medicine in Twentieth-Century North America*. New York: Routledge, 2004: 9–26.

Del Mar, David Peterson. "'His Face Is Weak and Sensual': Portland and the Whipping Post Law." In Karen Blair, ed. *Women in Pacific Northwest History*. Seattle: University of Washington Press, 2001: 59–89

Dilg, Janice. "'For Working Women in Oregon': Caroline Gleason / Sister Miriam Theresa and Oregon's Minimum Wage Law." *Oregon Historical Quarterly* 110 (Spring 2009): 96–129.

Foner, Eric. "Abolitionism and the Labor Movement in Antebellum America." In Christine Bolt and Seymour Drescher, eds. *Anti-Slavery, Religion, and Reform: Essays in Memory of Roger Anstey*. Folkestone, UK: Wm Dawson & Son, 1980. 254–71.

Glauber, Carole. "Eyes of the Earth: Lily White, Sarah Ladd, and the Oregon Camera Club." *Oregon Historical Quarterly* 108 (Spring 2007): 34–67.

Golia, Julia A. "Courting Women, Courting Advertisers: The Woman's Page and the Transformation of the American Newspaper, 1895–1935." *Journal of American History* 103 (December 2016): 606–628.

Hatch, Nathan O. "The Puzzle of American Methodism." *Church History* 63 (June 1994): 175–89.

Holden, Margaret K. "Gender and Protest Ideology: Sue Ross Keenan and the Oregon Anti-Chinese Movement." *Western Legal History* 7 (Summer/Fall 1994): 223–43.

Jensen, Kimberly. "'Neither Head Nor Tail to the Campaign': Esther Pohl Lovejoy and the Oregon Woman Suffrage Victory of 1912." Oregon Historical Quarterly 108 (Fall 2007): 350–83.

Johnson, Daniel P. "Anti-Japanese Legislation in Oregon, 1917–1923." *Oregon Historical Quarterly* 97 (Summer 1996): 176–210.

Kesselman, Amy. "The 'Freedom Suit': Feminism and Dress Reform in the United States, 1848–1875." *Gender and Society* 5 (December 1991): 495–510.

Koven, Seth and Sonya Michel. "Womanly Duties: Maternalist Politics and the Origins of Welfare States in France, Germany, and the United States, 1880–1920." *American Historical Review* 95 (October 1990): 1076–1108.

Lipin, Lawrence M. "Nature, the City, and the Family Circle: Domesticity and the Urban Home in Henry George's Thought." *Journal of the Gilded Age and Progressive Era* 13 (July 2014): 305–35.

Lipin, Lawrence M. and William Lunch. "Moralistic Direct Democracy: Political Insurgents, Religion, and the State in Twentieth-Century Oregon." *Oregon Historical Quarterly* 110 (Winter 2009): 514–43.

MacLean, Nancy. "The Leo Frank Case Reconsidered: Gender and Sexual Politics in the Making of Reactionary Populism." *Journal of American History* 78 (December 1991): 917–48.

McKanan, Dan. "The Implicit Religion of Radicalism: Socialist Party Theology, 1900–1934." *Journal of the Academy of Religion* 78 (September 2010): 750–89.

Messing, John. "Public Lands, Politics, and Progressives: The Oregon Land Fraud Trails, 1903–1910." *Pacific Historical Review* 35 (February 1966): 35–66.

Montgomery, David. "The Shuttle and the Cross: Weavers and Artisans in the Kensington Riots of 1844." *Journal of Social History* 5 (Summer 1972): 411–46.

Olsen, Deborah M. "Fair Connections: Women's Separatism and the Lewis and Clark Exposition of 1905." *Oregon Historical Quarterly* 109 (Summer 2008): 174–203.

Padget, Chris. "Hearing the Antislavery Rank-and-File: The Wesleyan Methodist Schism of 1843." *Journal of the Early Republic* 12 (Spring 1992): 63–84.

Roberts, Helene E. "The Exquisite Slave: The Role of Clothes in the Making of the Victorian Woman." *Signs* 2 (spring 1977): 554–59.

Saler, Michael. "Modernity and Enchantment: A Historiographic Review." *American Historical Review* 111 (June 2006): 692–716.

Scobey, David. "Boycotting the Politics Factory: Labor Radicals and the New York City Mayoral Election of 1886." *Radical History Review* (1984): 280–325.

Silberman, Marsha. "Leo Tolstoy's Use of Lucy Mallory's Moralistic Writing in the Circle of Reading." *Tolstoy Studies Journal* 23 (2011): 84–90.

Sleeth, Peter. "'Read you Mutt': The Life and Times of Tom Burns, the Most Arrested Man in Portland." Oregon Historical Quarterly 112 (Spring 2011): 58–81.

Stein, Harry Stein. "Printers and Press Operators: The *Oregonian* Remembered." *Oregon Historical Quarterly* 115 (Summer 2014): 208–23.

Strong, Douglas M. "Partners in Political Abolitionism: The Liberty Party and the Wesleyan Methodist Connection." *Methodist History* 23 (January 1985): 99–115.

Tanaka, Stefan. "The Toledo Incident: The Deportation of the Nikkei from an Oregon Mill Town." *Pacific Northwest Quarterly* 69 (September 1978): 116–26

Toy, Eckard V. "The Ku Klux Klan in Oregon." In G. Thomas Edwards and Carlos A. Schwantes, eds. *Experiences in a Promised Land: Essays in Pacific Northwest History*. Seattle: University of Washington Press, 1986, 269–86.

Weir, Robert Weir. "A Fragile Alliance: Henry George and the Knights of Labor." *American Journal of Economics and Sociology* 56 (October 1997): 421–39.

Williamson, Douglas J. "The Rise of the New England Methodist Temperance Movement, 1823–1836." *Methodist History* 21 (1982): 3–28.

Woodward, Robert C. "William S. U'Ren: A Progressive Era Personality." In G. Thomas Edwards and Carlos A. Schwantes, eds. *Experiences in a Promised Land: Essays in Pacific Northwest History*. Seattle: University of Washington Press, 1986.

Zeien–Stuckman, Emily. "Creating New Citizens: The National Council of Jewish Women's Work at Neighborhood House in Portland, 1896–1912." *Oregon Historical Quarterly* 113 (Fall 2012): 312–33.

BOOKS

Abbott, Carl. *The Great Extravaganza: Portland and the Exposition*. Portland: Oregon Historical Society, 1981.

Abrams, Paula. *Cross Purposes: Pierce v. Society of Sisters and the Struggle over Compulsory Public Education*. Ann Arbor: University of Michigan Press, 2009.

Aiken, Katharine G. *Harnessing the Power of Motherhood: The National Florence Crittenton Mission*. Knoxville: University of Tennessee Press, 1998.

Alonso, Harriet Hyman. *Peace as a Woman's Issue: A History of the U.S. Movement for World Peace and Women's Rights*. Syracuse, NY: Syracuse University Press, 1993.

Albanese, Catharine L. *A Republic of Mind and Spirit: A Cultural History of American Metaphysical Religion*. New Haven, CT: Yale University Press, 2008.

Barber, Katrine and William Robbins. *Nature's Northwest: The North Pacific Slope in the Twentieth Century*. Tucson: University of Arizona Press, 2011.

Bederman, Gail. *Manliness and Civilization: A Cultural History of Gender and Race in the United States, 1880–1917*. Chicago, IL: University of Chicago Press, 1996.

Benson, Susan Porter. *Counter Cultures: Saleswomen, Managers, and Customers in American Department Stores, 1890–1940*. Urbana: University of Illinois Press, 1988.

Blee, Kathleen M. *Women of the Klan: Racism and Gender in the 1920s*. Berkeley: University of California Press, 1991.

Blocker, Jack S. jr., *"Give to the Wind Thy Fears": The Women's Temperance Crusade, 1873–1874*. Westport, CT: Praeger, 1985.

Boag, Peter. *Same-Sex Affairs: Constructing and Controlling Homosexuality in the Pacific Northwest*. Berkeley: University of California Press, 2003.

Bordin, Ruth. *Women and Temperance: The Quest for Power and Liberty, 1873–1900*. Philadelphia, PA: Temple University Press, 1981.

Boris, Eileen. *Art and Labor: Ruskin, Morris, and the Craftsman Ideal in America*. Philadelphia, PA: Temple University Press, 1986.

Bowler, Kate. *Blessed: A History of the American Prosperity Gospel*. New York: Oxford University Press, 2013.

Braude, Anne. *Radical Spirits: Spiritualism and Women's Rights in Nineteenth-Century America*. Boston, MA: Beacon Press, 1989.

Browne, Sheri Bartlett. *Eva Emery Dye: Romance with the West*. Corvallis: Oregon State University Press, 2004

Buhle, Mari Jo. *Women and American Socialism, 1870–1920*. Urbana: University of Illinois Press, 1981.

Coben, Stanley. *Rebellion against Victorianism: The Impetus for Cultural Change in 1920s America*. New York: Oxford University Press, 1991.

Cohen, Nancy. *The Reconstruction of American Liberalism, 1865–1914*. Chapel Hill: University of North Carolina Press, 2002.

Cott, Nancy. *The Grounding of Modern Feminism*. New Haven, CT: Yale University Press, 1989.

Cronon, William. *Nature's Metropolis: Chicago and the Great West*. New York: W. W. Norton, 1991.

Currarino, Rosanne. *The Labor Question in America: Economic Democracy in the Gilded Age*. Urbana: University of Illinois Press, 2011.

Dana, Marshall N. *The First 50 Years of the Oregon Journal: A Newspaper Story*. Portland, OR: Binford & Morts, 1951.

Daniels, Roger. *The Politics of Prejudice: The Anti-Japanese Movement in California and the Struggle for Japanese Exclusion*. Second edition. Berkeley: University of California Press, 1978.

Davis, Sue. *The Political Thought of Elizabeth Cady Stanton: Women's Rights and the American Political Traditions*. New York: New York University Press, 2008.

Dawley, Alan. *Changing the World: American Progressives in War and Revolution*. Princeton, NJ: Princeton University Press, 2003.

Dawley, Alan. *Struggles for Justice: Social Responsibility and the Liberal State*. Cambridge, MA: Belknap Press of Harvard University Press, 1991.

Dinnerstein, Leonard. *Antisemitism in America*. New York: Oxford University Press, 1994.

Donohue, Kathleen. *Freedom from Want: American Liberalism and the Idea of the Consumer*. Baltimore: Johns Hopkins University Press, 2003.

Edwards, G. Thomas. *Sowing Good Seeds: The Northwest Suffrage Campaigns of Susan B. Anthony*. Portland: Oregon Historical Society Press, 1990.

Edwards, Rebecca. *New Spirits: Americans in the Gilded Age, 1865–1905*. New York: Oxford University Press, 2006.

Epstein, Barbara Leslie. *The Politics of Domesticity: Women, Evangelism, and Temperance in Nineteenth-Century America*. Middletown, CT: Wesleyan, 1981.

Ewen, Stuart. *Captains of Consciousness: Advertising and the Social Roots of the Consumer Culture*. New York: McGraw Hill, 1976.

Fahs, Alice. *Out on Assignment: Newspaper Women and the Making of Modern Public Space*. Chapel Hill, N.C.: University of North Carolina Press, 2011.

Faue, Elizabeth. *Writing the Wrongs: Eva Valesh and the Rise of Labor Journalism*. Ithaca, New York: Cornell University Press, 2002.

Fink, Leon. *Workingmen's Democracy: The Knights of Labor and American Politics*. Urbana: University of Illinois Press, 1985.

Flanagan, Maureen A. *Seeing with Their Hearts: Chicago Women and the Vision of the Good City, 1871–1933*. Princeton, NJ: Princeton University Press, 2002.

Fowler, Henry E. *A Century of Teacher Education in Connecticut: The Story of the New Britain State Normal School and the Teachers College of Connecticut, 1849–1949*. New Britain: Teachers College of Connecticut, 1949.

Foner, Eric. *Free Soil, Free Labor, Free Men: The Ideology of the Republican Party before the Civil War*. New York: Oxford University Press, 1970.

Forbath, William E. *Law and the Shaping of the American Labor Movement*. Cambridge, MA: Harvard University Press, 1991.

Friedman, Milton and Anna Jacobson Schwartz. *A Monetary History of the United States, 1867–1960*. Princeton, NJ: Princeton University Press, 1963.

Garrison, Dee. *Mary Heaton Vorse: Life of an American Insurgent*. Philadelphia, PA: Temple University Press, 1989.

Ginzburg, Lori. *Women and the Work of Benevolence: Morality, Politics, and Class in the Nineteenth-Century United States*. New Haven, CT: Yale University Press, 1992.

Glickman, Lawrence. *A Living Wage: American Workers and the Making of Consumer Society*. Ithaca, NY: Cornell University Press, 1999.

Goodwyn, Lawrence. *Democratic Promise: The Populist Movement in America*. New York: Oxford University Press, 1976.

Gordon, Robert J. *The Rise and Fall of American Growth: The U.S. Standard of Living Since the Civil War*. Princeton, NJ: Princeton University Press, 2016.

Green, Constance McLaughlin. *History of Naugatuck, Connecticut*. New Haven, CT: Yale University Press, 1948.

Green, James. *Death in the Haymarket: A Story of Chicago, the First Labor Movement and the Bombing That Divided Gilded Age America*. New York: Pantheon Books, 2006.

Gutman, Herbert. *Work, Culture and Society in Industrializing America*. New York: Vintage Books, 1977.

Haarsager, Sandra. *Organized Womanhood: Cultural Politics in the Pacific Northwest, 1840–1920*. Norman, Oklahoma: University of Oklahoma Press, 1997.

Hammond, Bray. *Banks and Politics in America from the Revolution to the Civil War*. Princeton, NJ: Princeton University Press, 1957.

Harper, Ida Husted, ed. *The History of Woman Suffrage*. Volume 5. New York: J. J. Little and Ives, 1922.

Hays, Samuel P. *Conservation and the Gospel of Efficiency: The Progressive Conservation Movement, 1890–1920*. Cambridge, MA: Harvard University Press, 1959.

Helquist, Michael. *Marie Equi: Radical Politics and Outlaw Passions*. Corvallis, OR: Oregon State University Press, 2015.

Higham, John. *Strangers in the Land: Patterns of American Nativism*. New Brunswick, NJ: Rutgers University Press, 1955.

Hill, Mary A. *Charlotte Perkins Gilman: The Making of a Radical Feminist, 1860–1896*. Philadelphia, PA: Temple University Press, 1980.

Hodges, Adam. *World War I and Urban Order: The Local Class Politics of National Mobilization.* New York: Palgrave Macmillan, 2016.

Hofstadter, Richard. *Age of Reform: From Bryan to FDR.* New York: Vintage Books, 1960; originally published in 1955.

Hoganson, Kristin. *Consumers' Imperium: The Global Production of American Domesticity, 1865–1920.* Chapel Hill: University of North Carolina Press, 2007.

Holt, Michael F. *The Fate of Their Country: Politicians, Slavery Extension, and the Coming of the Civil War.* New York: Hill and Wang, 2004.

Horowitz, Daniel. *The Morality of Spending: Attitudes toward the Consumer Society in America, 1875–1940.* Chicago, IL: Ivan R. Dee, 1985.

Horwitz, Morton. *The Transformation of American Law, 1870–1960.* Oxford: Oxford University Press, 1992.

Howe, Daniel Walker, ed. *American Victorianism.* Philadelphia, PA: University of Pennsylvania Press, 1976.

Howe, Daniel Walker. *What Hath God Wrought: The Transformation of America, 1815–1848.* New York: Oxford University Press, 2009.

Huyssen, David. *Progressive Inequality: Rich and Poor in New York, 1890–1920.* Cambridge, MA: Harvard University Press, 2014.

Jackson, Kenneth T. *The Klan in the City, 1915–1930.* New York: Oxford University Press, 1967.

Jensen, Kimberly. *Oregon's Doctor to the World: Esther Pohl Lovejoy and a Life in Activism.* Seattle, WA: University of Washington Press, 2012.

Johns, Adrian. *Piracy: The Intellectual Property Wars from Gutenberg to Gates.* Chicago, IL: University of Chicago Press, 2009.

Johnson, Jeffrey A. *"They Are All Red Out Here": Socialist Politics in the Pacific Northwest.* Norman: University of Oklahoma Press, 2008.

Johnston, Robert D. *The Radical Middle Class: Populist Democracy and the Question of Capitalism in Progressive Era Portland, Oregon.* Princeton, NJ: Princeton University Press, 2003.

Karsten, Peter. *Heart versus Head: Judge-Made Law in Nineteenth-Century America.* Chapel Hill: University of North Carolina Press, 1997.

Kessler-Harris, Alice. *In Pursuit of Equity: Women, Men, and the Quest for Economic Citizenship in 20th-Century America.* New York: Oxford University Press, 2001.

Kolko, Gabriel. *The Triumph of Conservatism: A Reinterpretation of American History, 1900–1916.* New York: Free Press, 1963.

Kraditor, Aileen. *The Ideas of the Woman Suffrage Movement, 1890–1920.* New York: Columbia University Press, 1965.

Ladd-Taylor, Molly. *Mother-Work: Women, Child-Welfare, and the State, 1890–1930.* Urbana: University of Illinois Press, 1994.

Larson, John Lauritz. *The Market Revolution in America: Liberty, Ambition, and the Eclipse of the Common Good.* Cambridge: Cambridge University Press, 2009.

Laurie, Bruce. *Working People of Philadelphia, 1800–1850.* Philadelphia, PA: Temple University Press, 1980.

Lay, Shawn, ed. *The Invisible Empire in the West: Toward a New Historical Appraisal of the Ku Klux Klan of the 1920s.* Urbana: University of Illinois Press, 1992.

Leach, William. *Land of Desire: Merchants, Power, and the Rise of a New American Culture.* New York: Vintage Books, 1993.

Lears, Jackson. *No Place of Grace: Antimodernism and the Transformation of American Culture, 1880–1920.* New York: Pantheon, 1981.

Lears, Jackson. *Rebirth of a Nation: The Making of Modern America, 1877–1920*. New York: HarperCollins, 2009.

Levine, Lawrence. *Defender of the Faith: William Jennings Bryan, the Last Decade 1915–1925*. Cambridge, MA: Harvard University Press, 1963.

Lipin, Lawrence M. *Workers and the Wild: Conservation, Consumerism, and Labor in Oregon, 1910–30*. Urbana: University of Illinois Press, 2007.

Livingston, James. *Origins of the Federal Reserve System: Money, Class and Corporate Capitalism, 1890–1913*. Ithaca, NY: Cornell University Press, 1986.

MacColl, E. Kimbark. *Merchants, Money and Power: The Portland, 1843–1913*. Portland, OR: Georgian Press, 1988.

MacLean, Nancy. *Behind the Mask of Chivalry: The Making of the Second Ku Klux Klan*. New York: Oxford University Press, 1994.

Mangun, Kimberly. *A Force for Change: Beatrice Morrow Cannady and the Struggle for Civil Rights in Oregon, 1912–1936*. Corvallis, OR: Oregon State University Press, 2010.

Marchand, C. Roland. *The American Peace Movement and Social Reform, 1898–1918*. Princeton, NJ: Princeton University Press, 1972.

Mathewson, Worth. *William L. Finley: Pioneer Wildlife Photographer*. Corvallis: Oregon State University Press, 1986.

May, Henry F. *The End of American Innocence: The First Years of Our Own Time, 1912–1917*. New York: Oxford University Press, 1959.

McAdams, Elizabeth E. and Raymond Bayless. *Life after Death: Parapsychologists Look at the Evidence*. Chicago, IL: Nelson-Hall, 1981.

McCartin, Joseph A. *Labor's Great War: The Struggle for Industrial Democracy and the Origins of Modern American Labor Relations, 1912–1921*. Chapel Hill: University of North Carolina Press, 1998.

McMath, Robert C., Jr. *American Populism: A Social History 1877–1898*. New York: Hill and Wang, 1993.

McNeur, Catherine. *Taming Manhattan: Environmental Battles in the Antebellum City*. Cambridge, MA: Harvard University Press, 2014.

Mead, Rebecca. *How the Vote Was Won: Woman Suffrage in the Western United States, 1868–1914*. New York: New York University Press, 2004.

Minh, Steven. *A Nation of Counterfeiters: Capitalists, Con Men, and the Making of the United States*. Cambridge, MA: Harvard University Press, 2009.

Modern, John Lardas. *Secularism in Antebellum America, with Reference to Ghosts, Protestant Subcultures, Machines, and Their Metaphors*. Chicago, IL: University of Chicago Press, 2011.

Moore, Leonard J. *Citizen Klansmen: The Ku Klux Klan in Indiana, 1921–1928*. Chapel Hill: University of North Carolina Press, 1991.

Moore, R. Laurence. *In Search of White Crows: Spiritualism, Parapsychology, and American Culture*. New York: Oxford University Press, 1977.

Montgomery, David. *Beyond Equality: Labor and the Radical Republicans*. Urbana: University of Illinois Press, 1981.

Moynihan, Ruth Barnes. *Rebel for Rights: Abigail Scott Duniway*. New Haven, CT: Yale University Press, 1983.

Muncy, Robyn. *Creating a Female Dominion in American Reform, 1890–1935*. New York: Oxford University Press, 1991.

Murray, Robert K. *Red Scare: A Study in National Hysteria, 1919–1920*. Minneapolis: University of Minnesota Press, 1955.

Myers, Gloria E. *A Municipal Mother: Portland's Lola Greene Baldwin, America's First Policewoman*. Corvallis: Oregon State University Press, 1995.

Nissenbaum, Stephen. *Sex, Diet and Debility in Jacksonian America: Sylvester Graham and Health Reform*. Westport, CT: Greenwood Press, 1980.

Nord, David Paul. *Communities of Journalism: A History of American Newspapers and Their Readers*. Urbana: University of Illinois Press, 2001.

Nugent, Walter T. K. *Tolerant Populists: Kansas Populism and Nativism*. Chicago, IL: University of Chicago, 1963.

Orren, Karen. *Belated Feudalism: Labor, the Law, and Liberal Development in the United States*. Cambridge: Cambridge University Press, 1991.

Pascoe, Peggy. *What Comes Naturally: Miscegenation Law and the Making of Race in America*. New York: Oxford University Press, 2009.

Parker, Gail Thain. *Mind Cure in New England: From the Civil War to World War I*. Hanover, NH: University Press of New England, 1973.

Piketty, Thomas. *Capital in the Twenty-First Century*. Cambridge, MA: Harvard University Press, 2014.

Pollack, Norman. *The Populist Response to Industrial America: Midwestern Populist Thought*. Cambridge, MA: Harvard University Press, 1976.

Postel, Charles. *The Populist Vision*. New York: Oxford University Press, 2007.

Price, Jennifer. *Flight Maps: Adventures with Nature in Modern America*. New York: Basic Books, 1999.

Remini, Robert V. *Andrew Jackson and the Bank War*. New York: W. W. Norton, 1967.

Ritter, Gretchen. *Goldbugs and Greenbacks: The Antimonopoly Tradition and the Politics of Finance in America*. Cambridge: Cambridge University Press, 1997.

Robertson, Stacey M. *Parker Pillsbury, Radical Abolitionist, Male Feminist*. Ithaca, NY: Cornell University Press, 2000.

Rohrbaugh, W. J. *The Alcoholic Republic*. New York: Oxford University Press, 1981.

Rosenberg, Carroll Smith. *Disorderly Conduct: Visions of Gender in Victorian America*. New York: Oxford University Press, 1986.

Rousmaniere, Kate. *Citizen Teacher: The Life and Leadership of Margaret Haley*. Albany: State University of New York Press, 2005.

Ryan, Mary P. *Cradle of the Middle Class: The Family in Oneida County, New York, 1790–1865*. Cambridge: Cambridge University Press, 1981

Rydell, Robert W. *All the World's a Fair: Visions of Empire at American International Expositions, 1876–1916*. Chicago, IL: University of Chicago, 1984.

Sattler, Beryl. *Each Mind a Kingdom: American Women, Sexual Purity, and the New Thought Movement, 1875–1920*. Berkeley: University of California Press, 2001.

Saxton, Alexander. *Indispensable Enemy: Labor and the Anti-Chinese Movement in California*. Berkeley: University of California Press, 1975.

Sellers, Charles. *The Market Revolution: Jacksonian America, 1815–1846*. New York: Oxford University Press, 1994.

Shi, David. *The Simple Life: Plain Living and High Thinking in American Culture*. New York: Oxford University Press, 1985.

Sklansky, Jeff. *The Soul's Economy: Market Society and Selfhood in American Thought, 1820–1920*. Chapel Hill: University of North Carolina Press, 2002.

Sklar, Kathryn Kish. *Catharine Beecher: A Study in American Domesticity*. New York: W. W. Norton, 1976.

Sklar, Kathryn Kish. *Florence Kelley and the Nation's Work*. New Haven, CT: Yale University Press, 1995.

Spiro, Jonathan Peter. *Defending the Master Race: Conservation, Eugenics, and the Legacy of Madison Grant*. Burlington: University of Vermont Press, 2009.

Stansell, Christine. *City of Women: Sex and Class in New York, 1789–1860.* New York: Alfred A. Knopf, 1982.

Sutton, William R. *Journeymen for Jesus: Evangelical Artisans Confront Capitalism in Jacksonian Baltimore.* University Park: Pennsylvania State University Press, 1998.

Taves, Ann. *Fits, Trances, and Visions: Experiencing Religious and Explaining Experience from Wesley to James.* Princeton, NJ: Princeton University Press, 1999.

Taylor, George Rogers. *The Transportation Revolution, 1815–1860.* New York: M. E. Sharpe, 1977.

Taylor, Marlene. *A History of the Naugatuck Methodist Church in Connecticut.* Naugatuck, CT: Naugatuck United Methodist Church, 1988.

Thernstrom, Stephen. *Poverty and Progress: Social Mobility in a Nineteenth Century City.* Cambridge, MA: Harvard University Press, 1964.

Turnbull, George S. Turnbull, *History of Oregon Newspapers.* Portland, OR: Binfords & Mort, 1939.

Unger, Irwin. *The Greenback Era: A Social and Political History of American Finance, 1865–1879.* Princeton, NJ: Princeton University Press, 1964.

Watts, Steven. *The People's Tycoon: Henry Ford and the American Century.* New York: Knopf, 2005.

Waugh, Joan. *Sentimental Reformer: The Life of Josephine Shaw Lowell.* Cambridge, MA: Harvard University Press, 1998.

Weinstein, James. *The Corporate Ideal in the Liberal State, 1900–1918.* Boston: Beacon Press, 1968.

Weiss, Richard. *The American Myth of Success: From Horatio Alger to Norman Vincent Peale.* Urbana: University of Illinois Press, 1988.

Wilentz, Sean. *Chants Democratic: New York City and the Rise of the American Working Class.* New York: Oxford University Press, 1984.

Witt, John Fabian. *The Accidental Republic: Crippled Workingmen, Destitute Widows, and the Remaking of American Law.* Cambridge, MA: Harvard University Press, 2004.

Woeste, Victoria Saker. *Henry Ford's War on Jews and the Legal Battle against Hate Speech.* Stanford, CA: Stanford University Press, 2012.

Woloch, Nancy. *Women and the American Experience.* New York: Knopf, 1984.

Wood, Gordon. *The Radicalism of the American Revolution.* New York: Alfred Knopf, 1991.

Woodward, C. Vann. *Tom Watson: Agrarian Rebel.* New York: Oxford University Press, 1963.

THESES AND DISSERTATIONS

Barefoot, Martha Killian. "Between 'True Women' and 'New Women': Oregon's Women's Clubs, 18901916. Master's Thesis, University of Oregon, 1994.

Index